Proud and Angry

Proud and Angry

Political Culture in Post-British Hong Kong

Wenfang Tang
Ying Xia

OXFORD
UNIVERSITY PRESS

Oxford University Press is a department of the University of Oxford.
It furthers the University's objective of excellence in research, scholarship,
and education by publishing worldwide. Oxford is a registered trade mark of
Oxford University Press in the UK and in certain other countries.

Published in the United States of America by Oxford University Press
198 Madison Avenue, New York, NY 10016, United States of America.

© Oxford University Press 2025

All rights reserved. No part of this publication may be reproduced, stored in a retrieval system, transmitted, used for text and data mining, or used for training artificial intelligence, in any form or by any means, without the prior permission in writing of Oxford University Press, or as expressly permitted by law, by license or under terms agreed with the appropriate reprographics rights organization. Inquiries concerning reproduction outside the scope of the above should be sent to the Rights Department, Oxford University Press, at the address above.

You must not circulate this work in any other form
and you must impose this same condition on any acquirer.

CIP data is on file at the Library of Congress.

ISBN 9780197831557

ISBN 9780197831540 (hbk.)

DOI: 10.1093/9780197831588.001.0001

The manufacturer's authorized representative in the EU for product safety is
Oxford University Press España S.A. of Parque Empresarial San Fernando de Henares,
Avenida de Castilla, 2 – 28830 Madrid (www.oup.es/en or product.safety@oup.com).
OUP España S.A. also acts as importer into Spain of products made by the manufacturer.

Contents

List of Figures	viii
List of Photos	ix
List of Tables	x
Preface	xi

1. The Study of Political Culture — 1
   What Is Political Culture? — 1
   How to Measure Political Culture? — 4
   How Does Political Culture Change? — 12
   Measurement Errors — 17
   Why Does Political Culture Matter? — 19
   Studying Political Culture of Hong Kong in the Postcolonial Era — 20

2. Detecting Social Desirability in Public Opinion Surveys — 23
   Introduction — 23
   Social Desirability in Public Opinion Surveys — 23
   Traditional Methods of Dealing with Social and Political Desirability — 25
   New Tools to Study Social and Political Desirability — 26
   Political and Social Desirability in Hong Kong Public Opinion Surveys — 27
   List Experiments — 29
   Hong Kong Political Culture Survey — 32
   Detecting Opposite Social Desirability Effects — 34
   Statistical Weighting with an Activator Variable — 36
   Discussion and Implications — 39

3. Indigenization of Political Identity — 42
   Introduction — 42
   Competing Theories of Postcolonial Identity — 42
   Indigenization of Political Identity in Postcolonial Hong Kong — 45
   Data and Measures of Political Identity — 49
   Levels of Political Identities in Hong Kong — 52
   Sources of Political Identity — 57
   Robustness Check — 66
   Conclusions — 68

4. Political Trust Under One Country, Two Systems — 70
   Introduction — 70
   The Evolving Political Landscape in Postcolonial Hong Kong — 70
   Political Trust in Democratic and Authoritarian Societies — 80

Measuring Political Trust in Hong Kong	82
Trust of Officials and Dissidents	89
Policy Satisfaction	91
Sources of Political Trust and Policy Satisfaction	92
Summary and Discussions	101

5. Political Contention — 103
Introduction	103
Political Participation in Post-British Hong Kong	103
Theories of Social Protests	110
Channels of Political Action	113
Sources of Political Action	118
Summary and Discussions	120

6. The "Apple-Lization" of Hong Kong Media — 125
Introduction	125
Media Environment in Hong Kong	126
Existing Studies on Media Freedom in Hong Kong	128
Media Narratives of CCP: Evidence from *Apple Daily* and *Wen Wei Po*	129
Measuring Media Slant of Major Newspapers	136
Reader Preference: Evidence from Survey Data	138
Conclusions and Discussion	143

7. Conclusions and Discussion — 144
Summary of Main Findings	144
Broader Implications for Political Culture Studies	146

Appendices — 149
Appendix 2.1	149
Appendix 2.2	150
Appendix 2.3	151
Appendix 3.1	153
Appendix 3.2	154
Appendix 3.3	156
Appendix 4.1a	158
Appendix 4.1b	158
Appendix 4.1c	158
Appendix 4.2	162
Appendix 4.3	165
Appendix 4.4	167
Appendix 4.5	180
Appendix 4.6	187
Appendix 5.1	188
Appendix 5.2	190

Appendix 6.1	192
Appendix 6.2	196
Appendix 6.3	199
Bibliography	201
Index	223

List of Figures

2.1.	Social desirability by political leaning (direct questioning minus list experiments)	35
2.2.	Support for politically sensitive questions: Proportions after weighting and social desirability	39
3.1.	Hong Kong residents' feelings toward Chinese culture and the Chinese state (weighted by social desirability)	53
3.2.	Hong Kong residents' feelings toward people from other countries and regions	54
3.3.	Two-way interaction between education and age on cultural nationalism (a), political nationalism (b), and immigration intention (c)	62
4.1.	Institutional trust in China before and after weighting	84
4.2.	Institutional trust in Hong Kong before and after weighting	87
4.3.	Comparing level of trust in key institutions of Asian countries in 2016 and Hong Kong's change over time	89
4.4.	Proportion of trust in government officials before and after weighting	90
4.5.	Rating of Hong Kong chief executives and political activists before and after weighting	92
4.6.	Social policy satisfaction and its change over time, 9 weighted areas	93
4.7.	Political policy satisfaction and its change over time, 8 weighted areas	94
5.1.	Problem-solving channels: 1st, 2nd, and 3rd choices (% weighted by social desirability)	115
5.2.	"Will not do business if political view is different" by political leaning (weighted %)	117
6.1.	Media slant of Hong Kong newspapers, 2002–2020	137
6.2.	Reader preference of print media in Hong Kong, 2021	140

List of Photos

3.1. Protest slogan: Light up Hong Kong, arouse the public. Hong Kong Island. Photo by Wenfang Tang, 8/24/2019.   47

3.2. Taiwan became the biggest beneficiary of the Hong Kong protest. Tsai Yin-wen rode on the anti-China sentiment and easily won her presidential reelection in 2020. Tamkang University, Taiwan. Photo by Wenfang Tang, 12/22/2023.   55

3.3. Wall slogan: Protect Hong Kong and kick out the disease-carrying Mainland locusts. Hang Hau MRT station. Photo by Wenfang Tang, 1/20/2020.   61

4.1. The total number of protesters reached an estimated 2 million people. Central, Hong Kong Island. Photo by Wenfang Tang, 7/1/2019   74

4.2. Poster against Chief Executive Carrie Lam. Hong Kong University of Science and Technology, Clear Water Bay. Photo by Wenfang Tang, 7/21/2019.   77

4.3. A poster referring to "the local police force as CCP officials and mafia." Central, Hong Kong Island. Photo by Wenfang Tang, 8/24/2019.   86

5.1. The closed Hang Hau MRT station entrance after being destroyed by the protesters. Sai Kung District. Photo by Wenfang Tang, 10/10/2019.   110

5.2. Protest leaders Pang Ka-ho (*far left*), Wong Chi-fong (*second from left*), Nathan Law (*second from right*), and Zhang Kunyang (*far right*) meeting with Julie Eadeh (*front*), suspected political chief at the US Consulate General in Hong Kong, in the lobby of the Golden Bell Marriott Hotel in Hong Kong. Published by *Ta Kung Pao*, 8/8/2019.   113

5.3. An elderly protester wearing a poster supporting young protesters. Hong Kong Island. Photo by Wenfang Tang, 8/24/2019.   122

5.4. A protester's last effort at continuing the social movement by distributing flyers after the passage of the National Security Law. Hong Kong Island. Photo by Wenfang Tang, 12/25/2021.   123

6.1. Newsstand outside a convenience store in Hong Kong on a Sunday around noon in Wan Chai. Newspapers that were sold out included *Oriental Daily*, *Sing Tao Daily*, and *South China Morning Post*. At the bottom were Chinese government-sponsored papers, *Wen Wei Po*, *Ta Kung Pao*, and *China Daily*. Photo by Wenfang Tang, 12/10/2023.   142

List of Tables

2.1. Ratios of List Experiment to Direct Questioning by Political Leaning (ratio=list experiment/direct questioning)	38
3.1. Three Selected Identity Measures (weighted by social desirability)	56
3.2. Sources of Hong Kong Ethnic and Political Identity (multilevel OLS regression)	58
3.3. Robustness Check (two-stage IV regression)	67
4.1. Sources of Political Trust and Policy Satisfaction (multilevel OLS regression)	97
5.1. Major Public Events in Post-British Hong Kong	105
5.2. Voted in 2019 and Plan to Vote in 2021 (weighted %)	118
5.3. Sources of Political Action (OLS)	121
6.1. Top-10 Topic Keywords Used by *Apple Daily* and *Wen Wei Po* in Selected Years	131
6.2. Ideological Categories of Major Newspapers in Hong Kong	139

Preface

The idea of writing this book came from Professor Wenfang Tang's total surprise living in Hong Kong. In 2019, he moved to Hong Kong during the peak of the largest ever anti-China protests. On public buses, in shops and restaurants, his mandarin with a thick northern accent immediately drew dirty looks and even comments about him as a barbarian from the Mainland. He was simply ignored when he asked in Mandarin for directions on the streets. He never personally encountered such open discrimination based on his accent after working and living in the United States for more than three decades, although other people may think there is plenty of racism in that country.

Consequently, Professor Tang decided to conduct a public opinion survey and systematically examine the political sentiment in this postcolonial society. Thanks to two research grants from the General Research Fund (RGC Ref No. 16601820, and the Anti-Epidemic Fund 2.0), he was able to conduct the Hong Kong Political Culture Survey in 2021. This survey is valuable because it is based on a representative sample of 3,744 randomly selected Hong Kong residents. The face-to-face interviews provide a solid foundation for understanding the political attitudes and behavior of the Hong Kong population. The survey is also valuable because of its timing. It was conducted one year after China passed the Hong Kong National Security Law (NSL). This was perfect timing for checking the immediate impact of the NSL in the aftermath of the largest protests in Hong Kong society.

The Hong Kong Political Culture Survey is also valuable to the field of survey research in general. By embedding a series of list experiments with an innovative and pioneering statistical weighting technique, the survey was able to detect a large amount of social desirability in which the respondents hide their resentment of China due to concerns of political incorrectness (Chapter 2). This technique will be helpful for other survey researchers in dealing with the similar and common problems in their own surveys.

Chapter 1 of this book develops a comprehensive approach to studying political culture with quantitative data. It is hoped that this chapter will be helpful in providing theoretical and methodological guidelines for future researchers in the field of comparative quantitative studies of political culture. One focus of this chapter is about how to avoid incorrect measurement of key concepts in political culture that can lead to erroneous conclusions. This chapter also helps the reader to understand the political culture in Hong Kong in a comparative framework.

Chapter 3 shows that in the political vacuum left by the departure of the British colonists and the inability of China to intervene under the One Country, Two Systems framework, Hong Kong residents established a new political identity that is neither Chinese nor Western, but it is based on its indigenous culture.

In Chapters 4 and 5, Hongkongers' distrust in Chinese government and their tendency to protest remain surprisingly high. Unlike being feared by the West or hoped by China, there is a long way to go for Hong Kong to be fully integrated into the Chinese system.

Chapter 6 finds another interesting surprise. Hongkongers' anti-China sentiment was provoked by Hong Kong's media, which have been incorrectly described in the existing literature as "pro-China." This chapter suggests that Hong Kong media were overwhelmingly anti-China during the 2019 protests, except for two China-sponsored newspapers.

In 2022, Professor Tang moved to the Chinese University of Hong Kong, Shenzhen, and teamed up with Professor Ying Xia at Sun Yat-Sen University. Professor Xia is a veteran scholar of contemporary Hong Kong politics and Hong Kong's colonial legacy. She made valuable contributions to the manuscript, particularly in Chapters 1, 3, and 5. Most importantly, she is the mastermind behind Chapter 6. With her knowledge and understanding of Hong Kong's media environment and her help with applying machine learning to analyzing a large amount of media materials, Chapter 6 makes an important contribution to this volume by strengthening and enriching its empirical foundation.

In preparing this book, we received help from several organizations and many individuals. In addition to the two GRF grants, Professor Wenfang Tang received generous financial support from the Chinese University of Hong Kong, Shenzhen, including the Presidential Chair Fund, the University Development Fund, the Peacock Talent Fund, the Peacock Startup Research Fund, and a grant from the Shenzhen Key Lab of Computational Social Science. Professor Xia Ying received financial support from the Institute of Guangdong, Hong Kong and Macao Development Studies, Sun Yat-sen University.

We would like to express our sincere appreciation for several research assistants, including Tianzhu Nie, Jennifer Hung, Brian Ho, and Jingyin Chia at the Hong Kong University of Science and Technology, ZUO Yihang and LIN

Kuo at the Chinese University of Hong Kong, Shenzhen, and LI Yujie at the Chinese University of Hong Kong, Shatin.

Some materials in this book were presented at several institutions, including the Faculty of Social Science at the Chinese University of Hong Kong Shatin, Division of Social Science at the Hong Kong University of Science and Technology, the Department of Political Science at the National Taiwan University, School of Humanities and Social Science at the Chinese University of Hong Kong Shenzhen, and School of Government at Sun Yat-sen University. We would like to thank the participants at these institutions for their helpful comments and suggestions.

The anonymous reviewers at the Oxford University Press made many helpful comments and suggestions that have been incorporated in the manuscript. The authors would also like to express their appreciation for David McBride, Editor in Chief, Social Sciences, Oxford University Press, for his suggestions and support during the review process.

Wenfang Tang
Ying Xia
New Territories, Hong Kong, 2025

1
The Study of Political Culture

Political culture can provide answers to some seemingly puzzling questions. For example, why do people still rebel when their basic needs in life are being met? Why do some people pay more attention to the legal procedure regardless of the outcome, while others pay more attention to the outcome regardless of the procedure? Why do people in some societies have higher expectations of their governments to provide public services, while people in other societies would rather rely on their own efforts? Why are social trust and political confidence so much lower in some democracies than in authoritarian societies? Why do some people have more tolerance of different political views than others? These questions are related to the different dimensions of political culture.

Although the popularity of the concept of political culture has waxed and waned since Gabriel Almond's 1956 classic essay "Comparative Political Systems,"[1] it has been one of the featured concepts in the field of political science. The purpose of this chapter is to develop a general guideline in the quantitative study of political culture. The reader is reminded that the materials in this chapter include but are not limited to the political culture in Hong Kong. It is intended to embed Hong Kong in a comprehensive and comparative framework.

What Is Political Culture?

Political culture is a subfield of political science. It is about how the dominant ideology in a society is reflected in the values, attitudes, and behavior of its members and in their ways of interacting with political institutions.[2] The term "ideology" is used in a broad sense. It includes specific social science theories such as democracy, capitalism, communism, socialism, authoritarianism, populism, as well as broadly defined civilizations, such as liberalism, Confucianism, and Islamism, among others.[3] Political institutions, which are

---

[1] Almond 1956.
[2] Almond and Verba 1963; Pye 1991.
[3] Huntington 1996.

shaped under the influence of the dominant ideology, include government agencies, electoral systems, legal systems, social organizations, and other channels for citizens to interact with and influence government decision-making, such as voting, contacting government offices, informal ties with government officials, social media posts, petitions, and protests.[4] The dominant mode of political participation or interaction reflects the dominant political culture.

The study of political culture relies on knowledge about ideology and political institutions, but the focus of political culture is not about ideologies and political institutions per se. It is about the societal consequences of ideologies and institutions. It is about how these ideologies and institutions are perceived by ordinary people. Political theorists made great contributions in describing and interpreting the philosophical meaning of ideologies and the likely function of political institutional designs.[5] The study of political culture, on the other hand, pays more attention to people's perception. It believes that ultimately ordinary people's perception provides an equally if not more accurate description of the dominant ideologies and political institutions in their society. The continuation of an ideology and political system depends on whether people support them. Without popular acceptance, government can lose support, political institutions can become unstable, and political crisis will follow, which will be discussed further below.

Gabriel Almond's 1956 article "Comparative Political Systems" is usually credited with introducing the concept of political culture into the study of politics.[6] In that article, Almond defines political culture as a "particular pattern of orientation to political action" and orientations as "attitudes towards politics." Almond and Verba further defined political culture in *The Civic Culture* as "the political system as internalized in the cognitions, feelings, and evaluations of its population."[7] Based on this definition, the authors of *The Civic Culture* categorize political culture as parochial, subject, and participant. A participant-based political culture can qualify to be a civic culture that sustains the political stability in a Western-style liberal democratic society. The civic culture must include, among other things, national pride, equal treatment by the legal system, freedom to voice political opinions, voluntary voting, tolerance of opposing opinions, political activism, sense of political efficacy, and civic cooperation and trust. In their study completed in the early 1960s, Almond and Verba found more civic culture in Britain and the US than

---

[4] Verba, Nie, and Kim 1978.
[5] Freeden 1996; McLellan 1986; Rothstein 1998.
[6] Almond 1956: 396.
[7] Almond and Verba 1963: 13–14.

in Germany, Italy, and Mexico, and they concluded that civic culture is the reason for better democratic governance in the UK and the US.

Political culture has been closely linked to explaining different types of political systems. In addition to how civic political culture contributes to the smooth functioning of democratic political systems,[8] other studies have demonstrated how a "mass society" political culture encouraged the rise of Nazi Germany[9] and how Confucian culture contributed to the development of Asian authoritarianism and state capitalism by focusing on the role of the state and by encouraging social hierarchy and political obedience.[10] Yet other studies found that economic modernization could promote an anti-authoritarian political culture and lead to democratic transition in non-liberal societies.[11] In later years, some studies[12] found the rise of postmaterialist political culture represented by individualism, equality of sexual orientation, and environmentalism, among other things, in advanced industrial societies. Others showed that such postmaterialist political culture has led to the fragmentation of American society and caused detrimental effects on social trust and cooperation and the smooth functioning of democratic institutions.[13]

In the post-globalization era, a new trend of political culture, namely populist authoritarianism, has been on the rise in Asia, North America, Latin America, and Europe. This new trend of political culture is characterized as anti-elitism, anti-institutionalism, direct interaction between the top leadership and society, strong feelings of nationalism, government responsiveness, and strong regime support.[14] In China, populist authoritarianism was witnessed under Xi Jinping who revived the Maoist concept of "mass line" as a tool of direct political mobilization.[15] In the US, Donald Trump's successful election campaigns triggered a strong rise of populist authoritarianism when he tried to directly reach his voters by bypassing the established political institutions.[16] In Europe, the so-called right-wing political parties try to gain popular support by waving nationalist flags, shouting anti-immigration slogans, and overwriting the existing state welfare policies and their institutions.[17] In Hong Kong, during the anti-extradition movement, Western governments reached the street protesters with their repeated calls for action against China

---

[8] Putnam, Leonardi, and Nonetti 1994; Verba, Kay, and Henry 1995.
[9] Berman 1997; Kornhauser 1960.
[10] E.g., Huang 2024; Huntington 1996.
[11] Inglehart and Baker 2000; Inkeles and Smith 1974.
[12] E.g., Inglehart 1990.
[13] Putnam 2000.
[14] Adler et al. 2023; Morelock 2018.
[15] Tang 2016.
[16] Weyland and Madrid 2019.
[17] Fitzgerald 2018.

and through local agents and even diplomats (Chapter 5). Some people think that populist authoritarianism has the tendency of returning to fascism.[18] Others argue that it is a return to democracy by mobilizing ordinary people to be involved in government decision-making, and it is a slap in the face of the arrogant political elites.[19]

Political culture is an ongoing subject as societies are evolving and being replaced by new generations who are raised in the constantly changing technological, global, economic, social, and political environments. Any study of political culture is only a snapshot of a society or at best the result of historic developments in that society. It requires continuing scholarly efforts to understand the ever-emerging new trends in a society and their social and political consequences.

How to Measure Political Culture?

Political culture can be studied qualitatively and through historical archives, such as Theda Skocpol's comparative study of why revolutions took place in France, Russia, and China,[20] and Benedict Anderson's study of nationalism as imagined communities.[21] These studies are intellectual attempts to understand how certain aspects of political culture, such as rebellious political behavior and national identity, are formed through historical events.

In addition to historical, archival, and qualitative methods, another approach to studying political culture is quantitative. One example of the quantitative approach is public opinion surveys.[22] In conducting public opinion surveys, the researcher first designs a questionnaire including a series of questions related to various dimensions of political culture (to be discussed below). After face-to-face or increasingly popular online interviews, the researcher would then assign numeric values to the respondents' answers based on their degrees of agreement or disagreement with the questions. For example, 1 is assigned as strongly disagree, 2 as disagree, 3 as agree, and 4 as strongly agree. The researcher will use the quantitative data to conduct statistical analysis and determine the characteristics of the political culture in a given society.

One common criticism of the quantitative approach is that it is only skin deep; it does not reveal the complexity between different phenomena. One of

[18] Finchelstein 2022.
[19] Liddiard 2019.
[20] Skocpol 1979.
[21] Anderson 2016.
[22] Almond and Verba 1963.

the most important advantages of the quantitative approach, however, is that it allows cross-country and cross-society comparisons of political cultures because similar survey questions can be asked and their answers can be compared in different societies. In addition, even if the numeric values based on people's attitude are by no means as precise as in engineering, they nevertheless provide categorically measurable information that qualitative methods cannot.

While political culture has been variously defined, its conceptual core is widely shared by different understandings. On one hand, political culture is fundamentally the subjective reflection of two major sets of relationship—the relationship between the individual citizen and the political system as a whole—and the relationship between fellow citizens under a particular political configuration. On the other hand, political culture can be observed from both people's self-reported political orientation and the political behavior they are actually practicing.

Below are nine examples of the indicators or measures of political culture that have been widely used by researchers: social and political tolerance, social trust, political trust, modes of political participation and political activism, political efficacy, political identity and nationalism, postmaterialism, individualism, and sense of social justice. These popularly used measurements are a result of the operationalization of the concept of political culture.

Social and Political Tolerance

The level of social and political tolerance is one measure of political culture in a society. The conventional view holds that social and political tolerance is necessary for civic culture and democracy.[23] Survey questions related to such tolerance have been developed by survey researchers. For example, in the seventh wave of the World Values Survey, the respondents were asked if they would like to have certain people as their neighbors, including drug addicts, people of a different race, people who have AIDS, immigrants/foreign workers, homosexuals, people of a different religion, heavy drinkers, unmarried couples living together, and people who speak a different language.[24]

---

[23] Gibson 2009.
[24] See World Values Survey (WVS): WVS-7 Master Questionnaire 2017–2020, Q18–Q26, p. 5, https://www.worldvaluessurvey.org/WVSDocumentationWV7.jsp.

These items can be examined individually according to the researcher's interests, or they can be combined into one or several indices, measuring the total or different aspects of social and political tolerance in a society.

In addition to the standard questions in cross-regional surveys, researchers can develop their own measures of social and political tolerance. For example, in the 2021 Hong Kong Political Culture Survey (see Chapter 2 for details), the respondents were asked if they would do business with people holding different political views. The anti-China respondents were much less willing to do so than the pro-China respondents, suggesting a lack of political tolerance in the anti-China camp (see Chapter 5).

Social Trust

Social trust is another necessary component of political culture. In the civic culture literature, interpersonal trust promotes social capital, which is necessary for the smooth functioning of democratic political systems because it allows people to cooperate with each other and to cast their vote and trust that the elected officials will protect the voters' interests.[25]

Many surveys today continue to use the same measure of general social trust from Almond and Verba's 1963 study: Generally speaking, would you say that most people can be trusted or that you need to be very careful in dealing with people?[26], labor unions, the police, the courts, the government, political parties, parliament, civil service, universities, elections, major companies, banks, environmental organizations, women's organizations, and charitable or humanitarian organizations.[27]

In addition, others have developed more measures of political trust by asking people's opinion about their political leaders and about governments at different levels, including central, provincial, county, urban district, and village governments.[28] In China, for example, political trust in central government was found significantly higher than in local governments.[29] In contrast, in the 2021 Hong Kong Political Culture Survey, political trust in local political institutions was much higher than in the central government (Chapter 4).

---

[25] Almond and Verba 1963.
[26] Hu Fu Center for East Asia Democratic Studies 2023; National Survey Research Center 2023; NORC 2023; see Wenfang Tang, Hong Kong Political Culture Survey 2021 in this book.
[27] See WVS-7 Master Questionnaire 2017–2020, Q64–Q81, p. 7.
[28] National Survey Research Center 2023.
[29] Dickson et al. 2016.

Modes of Political Participation and Political Activism

The modes of political participation represent the channels through which people take action when they try to influence government decision making.[30] These channels may include voting; contacting government officials or offices; using the media or the courts; petitioning; protesting; or simply taking no action. Different modes of participation suggest different political cultures. For example, the dominant mode may be voting in one society but protesting in another, representing very different ways of political problem-solving.

Political participation is easy to measure when it takes the form of voting because it is a relatively popular behavior. When a political behavior is relatively rare, such as protesting, it becomes difficult to detect such behavior in public opinion surveys because very few people take such action, and when they do, they do so only occasionally. Sometimes only a handful of survey respondents are protesters in a sample of several thousand respondents, making it difficult to conduct further statistical analysis.

To solve the problem of rare political behavior, some researchers propose asking hypothetical questions. Instead of asking people if they have taken a certain action, the researcher would ask them if they would take such action if they felt unhappy with their government. For example, in the 2021 Hong Kong Political Culture Survey, the respondents were asked what would be the first political action they would take if they felt mistreated by the government and the second and the third actions if their problems were not solved. Interestingly, very few Hong Kong respondents would protest as their first choice, but many more of them would do so if their problems were not solved, suggesting a contentious political culture in Hong Kong society (see Chapter 5).

Political participation is closely related to political activism. A high level of political participation suggests a high level of political activism. Some studies show that political activism is high in Western liberal democratic political culture, or civic culture.[31] Other studies find it high in non-Western societies like China.[32] One common way to measure political activism is a survey question about one's political interest, i.e., how interested are you in politics?

---

[30] Verba, Nie, and Kim 1978.
[31] Almond and Verba 1963.
[32] Chen 2004.

Political Efficacy

Closely related to political participation is political efficacy, which is another dimension of political culture. Political efficacy means the feeling of effectiveness of the individual's political action or the effectiveness of the political institutions that are designed to safeguard their interests. Political efficacy is important because it is the precondition for political participation. Often people participate only if they think that their participation is effective. Some civic culture scholars think that in a democratic system, people may not feel the need to participate in politics as long as they believe that their participation would make a difference.[33]

One way to measure political efficacy is by looking at the number of people who would not take political action when they feel they are being mistreated by their government, as described above about the possible channels of political participation. If the number of respondents who would not take action is large, it may suggest a lack of political activism and a low level of political efficacy. In contrast, when the percentage of no action takers is low, it may indicate a high level of political activism (Chapter 5).

Political efficacy can be further defined as internal efficacy and external efficacy.[34] Internal efficacy means people's feeling about their ability to influence government decision-making through their own actions. External efficacy is people's belief that political institutions in their societies are capable of functioning based on their best interests. Examples of commonly used survey questions include "ordinary people like us can influence government decision-making as long as we voice our opinion," and "we should let the government make decisions for our country." The first question may be a measure of internal efficacy, and the second question is more about external efficacy.

Political Identity and Nationalism

Political identity is another commonly studied dimension of political culture. It measures people's feelings about the political entity they live in or associate with. The most obvious such identity is the nation-state. In this sense, political identity and nationalism are sometimes used interchangeably. One set of questions commonly used is in the National Identity Survey conducted by the International Social Survey Programme (ISSP).[35] These questions include

---

[33] Arts, Hagenaars, and Halman 2003; Dekker and Uslaner 2001.
[34] OECD 2021.
[35] ISSP Research Group 2015.

the following: (1) I would rather be a citizen of my country than of any other country. (2) The world would be a better place if other countries were more like my country. (3) My country is a better country than most other countries. (4) It makes me proud when my country does well in international sports. The World Values Survey added another question about people's willingness to fight for their country: "Of course, we all hope that there will not be another war, but if it were to come to that, would you be willing to fight for your country?"[36] Together these questions measure nationalism or national identity.

In addition to the nation-state, political identity can be further defined as political partisanship, religious affiliation, or ethnic and regional identity. For example, in the World Values Survey, respondents were asked about their feelings of belonging to their continent, their country, their region, and their ethnic group(s).[37] Other times survey researchers try to measure political identity by xenophobia, which is about people's attitude toward immigration or foreigners.[38].

The 2021 Hong Kong Political Culture Survey examines several subdimensions of political identity among Hong Kong residents. These subdimensions include cultural and political identity, public images of selected countries and regions, political orientation toward Mainland China, local ethnic identity, East/West value preferences, and intention of immigration. The findings suggest a strong identity with traditional Chinese culture but a lukewarm feeling toward the West and a strong resentment toward Mainland China (see Chapter 3).

Postmaterialism

Postmaterialism is a relatively new trend in studying political culture, and it was popularized by the late Ronald Inglehart.[39] It is a consequence of sustained economic development and industrialization.[40] It states that when people's basic needs in life are satisfied, they begin to think about higher level needs, such as individual political rights, challenging the political establishment, decentralized community oriented social networking,

---

[36] See WVS-7 Master Questionnaire 2017–2020, Q151, p. 13.
[37] See World Values Survey: WVS-4 2000 Questionnaire, V39–V53, pp. 4–5, https://www.worldvaluessurvey.org/WVSDocumentationWV4.jsp.
[38] See WVS-7 Master Questionnaire 2017–2020, Q122–Q126, p. 11.
[39] Inglehart and Welzel 2001.
[40] Inkeles and Smith 1974.

environmentalism, feminism, and alternative sexual orientations, among other things.

Public opinion surveys measure postmaterialism by asking people's attitudes about the above questions. In addition, the World Values Survey includes questions regarding people's perception of their country's national priorities: "In your opinion, which is the most important in your country: 1) A stable economy, 2) Progress toward a less impersonal and more humane society; 3) Progress toward a society in which ideas count more than money; 4) The fight against crime."[41] (1) and (4) suggest more materialist values, while (2) and (3) indicate postmaterialist values.

Some studies show that postmaterialism played a negative role in some liberal democratic societies, such as the US, because it tends to fragment a society by focusing on the interests of individuals and small groups, making political mobilization very difficult.[42] Others think postmaterialism may contribute to a "silent revolution" that would make authoritarian societies more democratic.[43]

Relationship Between the Individual and the State

The relationship between the individual and the state is another dimension of political culture. Some societies focus more on the individual by prioritizing individual interests over group interests. Other societies tend to emphasize group interests over individual rights.[44]

People's attitude toward government surveillance may indicate their understanding of the boundary between individual citizens and the society. In the World Values Survey,[45] for example, the respondents were asked to report their support for the following government policies: (1) Keep people under video surveillance in public areas; (2) monitor all emails and any other information exchanged on the internet; and (3) collect information about anyone living in this country without their knowledge. The first question is about government surveillance in public spaces, and the second and third questions are about government surveillance in private spaces.

The conventional view suggests that people living in liberal democracies are more aware of their individual rights and take their privacy more seriously

---

[41] See WVS-7 Master Questionnaire 2017–2020, Q156–Q157, p. 12.
[42] Putnam 2000.
[43] Chen, Huhe, and Yan 2022.
[44] Hofstede 1980.
[45] See WVS-7 Master Questionnaire 2017–2020, Q196–Q198, p. 14.

than those in non-liberal democracies.[46] Interestingly, Chinese respondents in the seventh World Values Survey demonstrated a strong support for government surveillance in public spaces for public safety but significantly less support for private space surveillance.[47] This finding suggests that the Chinese respondents living in a non-Western society seem to be equally aware of their privacy and individual rights.[48]

Another frequently used measure of individual versus the state is welfare policy support. Some societies are more likely to encourage individual effort while allowing those who are less capable to fall behind. Other societies tend to provide more welfare support for their citizens by allowing the government to collect more taxes and provide more subsidies. Finally, people's attitude toward crime control versus individual freedom can also be used to measure individualism and group interest.[49] Crime control requires more government effort, but it can potentially curb individual freedom.

Sense of Social Justice

People living under different political cultures develop different attitudes toward justice. One such example is public support for procedural or substantive justice in legal issues. Those in favor of following the correct legal procedures are less concerned about the substantive outcome of a legal trial. Others think that paying too much attention to following legal procedures may let a guilty person free.[50]

Another example related to procedure is about the selection of political leaders. In some political cultures the electoral procedure is very important in determining who should be the leader. In other societies, individual ability is more important in leadership selection, regardless of the specific procedure. Public support for either of these two options is often used in public opinion surveys.[51]

The third example of the sense of justice is related to the public attitude toward income inequality. Some political cultures are more acceptable of income inequality. Others tend to think it is unjust to have a large income gap

---

[46] Westin 1966.
[47] World Value Survey Association 2023.
[48] Tang 2024.
[49] See WVS-7 Master Questionnaire 2017–2020, Q149–Q151, p. 11.
[50] See 2004 China Legal Survey quoted in Tang 2009.
[51] See WVS-7 Master Questionnaire 2017–2020, Q235–Q239, p. 16.

and government action is required to collect taxes and redistribute income by providing subsidies for the poor.[52]

In short, the above are some examples of different dimensions of political culture. They can be studied individually or together. Since they can be measured quantitatively and by the same survey questions in different societies, political cultures can be studied more precisely than with qualitative and archival information, and they can be compared cross-nationally and over time.

How Does Political Culture Change?

Political cultures are maintained, and new trends are developed in societies through multiple channels. These channels can be divided into two groups—environmental conditions and demographic factors.

Environmental Conditions

Environmental conditions include political institutional design, social and economic development, traditional cultural values and practices, technological development, and so on. These conditions can play a powerful role in shaping people's political attitudes and behaviors.

The most obvious environmental factor is the political system people live in. A political system is represented by the political institutions and the rules, policies, regulations, and laws it develops. Understanding the nature of these institutions and their rules can provide clues to why people think and behave in a given way in their political life.

One of the most popular measures of political institutional environment is by Freedom House. It publishes annual reports assessing the degrees of freedom and democracy around the world by assigning a score to each country or region.[53] It determines the scores by examining if the political institutions and the rules and policies protect people's political rights and civil liberties in these societies. Political rights are defined as free and fair elections; political party competitiveness; public involvement in political decision-making; and the representativeness, integrity, and accountability of the government. Civil liberties include freedom of expression and belief, freedom of association, rule of law, individual autonomy, individual freedom to travel and to own

---

[52] See WVS-7 Master Questionnaire 2017–2020, MN5–MN9, p. 27.
[53] Freedom House 2023.

property, and social justice and minority rights. Together these items form a Freedom House index that measures the political environment that can be used to study how it helps develop certain values, attitudes, and behavior among the citizens in a society.

The second environmental factor is socioeconomic development. As the above discussion of postmaterialism suggests, economic development and industrialization promote people's awareness of needs beyond their immediate everyday survival such as food and lodging. The most common indicator for socioeconomic development is a living standard measured by a country's or society's per capita income. Sometimes researchers also use the pace of economic growth in a given time frame in a society as another measure of socioeconomic development and compare the difference in political attitudes among high-growth and low-growth societies. Other commonly used measures are social indicators such as healthcare, life expectancy, infant mortality, average level of education, status of women, income gap, poverty ratio, and so on. Finally, geographic location in the world or within a country or region is often included when examining a political culture. One difficulty of geographic location is its meaning. Many researchers correctly use location to measure regional socioeconomic development, but location can also mean differences in local cultural practices, which will be discussed below.

The third environmental factor shaping political values and behavior is traditional cultural practices. Studies have shown that different civilizations are associated with different political cultures.[54] For example, Protestantism is related to the development of individualism.[55] Latin American revolution theology is associated with the anti-imperialist social movements in the region in the 1960s.[56] Catholicism is sometimes described as politically conservative in the US.[57] Islamism is sometimes coupled with political violence.[58] Confucianism is described as the reason for political obedience and the development of authoritarianism.[59] To understand the consequences of these cultural traditions, it is necessary to examine and compare the different measures of political culture described in the previous section, say, protest behavior, among survey respondents in societies carrying these different cultural traditions.

The final environmental factor is technology. Technology has played an important role not only in economic development but also in people's social

---

[54] Huntington 1993a and 1996; Inglehart and Welzel 2001.
[55] Weber 2013.
[56] Zolov 2014.
[57] Greeley 1977.
[58] Lia and Kjøk 2001.
[59] Watkins and Biggs 2001.

and political lives. In the 21st century, no other technological innovation can surpass the development of digital technology and artificial intelligence in profoundly changing the way people live. Digital technology has revolutionized information gathering, processing, and distribution, and making them much faster, much more efficient, in much larger quantities, and with much more diverse sources. Traditional political mobilization based on face-to-face interaction carried out by political party organizations has been replaced by online social networking. Digital technology has facilitated the public's ability to voice their opinion more easily and compelled the government to respond to public opinion more promptly. Social scientists need to pay sufficient attention to how new technologies shape people's political attitudes and behaviors.

Individual Characteristics

In addition to the environmental factors discussed above, political culture can also be influenced by demographic and socioeconomic characteristics at the individual level. The most commonly used variables are age, gender, education, occupation, income, marital status, family background, language and dialect, religious background, media consumption, and political party affiliation.

Age is one of the most important factors in shaping individual political attitude and behavior. Younger generations are more open to new ideas and new technologies, and they tend to be more politically radical and confrontational. Age cohorts also carry the social and political characteristics in which they grow up. For example, people who grew up in the 1960s antiwar culture in the US continue to hold such political attitude even when they get older.[60]

Gender difference may lead to different political attitude and behavior. In some traditional societies, women may be less politically assertive and less radical. They tend to be more politically conservative. In other societies with more government effort at promoting gender equality, women may be more politically assertive, particularly regarding issues related to the treatment of women, such as gender equality in healthcare, education, and employment.

Education can be a double-edged sword. It can open up people's perception by providing more information and new ideas, causing them to develop regime-challenging attitudes and behaviors. On the other hand, education is an instrument of the government through which ideological indoctrination is

---

[60] Schreiber 1976.

carried out, encouraging people to develop more regime-supporting attitudes and behaviors.

People working in different occupations may develop different values and attitudes. For example, government employees may be more pro-government. People in the financial sector may be against government intervention in economy. Farmers in some societies tend to be more conservative such as in France,[61] but they can be more radical and rebellious in other societies such as in China in the first half of the 20th century.[62]

Income may lead to different political attitudes and behaviors. For example, high-income earners may be more politically conservative and more pro-government because they want political stability and the government to protect their wealth. It should be noted that individual income should be treated separately from socioeconomic development in a society. High-income earners can live in a low-income society, and low-income earners can exist in a highly developed economy.

Marital status sometimes can also make a difference in people's social and political attitudes and behaviors. Marriage means family responsibilities and increased need for government services, which may make people more supportive of the government's welfare policies and increases in taxation. Marriage may make people feel more need for social stability and less supportive of any radical political change.

Family background means one's parental socioeconomic status. Family is one of the most important venues of political socialization in addition to education and career. The family environment, including parental education, occupation, income, and other factors, provides important ways for one to learn about society and politics at young age. Dinner table conversations between parents can leave long-lasting impact on one's attitude toward the government and its policies in one's later life.

Language can shape political culture. For example, collective memory based on a written language plays a crucial role in formulating national identity in Benedict Anderson's *Imagined Community*.[63] Spoken language often leads to different political attitudes. In Hong Kong, Cantonese speakers demonstrated significantly more anti-China sentiment than Mandarin speakers in the 2021 Hong Kong Political Culture Survey (see Chapter 3). In China, Mandarin speakers showed more regime support than speakers of the local dialects.[64]

---

[61] Scoones et al. 2018.
[62] Mao 1965.
[63] Anderson 2016.
[64] Hu 2020.

Religion is another channel of political socialization through which people develop norms in dealing with the outside world. In addition to religious denomination described above as an environmental factor, the intensity of one's religiosity can be more easily measured at the individual level through survey questions such as one's frequency of religious practice. Religious denomination sometimes needs to be studied together with the larger religious environment in a society. For example, a study found that Christianity and Islamism in China carry characteristics of traditional Chinese practices such as ancestor worship.[65]

Media consumption is a way of information dissemination and political mobilization. All governments throughout the world try to spread their political messages and gain popular support through media, whether or not they own or control the media. It is easy to see how governments own and control media in some non-liberal democracies, but governments in liberal democracies are also savvy about media manipulation through information control and through media self-censorship.[66] With the rise of digital technology, social media has become an alternative for information transmission and political mobilization. Studies have found that traditional media users and social media users tend to develop different political attitudes.[67]

Finally, political party affiliation can play a role in formulating one's political attitudes and behaviors. Political parties are important instruments for political mobilization. They recruit party members by indoctrinating them with party ideology and mobilize ordinary citizens to participate in politics activities such as voting and government-sponsored campaigns. In China, membership in the Chinese Communist Party is necessary for one's career advancement.[68]

In sum, the above environmental and individual factors can all affect people's attitudes toward the different dimensions of political culture, including people in Hong Kong. Many researchers have included as many of them as possible as independent variables in their multivariate statistical analysis. To consider both environmental and individual factors, or macro and micro conditions in the same analysis, researchers often use multilevel regression analysis.

Sometimes researchers can gain interesting and unexpected insight by considering the interaction between two variables. For example, when region and

---

[65] Tang 2014.
[66] Khan 2017.
[67] Gainous, Abbott, and Wagner 2019.
[68] Tang and Lin 2020.

gender were examined separately, Mainland Chinese showed more sexist attitudes than Taiwanese respondents, and older respondents in both regions were more sexist because they experienced a more traditional upbringing. Yet when the interaction effect of age and gender was examined in the two societies, older Mainland female respondents showed much less sexism than their Taiwanese counterparts, suggesting the effect of the egalitarian political socialization in China during the Cultural Revolution in the 1960s.[69]

Measurement Errors

In the comparative study of political culture based on survey data, sometimes researchers can make mistakes by creating measurement errors. A measurement error is when the quantitative data do not measure the intended concept. Below are some examples.

One of the most difficult tasks in survey research is to overcome the problem of social desirability. That is, survey respondents hide their true attitudes due to their desire to be politically correct in front of the interviewer. For example, in a survey a white American respondent may hide their true feelings about black people if the interviewer is black. Other socially and politically sensitive survey questions include drug use, sexual behavior, bribery, anti-establishment feelings, and so on.

Various attempts have been made to solve the problem of social desirability. One such attempt is list experiment.[70] This is a technique in which the respondent is made to feel safe to answer sensitive questions truthfully because the interviewer does not know what the answer is. The researcher can estimate the answer through statistical analysis after the survey. This is the technique used in the 2021 Hong Kong Political Culture Survey. By embedding eight list experiments in the questionnaire and with additional statistical weighting methods, the survey was able to detect a large amount of social desirability related to sensitive questions (Chapter 2), and this technique is applied to the statistical analysis in other chapters of this book.

Another example of measurement error is the democracy and freedom scores developed by Freedom House.[71] Freedom House assigns these scores based on whether political institutions and the related policies meet the

---

[69] Liu and Tang 2020.
[70] Kuklinski, Cobb, and Gilens 1997 and Kuklinski, Sniderman, et al. 1997.
[71] See Freedom House, *Countries and territories*, https://freedomhouse.org/countries/nations-transit/scores.

standards of Western liberal democracy. Yet when examining people's feelings about freedom and democracy in the World Values Survey, there is no relationship between Freedom Housing's ratings and people's feelings. In some societies with low Freedom House scores, people's feelings about democracy and freedom are much higher. In contrast, people living in societies with high Freedom House scores often feel not that free.[72] This gap suggests that Freedom House's rankings do not measure the true levels of freedom and democracy perceived by people living in these societies.

The third example of measurement error is about civil society. In the standard survey questions widely used in cross-national surveys such as the World Values Survey and the Barometer Surveys, respondents are typically asked if they belong to a set of voluntary social organizations, such as a church or religious organization; sport or recreational organization; art, music, or educational organization; labor union; political party; environmental organization; professional association; humanitarian or charitable organization; consumer organization; self-help group; mutual aid group; or women's group. In the Western political science literature, membership in these organizations suggests a lively civil society that serves as a buffer zone between the state and society.[73] In a non-Western society, there is little evidence of such group membership, yet studies have found that local interest groups are actively negotiating with their governments for policy favors, including environmental groups, migrant groups, HIV/AIDS groups, labor groups, and religious groups, among others.[74] Additional survey questions are needed to capture such dynamics of "civil society" in non-Western societies.

The final example of measurement error regards religiosity. Standard survey questions in the existing cross-national surveys typically ask about people's religious beliefs and behavior based on Western practices of institutionalized religion, such as frequency of visiting a church, frequency of praying, belief in God, and people's religious denomination. These questions can measure systematic religiosity, but they miss diffuse religiosity. In China, for example, standard survey questions reveal that more than 90% of the population are atheists, yet there is a temple on the corner of every street as described by one study,[75] and more than 70% of people engage in diffuse but non-institutional religious practices such as ancestor worship and geomancy,

---

[72] Tang and Yu 2015.
[73] Evers 1995.
[74] Xu 2021; Kennedy and Shi 2019.
[75] Yang 2020.

or feng shui.⁷⁶ Again, new survey questions need to be developed to avoid such measurement error.

Why Does Political Culture Matter?

In Huntington's book *The Clash of Civilizations and the Remaking of the World Order*,⁷⁷ the author predicted major conflicts between civilizations in the post–Cold War era because of the fundamental differences between Western liberal democratic cultures and the rest of the world, such as Islamism, Confucianism, the Russian Orthodox Church, and so on. In particular, this view holds that the noble principles held by the Western world such as democracy, freedom, and human rights are not respected in other political cultures. People holding this view often try to prove their point by citing the gap in the Freedom House scores between the West and the rest of the world. This dichotomous view of the West versus the Rest is one of the reasons for the conflicts in today's world.

Yet studying political culture based on public opinion surveys can contribute to the reduction of conflicts. Public opinion surveys provide a more realistic picture of the political culture in a society. In the real world, the perception gap is by far narrower than postulated by Huntington. For example, in China, which is not a standard Western-style liberal democracy, people are just as satisfied with their country's democracy, freedom, and human rights. The Chinese survey respondents also demonstrate a high level of social trust, and their confidence in their political institutions is among the highest in the world.⁷⁸ If the political cultures are not as black and white as feared by those who see the world as the West versus the Rest, military conflicts aimed at promoting one's values are no longer necessary.

The second reason why political culture matters is that it is important for governance. Understanding public expectations facilitates government decision-making, which in turn can promote a more regime-supporting political cultural environment. A regime-friendly political culture can serve as a healthy lubricant between the government and society. It is political capital that any government wants to have.

The third reason that political culture is worth studying is that it may provide clues for regime change. In the conventional view, political institutions

---

⁷⁶ Tang 2014.
⁷⁷ Huntington 1996.
⁷⁸ See various waves of WVS at https://www.worldvaluessurvey.org/WVSDocumentationWVL.jsp.

shape individual attitudes and behaviors.[79] For example, some people think that abolishing the death penalty may encourage violent crimes. Yet political culture may not always mirror political institutions. Sometimes public expectations reflected in a political culture can put pressure on institutions or even encourage regime change. For example, public resentment of immigration is partially responsible for the elections of populist leaders in the US and Europe.

Studying Political Culture of Hong Kong in the Postcolonial Era

Based on the general interest in political culture, this book attempts to develop existing theories of political culture by taking the unique case of the formation of Hong Kong's political culture after its return to China from British colonizers in 1997. While mainstream studies of political culture have focused on the nation-state with a stable central authority,[80] the case of Hong Kong has sparked theoretical interest in exploring the formation of political culture in a political system without a single central authority. In 1997, Hong Kong was formally returned to China, bringing an end to the century-long British colonial rule. However, the Chinese central authority didn't directly intervene in the local politics of Hong Kong but introduced a new governance structure called "One Country, Two Systems." Under this structure, although Hong Kong is part of China, it practices a political, economic, and social system different from that of the Mainland. Hong Kong was given a great deal of room for autonomy.

However, this autonomy has become the source of a vacuum in political authority, making it difficult for Hong Kong to develop a stable political culture that adapts to the new political framework since the handover. Hong Kong was caught between the legacy of the British colonial power and the rising Chinese empire. Neither of these two powers thinks very highly of the other. This tension is contagious. Hong Kong society is polarized, contentious, and emotionally charged with a high level of social and political distrust and discontent.

The level of political distrust (Chapter 4) and political activism (Chapter 5) against the central government of China and the Hong Kong local government had been rising rapidly since Hong Kong's reunification with China and reached its peak in the summer of 2019 when the anti-extradition bill

---

[79] March and Olsen 1983.
[80] Pateman 1971.

movements took place. The rising trend of political activism by and even political radicalism of the local society since the handover is surprising to some observers because Hong Kong used to be perceived as a "politically indifferent" society before its reunification with China.[81] One may expect that the end of the British rule and the reunion of Hong Kong with China would foster Hong Kong people's sense of belonging to the nation-state and encourage them to be more engaged with the national development movements. What happened afterward, however, seems to be the opposite.

Local identity has been on the rise (Chapter 3), of which the most radical segment defines Hong Kong as an independent region beyond China's sovereignty.[82] Instead of learning how to belong to the nation,[83] local society in the postcolonial era struggled to keep its distance from China and more recently even tried to separate from it.[84] Anger, despair, and anti-China sentiment grew in the social movements,[85] and the local government was incapable of comforting and pleasing the crowds.[86] This accelerating tension reached its peak in the summer of 2019 when an individual criminal case accidentally developed into the most chaotic and long-lasting social uprising in the contemporary history of Hong Kong (Chapter 5). Confrontations on the streets between angry protestors and the police force lasted for more than six months. The authority of the local government was so drastically eroded that the situation was on the brink of anarchy.

The central government eventually stepped in soon after the months-long unrest was finally silenced by the sudden outbreak of Covid-19 in early 2020. On June 30, 2020, China's top legislature passed the new National Security Law for Hong Kong that came into effect just before midnight on the same day, bypassing Hong Kong's local legislature. The law gives the central and local governments extensive powers to oversee and manage political activism in the territory, as well as the development of social organizations, media, and local schools. Further steps were taken by the central government to reshape multiple sectors and institutions in Hong Kong, including a controversial electoral reform law in March 2021 that ensured Beijing's control of the legislative branch (Chapters 4 and 5).

Against this background and one year after the enactment of National Security Law, we conducted the 2021 Hong Kong Political Culture Survey in Hong

---

[81] Hoadley 1970.
[82] Kwong 2016.
[83] Ku 2009.
[84] Tang, Hung, and Ho 2022.
[85] Ma 2015.
[86] Kuo 2019.

Kong, which is the empirical backbone of this book. The facts of almost unrestricted political activism followed by sudden tight control under the National Security Law set a perfect scenario of quasi-natural experiments. It provides us with a lens to look into the changing dynamics of Hong Kong's political culture during this unusual political stage. One of the main intentions of our survey is to test the true political orientations of the Hong Kong people who might be hiding their anger and pride in fear of the National Security Law.

***

In summary, this chapter describes political culture as individual perceptions about the ideology and political institutions in a given society, including civic culture, postmaterialism, postcolonialism, and populist authoritarianism, among others. It suggests different dimensions of political culture, including social and political tolerance, social trust, political trust, political participation, political efficacy, political identity, postmodern values, individualism, and a sense of justice. It discusses the environmental and individual factors that contribute to the development and change of political culture in a society. Further, it warns of the danger of measurement errors in studying political cultures, including the problem of social desirability, Freedom House scores that discount public opinion, and relying exclusively on Western concepts to measure interest group participation and religiosity. Finally, the chapter discusses how studying popular political culture can help reduce conflict between societies by identifying common human values and behavior. While many aspects of this chapter are related to the study of political culture in Hong Kong, the chapter also intends to provide a general framework in which Hong Kong can be examined and compared with other political cultures.

2
Detecting Social Desirability in Public Opinion Surveys

Introduction

Public opinion is an important subject that many people want to know about for different purposes. Government officials need to know it for designing and adjusting public policies. Polling companies want to know it to predict electoral outcomes. Grassroots activists need to understand the public mood and organize social movements. Scholars and researchers need to know it to test their theories and research hypotheses. Yet public opinion is notoriously difficult to gauge. People often simply can't tell what they think. In the US, for example, only about 12% of survey respondents can tell where they are on the liberal versus conservative ideological spectrum.[1] Even more challenging for public opinion researchers is the problem of social desirability. That is, people may guess the "correct" answer due to concerns of being perceived as politically incorrect. Consequently, survey findings can be distorted due to the effect of social desirability. This study uses new techniques of survey experiment and statistical weighting and successfully detects up to 40% of social desirability in politically sensitive questions in a survey conducted in Hong Kong. The findings will be useful to correct future survey findings and provide a more realistic picture of the public sentiment in Hong Kong. The technique that is used to correct social desirability can be further applied to survey findings in other societies.

Social Desirability in Public Opinion Surveys

The question to be addressed in this study is to what extent social and political desirability influences people's responses in public opinion surveys. In other words, to what extent do people attempt to accommodate the preferred social and political norms while hiding their true opinions? Concealing

[1] Campbell et al. 1980; Converse 1964.

opinions undermines the very purpose of public opinion surveys, causing major distortions in the portrait of the actual public mood in a society. Consequently, governments could enact wrong policies, election campaign managers could adopt ineffective strategies, political activists could miss opportunities to mobilize social movements, and scholars could prove false theories.

Social desirability is a common concern in public opinion survey research. In authoritarian societies where the government actively propagates its official values, citizens may be afraid of expressing opinions that deviate from the official views. Some Western scholars even carry the false belief that citizens do not really have any opinions in a hierarchically structured Asian country like China.[2]

Such a concern poses a serious challenge to the findings in public opinion surveys. For example, in the public opinion surveys in China, researchers found a very high level of political support of the Chinese government. In the World Values Surveys, the Asian Barometer Surveys, and the Pew surveys,[3] Chinese survey respondents have shown much higher levels of political support than in democratic societies. Such high levels stay consistent no matter how political support is measured, including trusting government institutions, trusting government officials, trusting the central government, national identity, and so on.[4] These findings have been frequently challenged by other researchers.[5]

The influence of social desirability is by no means an isolated problem in authoritarian societies. It is also common in democratic societies. In the United States, people are often reluctant to openly discuss certain socially sensitive issues, such as abortion, gun control, and race. For example, a white respondent may not truthfully reveal his/her racist attitudes because of the concern of being politically incorrect in a face-to-face interview.[6] Such a problem becomes even worse if the interviewer is an African American, resulting in severe underestimation of racism in American society due to the interviewer effect.[7]

This study will explore the social and political desirability problem in public opinion surveys in Hong Kong. Hong Kong is a unique postcolonial

---

[2] Fuchs 2007; Rose 2007.
[3] Hu Fu Center for East Asia Democratic Studies 2023; Pew Research Center 2023; World Values Survey Association 2022.
[4] Chen 2004; Dickson 2016; Lewis-Beck, Tang, and Martini 2014; Shi 2014; Tang 2016; Wang 2006.
[5] Truex 2017; Nicholson and Huang 2023.
[6] Redlawsk, Tolbert, and Franko 2010; Kuklinski, Cobb, and Gilens 1997; Kuklinski, Sniderman, et al. 1997.
[7] Landry 2019.

and postindustrial society where freedom of expression coexists with an authoritarian political system under China's framework of One Country, Two Systems. In this context, conventional wisdom about social and political desirability may require revision; a new understanding of the socially and politically sensitive issues needs to be identified; the extent to which respondents in public opinion surveys may over- or underreport their opinion should be determined; and survey and statistical techniques to correct such distortion need to be developed.

Traditional Methods of Dealing with Social and Political Desirability

As discussed in the previous section, social and political desirability can cause unreliable outcomes in public opinion surveys and lead researchers to draw wrong conclusions. Traditionally, survey researchers have used several methods to deal with the social desirability effect. For example, in the case of political support in China, there are at least three ways to cope with such a problem. The first is *missing value conversion*.[8] This method is useful when the respondents hide their opinion by declining to answer. For example, if there are a lot of "don't know" answers to a question about the respondents' willingness to support the government, the researcher may assume that the respondents are actually unwilling to support the government but do not want to reveal such a feeling due to the fear of negative political consequences. If such an assumption is correct, the researcher can convert the "don't know" responses, or missing values, into negative values. In other words, "don't know" answers are treated as the respondents' unwillingness to support the government.

The second traditional method of checking social desirability may be described as the *cross-country comparison* method. This is simply done by comparing the responses to a survey question that is socially sensitive in one country but not in another country. One example is the survey question "I would not support my government if it does bad things." Agreeing with such a statement in authoritarian China may be risky since it shows one's willingness to challenge the government.

In a 2008 China survey,[9] 54% of the Chinese respondents said they would not support their government if it made wrong policies, which was about the same level as several democracies, including Australia, Denmark, and

[8] Shi 2014.
[9] Tang 2016.

the United States in the 2004 ISSP survey.[10] The level of willingness to challenge wrong government decisions in China in 2008 is even higher than in some democracies in the 2004 ISSP survey, such as Spain, Poland, Czech Republic, Switzerland, Portugal, South Korea, and Israel. These results suggest that this question in China may not be as socially and politically sensitive as people expect. The cross-country comparison of the politically sensitive question demonstrates that the Chinese survey respondents are just as open as people in other societies in expressing their willingness to challenge their government.

The third traditional method is *vertical comparison*.[11] Survey responses are compared within one country but between different levels of government support. For example, in the 2012 World Values Survey, Chinese respondents were asked about their trust in the central and local governments. The level of trust in the central government was on average 20% to 30% higher than in local governments. The respondents should be under more pressure not to express their distrust in local governments that may be more capable of punishing local dissidents. Yet these respondents were still willing to voice their distrust of local governments. The vertical comparison method suggests that political fear or social desirability may not be a serious problem in answering supposedly sensitive survey questions in China.

The above methods are helpful in detecting signs of social desirability effects in public opinion surveys. They are particularly helpful if the research project is constrained by funding. Yet they can at best provide indirect measures. Neither can they point to the precise level if such an effect exists.

New Tools to Study Social and Political Desirability

In recent years, researchers have developed new tools to study social desirability, noticeably the experimental method. Researchers in the United States used list experiments (to be described in more detail below) embedded in public opinion surveys and successfully detected fairly strong racism among survey respondents that were otherwise hidden due to social desirability. For example, when white Americans were asked if they did not vote for Barack Obama because he was black, as many as 30% of these respondents agreed with such statement in their mind but did not reveal that opinion in face-to-face interviews,[12] suggesting a relatively high level of social desirability effect in the US.

---

[10] ISSP Research Group 2012.
[11] Li 2013; Tang 2016.
[12] Redlawsk, Tolbert, and Franko 2010.

In China, researchers have also attempted to use experimental methods to detect social desirability effects. For example, the 2012 World Values Survey embedded several list experiments to test if the Chinese respondents were overreporting their trust of the government and found that only about 8% to 10% of them did so.[13] In a 2018 survey on grassroots bribery behavior, researchers embedded several list experiments and found a significant social desirability effect where people tried to hide their bribery behavior in face-to-face interviews.[14]

Sometimes social desirability works the opposite way. Instead of overreporting, people may underreport their attitude in face-to-face interviews. For example, in an implicit association test (IAT), Zhou and his coauthors found that Chinese university students purposely underreported their support for the government. The IAT experiment revealed that their actual support was significantly higher than they openly admitted.[15] This underreporting was perhaps due to the social desirability among college students to be critical of the government as an elite, educated group in Chinese society.

In sum, social desirability is a problem that exists in different societies whether they are authoritarian or democratic. Traditional methods of dealing with this problem have recently been replaced by new methods such as survey experiments.

Political and Social Desirability in Hong Kong Public Opinion Surveys

In the past years, many public opinion surveys were conducted in Hong Kong by both international and local researchers, including the World Values Surveys,[16] the Asian Barometer Surveys,[17] the Reuters surveys,[18] and many surveys conducted by Hong Kong scholars.[19] These surveys have provided valuable information about the distribution of and change in public opinion in the postcolonial society, but they have only begun to devote their attention to the social desirability effect. Even the rare few that tried to tackle the issue found no significant social desirability effect.[20]

---

[13] Tang 2016.
[14] Tang and Hu 2023.
[15] Huang, Intawan, and Nicholson 2023; Zhou, Tang, and Lei 2019.
[16] World Values Survey Association 2022.
[17] Hu Fu Center for East Asia Democratic Studies 2023.
[18] Reuters Graphics 2015.
[19] Chan and Lee 2007; Kuan and Lau 2002 and 1995; Lee 2010 and 2005; Lee and Chan 2011 and 2008; Lee, Chen, and Chan 2017; Lee, Tang, et al. 2019; Wu 2016.
[20] Wu 2016.

One reason that social desirability in Hong Kong has not been adequately examined is perhaps due to the argument that there is no need to do so since Hong Kong is a free and open society where people are not afraid of expressing their opinions. After all, hundreds of thousands of people went to the streets and demonstrated in recent years. This should be strong enough evidence to show that social and political desirability is not a concern.

Yet others have shown that people in Hong Kong are indeed concerned about exposing their individual identity and political views. For example, Hong Kong residents were concerned about expressing their desire to be autonomous from China.[21] Ethnic and sexual minorities never felt accepted and welcomed in Hong Kong.[22] Hong Kong residents with a Mainland background were afraid to speak publicly because their Mainland accents could be identified.[23] According to the repeated Western media reports during the protests in 2019, many protesters wore face masks to hide their identity from the undercover police.[24] They also destroyed public surveillance cameras because of the fear these cameras would capture evidence that would result in legal consequences.[25] Co-workers avoided talking about politics so that their employers wouldn't be able to identify the protesters and their sympathizers due to their companies' pressure to keep their businesses with China.[26] Many people have described such protests as faceless and leaderless,[27] suggesting the possibility of concealing one's true behavior and opinion in public opinion surveys. Since the passage of the Hong Kong National Security Law on July 1, 2020, and the political crackdown in the name of national security that followed, the concern of social desirability could be further worsened.[28]

The second possibility of the social desirability effect is rooted in the format of public opinion surveys, particularly when implemented via one-on-one interviews. In the case of public protests, people may not be as concerned when they join massive protests in a big crowd. Yet if they are interviewed one on one, there may be the psychological effect of fear of being identified. Such fear may lead to concealing individual protest behavior during public opinion surveys.

The third possibility of the social desirability effect may work in the opposite direction. That is, instead of underreporting one's radical protest

---

[21] Fewston 2019.
[22] Carvalho 2019.
[23] Huang 2019; Mathews 2019; Zhu 2019.
[24] Leicester 2019a and 2019b; Marcolini 2019.
[25] Wall Street Journal 2019.
[26] Bloomberg 2019; Wright and Stevens 2019.
[27] Hu 2019.
[28] Tsoi and Wai 2020.

behavior, survey respondents may overreport such action. This is possible when people sense that protesting itself is politically correct and not protesting may be looked down upon in a political atmosphere where anti-establishment sentiment is cherished. Previous studies have found that Chinese university students deliberately underreport their support for the government because they wanted to appear to be "thoughtful." This opposite effect is called "social desirability of dissent."[29]

The above reasons suggest that social desirability may exist in different forms and different degrees in Hong Kong's public opinion surveys, and it is necessary to detect such effect.

List Experiments

This study will examine social and political desirability in Hong Kong by using a series of list experiments embedded in a public opinion survey.[30] It begins with a description of the structure and mechanisms of the list experiment method.

The basic idea of list experiments is quite simple and can be described in the following steps:

1. The researcher draws a *random* sample that must be representative of the entire population.
2. The representative sample is further divided *randomly* into two roughly equal subsamples, or the control group and the treatment group.
3. The respondents in the control group will answer a question: "Please give a *number* to the items of a, b, and c that you agree with" (not to choose one or more specific items but simply give a number between 0 and 3).
4. The respondents in the treatment group are given the same set of items a, b, and c, with one additional item d, which is the treatment or the *sensitive item*.

---

[29] Zhu, Tang, and Lei 2019.
[30] Invented in the 1990s by James Kuklinski, a political science professor at the University of Illinois Urbana Champion (Sniderman 2011), the list experiment quickly became a popular research tool because of its ability to detect racial and religious biases among survey respondents in the United States (Kuklinski, Cobb, and Gilens 1997; Kuklinski, Sniderman, et al. 1997; Gilens, Sniderman, and Kuklinski 1998; Kane, Craig, and Wald 2004; Redlawsk, Tolbert, and Franco 2010; Tang 2016; Tang and Hu 2023). Before then, public opinion surveys were widely used among scholars of American politics, and survey respondents showed little racial and religious biases. When the above researchers embedded list experiments in these surveys, they found that a significant number of survey respondents would hide their racism and religious biases in face-to-face interviews due to their desire to be politically correct.

5. The average numbers of the two groups are compared and the difference between the two mean values becomes the *percentage* of respondents in the treatment agreeing with item d, the socially and politically sensitive item.
6. Respondents in both groups are asked a *direct question* about their agreement with the socially or politically sensitive question (item d). The difference between the percentages in this step and in step 5, or "difference-in-means,"[31] suggests the social desirability effect, or the percentage of people who hide their true attitude in step 6.

An example will further illustrate how list experiments are applied by researchers.[32] The survey question is why the respondents don't think Barak Obama is qualified to be the president of the United States. The answers given the respondents were as follows:

a. He is a smoker.
b. He doesn't have enough political experience.
c. He was born in Hawaii.
d. He is black. (Sensitive item)

The control group is only given a, b and c, and the treatment group is given a, b, c, and d. In the control group, the average number of items that the respondents agree on is 1.89. In the treatment group, that number is 2.20. The difference between the two numbers is 0.31, indicating that 31% of the respondents in the treatment group agree that Obama is not qualified to be the president because he is black.

The key to understanding why the value of 0.31 can be treated as a percentage is randomization. If none of the respondents or 0% in the treatment group agrees with d, the average number in this group should be 1.89, which is the same as the control group because the two groups are randomly divided and carry very similar characteristics. On the other hand, if everyone or 100% in the treatment groups agrees with d, the average number is 2.89. Since the difference between the two groups varies between 0 and 1, it can be interpreted as 0% and 100% and any value in between.

Finally, all the respondents in both groups are asked explicitly if they agree that Obama is not qualified to be the president because he is black, and if the percentage of agreement is 8%, then we know the proportion of the respondents who hide their racial bias is 31%−8%=23%, which is the social

---

[31] Blair and Imai 2012.
[32] Redlawsk, Tolbert, and Franco 2010.

desirability effect due to these respondents' fear of being politically incorrect in face-to-face surveys.

List experiments are so useful because they give the respondents an opportunity to hide their true opinion. Among a, b, c, and d, the respondents only need to give the interviewer a number, but not the specific item(s), and the interviewer has no idea which item(s) the number represents.

The idea of list experiments is simple, but its design can easily go wrong in at least three ways. The first problem is the *broadcast effect* when the respondents mistakenly mention the specific items instead of just giving a number.[33] Such a problem suggests that the respondents do not realize that it is possible to hide their politically incorrect opinion. To avoid the broadcast effect, interviewers must be well trained so that they can clearly explain the purpose of the list experiment to the respondents.

The second problem is the *ceiling and floor effects*.[34] This problem is caused when the respondents can easily agree or disagree with all or none of the items on the list, making it impossible for the respondents to hide their answer to the politically sensitive item. It is necessary to carefully design the control items (i.e., a, b, and c above) so that the ceiling and floor effects can be minimized.[35]

The third problem is the *fixed order effect* due to the particular order of the list experiment items.[36] For example, the respondents may make different decisions about how to answer if the politically sensitive item is positioned on top, at the bottom, or in the middle of the list. A similar fixed order problem can occur if the explicitly sensitive question is asked before or after the list experiment question. Such a problem of fixed order effect can be avoided by randomizing the order of the items of the list experiment and also by randomizing the order of the explicit question and the list experiment question.[37]

The results of difference in means can tell the extent of social desirability in the entire sample, but it is not capable of telling what types of respondents have more or less social desirability. In the following analysis, this study will consider individual characteristics and their impact on creating social desirability, similar to the method of multivariate analysis developed

---

[33] Tang and Hu 2023.

[34] Fox and Tracy 1986; Glynn 2013.

[35] A related minor problem is the design effect, meaning that the responses to control items might change when a sensitive item is added to the list, which can be detected using the technique proposed by Blair and Imai (2012).

[36] Sigelman 1981; McFarland 1981; Bishop, Oldendick, and Tuckfarber 1984; Schuman, Presser, and Ludwig 1981; Redlawsk, Tolbert, and Franko 2010; Imai 2011; Blair and Imai 2012; Glynn 2013.

[37] Druckman et al. 2011.

by other researchers.[38] This study is particularly interested in identifying any influential factor that may further trigger social desirability.

Hong Kong Political Culture Survey

To test social desirability with list experiments, the Hong Kong Political Culture Survey was conducted by Wenfang Tang and his research team May–August 2021.[39] A representative sample of 3,744 respondents was interviewed from 72 randomly selected electoral districts. Each interview lasted about 30 minutes. Such a representative sample is superior to other methods such as online and telephone surveys, and it will assure the generalizability of the survey findings (see Appendix 2.1 for a comparison between the sample and the population census).

To carry out the list experiments, the sample was further randomly divided into nine groups of about 416 respondents each (see Appendix 2.2 for group statistics). The 400 respondents in each group is the minimum number because a smaller number would not allow the researcher to conduct meaningful multivariate analysis. One group will serve as the control group, and the other eight will serve as treatment groups. A list experiment was embedded in each treatment group. Each of the eight treatment groups included one of the following eight carefully chosen politically sensitive questions:

1. 支持愛國不是選擇是義務 support the statement "It is not a choice but an obligation for Hong Kong people to love China" (patriotism)
2. 支持香港是中國不可分離的一部分 support Hong Kong is an inseparable part of China (sovereignty)
3. 支持將違法泛民主派人士判監 support the imprisonment of pan-democratic law-offenders, such as Jimmy Lai and Joshua Wong (imprison)

---

[38] See Blair and Imai 2012; Imai 2011. In general terms, the multivariate analysis is based on the following regression model:

$Y_i = X_i + T_i X_i \delta + i$, where (γ, δ) are the parameter estimates of the control and sensitive items using standard methods such as ordinary least square regression (OLS), and X_i are the respondent's characteristics. T_i represents whether a respondent is in the treatment group ($T_i=1$) or the control group ($T_i=0$). And Y_i indicates the probability of an affirmative response given the specific characteristics of the respondents. The form of the model is similar to that of the standard regression models, and the key difference is the addition of the term $T_i X_i$, where T_i serves as the switch to inform whether the respondent is in the control or treatment group. In doing so, the method can model the difference of response to the sensitive item between the control and treatment group given a set of respondent characteristics.

[39] This project was supported by a General Research Fund (RGC Ref No. 16601820) and the Anti-Epidemic Fund 2.0, awarded by the Research Grants Council of Hong Kong.

4. 支持解僱拒絕宣誓效忠的公務員 support the dismissal of civil servants who refuse to swear to uphold Basic Law and swear allegiance to HKSAR (allegiance)
5. 支持送中 support the extradition bill (extradition)
6. 支持完善選舉制度, 落實愛國者治港 support "improve electoral system, ensure patriots administering Hong Kong" (election)
7. 支持香港國安法 support Hong Kong National Security Law (NSL)
8. 支持警察止暴制亂 support the police force to "stop violence and curb disorder" (police)

The above eight items were selected as politically sensitive statements in the post–National Security Law Hong Kong. Since the summer of 2020, China had stepped up its rhetoric on patriotism[40] and China's sovereignty over Hong Kong.[41] In addition to passing the National Security Law,[42] China launched harsher measures: arresting anti-China activists,[43] firing civil servants who refused to pledge their allegiance to China,[44] strengthening the electoral system to ensure the dominance of pro-China candidates,[45] and denouncing the anti-extradition movement[46] and the violence during the movement,[47] should read the local news regularly.

The four items were carefully selected to avoid the ceiling and floor effects by which the respondents would have to answer 0 or 4, therefore defeating the purpose of hiding one's true but politically sensitive opinion.[48] The order of the items in each group was randomized to avoid the fixed order effect. Interviewers were trained to avoid the broadcast effect by making sure the respondents did not mention any specific item on the list but only give a number from 0 to 5. To further ensure that respondents do not mention the specific items, interviews were recorded with the consent of the interviewees.

In Figure 2.1 that presents the results of social desirability at the level of the overall sample (see bars labeled "overall"), only one treatment group,

---

[40] Luo 2020.
[41] LOCPG 2021.
[42] GHKSAR 2020.
[43] Human Rights Watch 2021.
[44] Chan and Lau 2021.
[45] Cheng and Alun 2021.
[46] Blanchard 2019; Cheng 2019; Zheng 2019.
[47] GHKSAR 2020.
[48] Indeed, using the method developed by Imai and Blair (2012), it is revealed that the percentages of liars who hide their opinion due to the floor effect are negligible (no more than 0.5% for each group), while the percentages of liars for most experimental groups because of the ceiling effect is around 5%, with the exception of the sovereignty group where the corresponding number is around 12%. Additionally, no design effect is found.

namely the extradition bill, generated a noticeable and statistically significant difference between direct questioning and the list experiment. In the treatment group that contains the sensitive item of supporting the extradition bill, the percentage of support is 51%. In direct questioning, only 39% expressed their agreement with the bill, and 12% concealed their agreement. In this case, the list experiment method was successful in detecting the 12% "hidden" opinion. Other items produced relatively small and insignificant differences. These results lead the researchers to doubt if there is indeed any social desirability effect in the survey.

Detecting Opposite Social Desirability Effects

The low level of social desirability in the first round of the list experiments may be rooted in the limitation of such a method if we only compute it on the level of an entire sample.[49] Specifically, it is not capable of detecting the opposite directions of social desirability for subgroups. For example, a list experiment will show no social desirability if the same numbers of respondents hide their opinions in opposite ways. Some people may overreport their support for the National Security Law in Hong Kong, while the same portion of people may underreport their support due to their different political orientations and their perceived political correctness within their own peer groups. Consequently, social desirability for the whole treatment group may be zero, but they are more noticeable at the subgroup level and in opposite directions.

To test the existence of opposite social desirability effects in the same treatment group, it is necessary to identify a variable that shows the respondents' opposite political orientations and then examine social desirability within each political orientation. In Figure 2.1, social desirability is further examined through such a variable: the respondents' political leaning as represented by one's reported political orientation. In Hong Kong's political culture, political orientation is often defined either by pro- or anti-establishment sentiment. Consequently, the blue color is used to show pro-establishment feelings, green as neutral, and yellow as anti-establishment. When the list experiment results are further examined through the respondents' reported political colors, some very interesting patterns of social desirability effects emerge.

In Figure 2.1, a negative number means that the list experiment result is greater than the result from direct questioning, suggesting underreporting of one's true support of a statement in direct questioning. In contrast, a positive number shows that the list experiment result is smaller than the

---

[49] Blair, Coppock, and Moor 2020; Blair and Imai 2012.

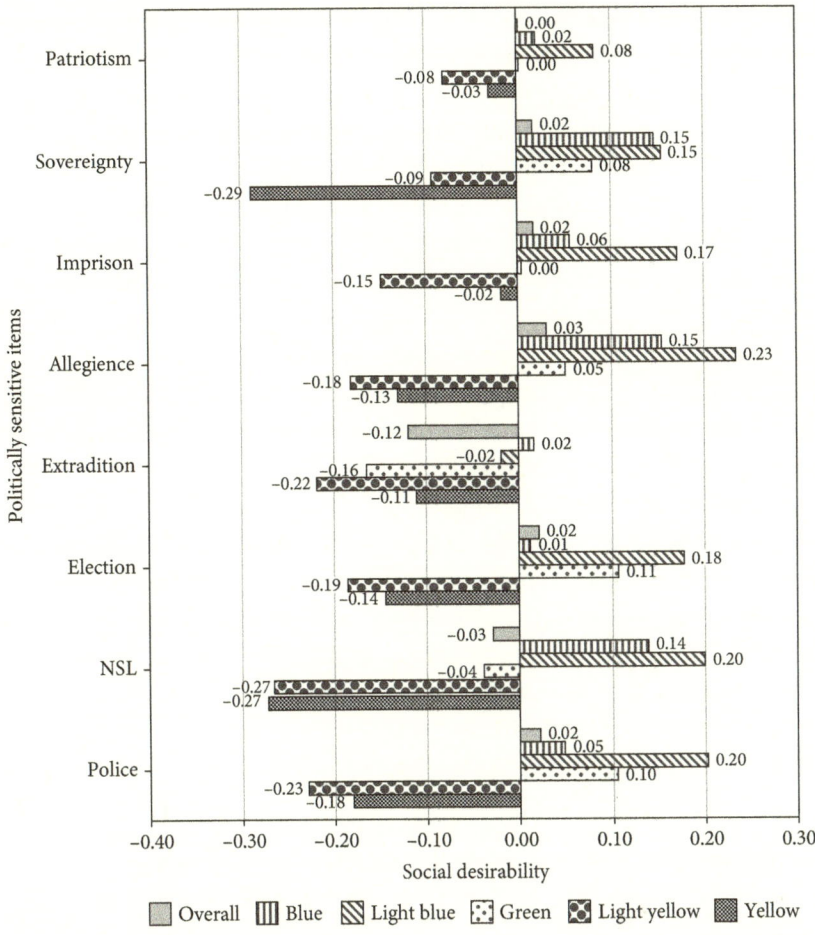

Figure 2.1 Social desirability by political leaning (direct questioning minus list experiments)

Main findings: The pro-democracy respondents (yellow and light yellow) tend to exaggerate their disapproval of the politically correct statements in direct questioning but showed significantly lower levels of disagreement in the list experiments. In contrast, the pro-China respondents (blue and light blue) tend to overreport their support of the politically correct statements in direct questioning but reveal significantly less support of political correctness in the list experiments. The neutral (green) respondents seem to be the "swing voters," overreporting their disapproval like the yellow in some cases (NSL and extradition), but for the most part, overreporting their support for the politically correct statements in direct questioning, like the blue and light-blue respondents.

Notes: Results are based on multivariate analysis controlling for socioeconomic factors (Blair and Imai 2012), including political leaning, age, education, gender, birthplace, connection with Mainland China, Mandarin level, household income per capita, house ownership, type of housing, political news exposure, and whether the interview is audio recorded. In the Hong Kong political context, the color blue is used to represent the political leaning of pro-establishment, green neutral, and yellow anti-establishment.

Source: 2021 Hong Kong Political Culture Survey.

result from direct questioning, implying overreporting or exaggeration of one's agreement with a statement in direct questioning.

As shown in Figure 2.1, the yellow and light-yellow respondents tend to exaggerate their disapproval of the politically correct statements in direct questioning but showed significantly lower levels of disagreement in the list experiments. In contrast, the blue and light-blue respondents tend to overreport their support of the politically correct statements in direct questioning but reveal significantly less support of political correctness in the list experiments. The green, or "neutral," respondents seem to be the "swing voters," overreporting their disapproval like the yellow in some cases (NSL and extradition), but for the most part, overreporting their support for the politically correct statements in direct questioning, like the blue and light-blue respondents.

These findings in Figure 2.1 suggest that opposite social desirability effects can be identified or activated through another variable, or an *activator*. These opposite effects can coexist in the same list experiment, and such effects cannot be detected by the traditional list experiment method. These findings also show that while it may be predictable that the blue respondents are under pressure to show their loyalty to the establishment, it is interesting to note that the yellow respondents are also under pressure to show their loyalty to the anti-establishment camp.

Statistical Weighting with an Activator Variable

With an activator variable, the previous section was able to "activate" the social desirability effects that were hidden in the first round of list experiment analysis. In this sense, the activator variable method is a step forward in overcoming the limitations and revealing the intricacies of the list experiment. The activator variable method, however, has its own limitation. The activator variable can tell us the levels of social desirability within each subgroup, but it cannot determine the extent of the true response in the entire sample.

The above limitation can be further described by the findings in Figure 2.1. In Figure 2.1, through the activator variable of political color, each of the five political colors leads to either overreporting or underreporting of support for the politically sensitive question in the list experiment. For instance, it shows that the respondents in the yellow subgroup underreported their support for the new pro-China election law by about 14% (see election/yellow in Figure 2.1). This finding can tell us how many people in the subgroup support a policy, but it cannot show the overall level of support of such policy in the entire sample, because it does not take into consideration the relative weight or proportion of this subgroup in the entire sample.

In fact, the sizes of the five political color subgroups in the survey are not equal: about 9% blue, 17% light blue, 44% green, 20% light yellow, and 10% yellow. The relative weights of these subgroups need to be considered in assessing their social desirability effects for the entire sample.

Weighting can be carried out in two steps. First, following the work of Tang and Hu, the ratios are calculated between the list experiment results and the direct questioning results for each color and in each list experiment.[50] For example, 100% of those in "blue" supported the new election law in direct questioning, but only 98% of them expressed the same support in the list experiment. The ratio is calculated as 0.98/1.00=0.98. Similarly, only 2% of the yellow respondents supported the same law in direct questioning, but 16% offered their support in the list experiment. The ratio is 0.16/0.02=8.00. Please see Appendix 2.3 for technical details.

Table 2.1 shows all the 40 ratios for the five political colors by eight list experiment groups. One potential problem with this method is the danger of not having enough observations in each of the 40 categories, which may lead to unreliable estimations. Fortunately, the Hong Kong Political Culture Survey has a relatively large sample of 3,744 observations, which ensures an adequate number of observations for each subcategory.

In the second step of weighting, the number of respondents in each subcategory is multiplied by its ratio. To continue with the above examples, if there are 50 respondents in the blue/election subcategory, they are counted as 50×0.98 = 49 respondents. Similarly, if there are 20 respondents in the subcategory of yellow/election, they are counted as 20×8.0 = 160 respondents. In this process, some subgroups are counted less, and others are counted more, depending on the value of the ratios. It is counted less if the ratio is less than 1 and more if the ratio is greater than 1. Consequently, the sample size will change because of undercounting and overcounting in different subgroups. The goal of statistical weighting, after all, is to estimate the more realistic levels of approval and disapproval of the politically sensitive questions for the entire sample rather than in each political color.

Figure 2.2 shows the proportions of support for politically sensitive questions after weighting and their gaps with unweighted proportions. Some questions, such as patriotism and Chinese sovereignty, are less sensitive to weighting. These questions only show about 5%–6% of inflated support, implying relatively low levels of social desirability effect. Other questions, however, result in a medium to strong impact of social desirability. Support

---

[50] Tang and Hu (2023) proposed the method that constructs a weight variable with the ratios between the list experiment and direct questioning results at the sample level but not at the subgroup level.

Table 2.1 Ratios of List Experiment to Direct Questioning by Political Leaning (ratio=list experiment/direct questioning)

		Patriotism	Sovereignty	Imprison	Allegiance	Extradition	Election	NSL	Police
Political leaning	Blue	.92/.94=.98	.83/.97=.86	.93/.98=.95	.83/.99=.84	.89/.91=.98	.98/1.00=.98	.85/.99=.86	.95/1.00=.95
	Light blue	.72/.80=.90	.76/.92=.83	.71/.88=.81	.66/.90=.73	.70/.68=1.03	.78/.96=.81	.69/.89=.78	.76/.96=.79
	Green	.51/.52=.98	.70/.78=.90	.48/.49=.98	.49/.54=.91	.51/.34=1.50	.57/.68=.84	.53/.49=1.08	.57/.68=.84
	Light yellow	.31/.23=1.35	.63/.54=1.17	.26/.11=2.36	.32/.14=2.29	.33/.11=3.00	.37/.18=2.06	.37/.10=3.70	.38/.15=2.53
	Yellow	.10/.07=1.43	.57/.28=2.04	.03/.01=3.00	.15/.02=7.5	.13/.02=6.50	.16/.02=8.00	.28/.01=28.00	.19/.01=19.00

This table shows all the 40 ratios for the five political colors by eight list experiment groups. Weighting is carried out in two steps. First, following the work of Tang and Hu (2023), the ratios are calculated between the list experiment results and the direct questioning results for each color and in each list experiment. For example, 100% of those in blue supported the new election law in direct questioning, but only 98% of them expressed the same support in the list experiment. The ratio is calculated as 0.98/1.00=0.98. Similarly, only 2% of the yellow respondents supported the same law in direct questioning, but 16% offered their support in the list experiment. The ratio is 0.16/0.02=8.00.

Note: Results are based on multivariate analysis controlling for socioeconomic factors (Blair and Imai 2012.) including political leaning, age education, gender, birthplace, connection with Mainland China, Mandarin level, household income per capita, house ownership, type of housing, political news exposure, and whether the interview is audio recorded.

Source: Hong Kong Political Culture Survey 2021

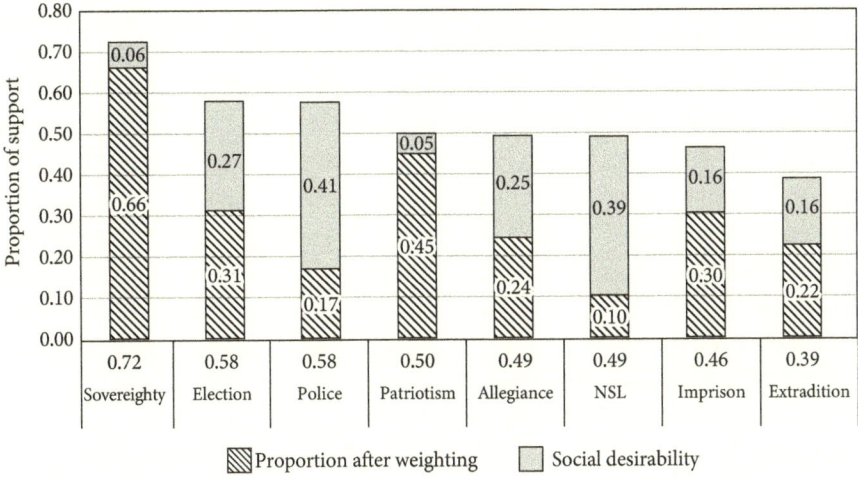

Figure 2.2 Support for politically sensitive questions: Proportions after weighting and social desirability

Main findings: Proportions of support for politically sensitive questions after weighting and their gaps with unweighted proportions. Some questions, such as patriotism and Chinese sovereignty, are less sensitive to weighting. These questions only show about 5%–6% of inflated support, implying relatively lower levels of social desirability effect. Other questions, however, result in a medium to strong impact of social desirability. Support is 16% less for jailing the anti-establishment activists, 16% less for the extradition agreement with China, 25% less for dismissing the civil servants who refuse to show their loyalty to Beijing, 27% less for the new pro-China election law, 39% less for Hong Kong's National Security Law, and 41% less for the police's effort at stopping violent protests.

Note: The number below each bar shows the proportion before weighting. Please see Appendix 2.3 for a formal presentation of statistical weighting.
Source: Hong Kong Political Culture Survey 2021.

is 16% less for jailing the anti-establishment activists, 16% less for the extradition agreement with China, 25% less for dismissing the civil servants who refuse to show their loyalty to Beijing, 27% less for the new pro-China election law, 39% less for Hong Kong's National Security Law, and 41% less for the police's effort at stopping violent protests.

Discussion and Implications

This study attempted to measure public opinion on politically sensitive issues in Hong Kong by conducting a public opinion survey on Hong Kong political culture. The survey embedded eight list experiments to detect any social desirability effect. In addition, this study developed new techniques to improve the list experiment method, including the activator variable method and statistical weighting based on the findings of the list experiments and the activator variable. The findings suggest that Hong Kong survey respondents are not completely truthful in answering politically sensitive questions and hide their anti-China sentiment on various issues. The levels of deception range from 5% to 40%.

If the findings in this study are reliable, the overall support for China and Chinese policies is low among Hongkongers. On the surface, without using antisocial desirability measures, the levels of support seem acceptable, at around 50% or higher. When the anti-deception measures are applied, such support drops to below 30% for most of the politically sensitive questions. These mostly negative results are probably caused by correcting the social desirability effect in the largest green subgroup that tended to overreport their support for the pro-China questions. For some people who did not support the violent anti-China protests in the second half of 2019 and who welcomed China's effort to stabilize Hong Kong society since then, these findings are probably not desirable. Yet this is the best available evidence for the time being.

One caveat about the low support is that social desirability is less noticeable for sovereignty and patriotism than for the other items in Figure 2.2. This gap suggests that Hongkongers were more supportive of the general principles of Chinese sovereignty over Hong Kong but less so of the specific policies.

The main contribution of this study is the development of the statistical weighting method. It improves and broadens the application of the traditional list experiment method. The advantage of statistical weighting through the activator variable is that it can go beyond subgroup and estimate social desirability for the entire sample. This is particularly useful when a list experiment produces little social desirability effects because it contains such effects in opposite directions.

The other advantage of the weighting technique developed in this study is that it can be applied to other politically sensitive questions that are not in the list experiment groups. For example, in the Hong Kong Political Culture Survey, there are two additional questions related to the respondents' opinion about the Hong Kong National Security Law (HKNSL): Do you think HKNSL will restrict people's freedom and rights? Do you think HKNSL will interfere with Hong Kong's self-governance under One Country, Two Systems? Only about 51% of the respondents agreed with both questions before applying weighting. When the two questions are re-examined with weighting, about 76% of the respondents said yes, a 25% increase in opposing the HKNSL if the social desirability effect is corrected.

The findings in this study should be taken with caution. Public mood is sensitive to timing. That is, it fluctuates according to the external political climate. If the survey was conducted two years earlier in 2019, political correctness would point to supporting the protesters rather than supporting the National Security Law. Anyone voicing disapproval during the peak of the antigovernment protests would be considered politically incorrect, and survey respondents during that time would be more likely to hide such a disapproval. In other words, social desirability must be considered together with what is politically correct at the time of the survey.

A final point is that caution should apply when using the weighting technique developed in this study. It should only be applied to questions of similar political sensitivity, such as in the above two examples about the Hong Kong National Security Law. It may cause inaccurate estimation if it is used for other unrelated questions. Future research needs to develop a more formal procedure regarding the exact conditions under which the weighting techniques can be applied to certain variables.

3
Indigenization of Political Identity

Introduction

In 2020, China passed the National Security Law (NSL) for Hong Kong, demanding its residents' political loyalty and outlawing any anti-China behavior.[1] The Hong Kong NSL was a turning point, and it symbolized the end of the first stage of postcolonial Hong Kong. This chapter examines Hong Kong residents' feelings of political identity during the first phase of the postcolonial era. It looks at such identity in three dimensions: Hongkongers' sentiments about China, the West, and traditional Chinese culture. It shows that while Hongkongers are predictably distant from China, they are also surprisingly indifferent to the West. In the meantime, they show a strong feeling of identity with Chinese traditional culture. This chapter further shows how Hong Kong's education system, media, and language policy played important roles in shaping Hongkongers' political identity in the first 23 years since Hong Kong's return to China in 1997.

Competing Theories of Postcolonial Identity

The study of postcolonial societies has gained momentum since the 1980s, following waves of decolonization and the detachment of former colonies from their European colonial powers. This emerged together with the rise of postindustrial, Western intellectual trends of critical race theory, feminism, globalization, and so on.[2] Many studies in this field examine the relationship between people in the former colonies and their former colonial rulers. Others focus more on the relationship between the former colonies and their new regimes and local leaders.

---

[1] An earlier version of this chapter was published as Tang, W. F., Hung, J. S. Y., and Ho, B. Y. Y. 2022. Indigenization of political identity in postcolonial Hong Kong. *Frontiers in Political Science* 4, 837992. DOI: 10.3389/fpos.2022.837992. In this new version but not in the original, statistical weighting based on political color (see Chapter 2) is used in the data analysis.
[2] Elam 2019; Gandhi 1998.

Some studies show the continuity of colonial rule and colonial mentality in postcolonial societies.[3] These scholars point out the stereotyping of the formerly colonized in the postcolonial present as inferior, "indolent, thoughtless, sexually immoral, unreliable and demented."[4] Some researchers attribute the identity construction to the colonial system and Western culture in light of political discourse and psychoanalytic theory. For example, Fanon postulates that the formation of identity is the product of a belief system of Western superiority,[5] whereas Said reminds us that the brainwashing by colonial powers ingrains a lopsided relationship, culture, and a low individual self-regard in the colonized society, resulting in the loss of identity.[6] To restrain from being debased and perceived as primitive, the colonized individuals reduce their native identity by wearing "white masks" to cope with the West, as Dizayi recapitulated.[7] Other studies examine the dominant class and foreign elite,[8] colonial government administration,[9] or education and language policy[10] as determinants for postcolonial identity. In short, these studies highlight the persistent effect of colonial power after its retreat.[11]

Other postcolonial theorists, however, describe postcolonial identity as a hybrid construct[12] that emerges as a new local identity.[13] They adopt the concept of "cultural identity," as Hall suggested, which undergoes continual renovation according to the interaction between colonial and local cultures.[14] Bhabha, a leading postcolonial theorist, argues that the hybridization of identities and cultures under colonial rule leads to the emergence of new sociopolitical identities of the colonizer and the colonized,[15] despite being wary of such hybridity as signifying an unstable colonized culture and potentially camouflaging colonial oppression and social inequalities.[16] Loomba and Young contend that such identity is not entirely new, nor does it replicate the old native culture.[17] Instead, it is "dislocated," fragmented, and hybrid under the conflictual interactions of the colonial hegemony and the colonized.

---

[3] Brysk, Parsons, and Sandholtz 2002; Chatterjee 2004; Fanon 1967 and 2004; Guha 1982; Paolini, Elliott, and Moran 1999; Said 1994; Spivak 1988.
[4] Bressler 2007: 204.
[5] Fanon 1967.
[6] Said 1994.
[7] Dizayi 2019.
[8] Guha 1982; Spivak 1988.
[9] Chatterjee 2004; Scott 1995; Young 2020.
[10] Bahri 2003; Ramanathan 2005; Venn 2000.
[11] Bahri 2003; Said 1994; Spivak 1988.
[12] Bhabha 1994; Young 2020.
[13] Ashcroft, Griffiths, and Tiffin 1995.
[14] Hall 1990.
[15] Bhabha 1990 and 1994.
[16] Gandhi 1998; Rukundwa and Aarde 2007.
[17] Loomba 1998; Young 2020.

Therefore, according to the constructivist view, identity is ever-changing and is shaped by externalities, such as international support,[18] rather than being settled or internalized completely, and through the related historical negotiation and renegotiation process, as Ang and Bammer summarized.[19]

Being a former British colony and reunified with China, its biological parent, Hong Kong has long been one of the atypical subjects of postcolonial identity for scholars[20] because they observed Hong Kong identity as neither British nor Chinese since the British colonial government had no intention of building a British identity for Hong Kong citizens[21] under its laissez-faire and de-ethnicization policy orientation.[22] Intellectuals argued that the identity of Hong Kong citizens in the colonial and postcolonial era was therefore ambiguous in a quasi-city-state, with high recognition of Chinese cultural or ethnic identity but a weak Chinese national identity.[23] Dynamic forces, including British colonial legacy, Hong Kong indigenization, and Chinese ideology, are accountable for identity formation in postcolonial Hong Kong.

Some scholars assume that the early Hong Kong identity emerged from its distinctive culture during the 1950s when the border closure policy between Hong Kong and China was enacted.[24] Such immigration policies that restrain Hong Kong from connecting with Mainland China marked the identity-building departure from China.[25] The British colonial government further constructed a sense of belonging and citizenship among Hong Kong residents through various policy reforms after the 1966 and 1967 riots, such as partially introducing elections; promoting Hong Kong's economic model and its achievements; bolstering the sense of pride of being Hong Kong citizens; and implanting Western liberal ideas of human rights, judicial independence, and freedom of speech.[26]

As a result, some studies argue that the Hong Kong identity was formed far from a Chinese identity due to different political, economic, and social experiences.[27] Even though the riots in the 1960s revealed a Chinese ethnic identity, these authors insist that the recognition of Chinese identity could hardly rise due to widespread condemnation of the pro-China leftist riots.[28]

---

[18] Han 2016 and 2019.
[19] Ang 2001; Bammer 1994.
[20] Kuan and Lau 1989; Lau 1992; So 2005 and 2015; Wong 1997.
[21] Chan 1994; Wong 1997.
[22] Leung 1997; Xiao 1997.
[23] Lau 2017; Wong 1997.
[24] Baker 1983; Carroll 2005; Lau and Kuan 1988; Lo 2015.
[25] Ku 2004; Lau 2017.
[26] Carroll 2005; King 1975; Lo 2015.
[27] Ku 2004; Lam 2018; Lau 2017; Lo 2018; So 1999; Mathews, Ma, and Lui 2008.
[28] Cheung 2012; Lau 2017.

On the other hand, such condemnation may serve as evidence of the existence of a pro-China sentiment in Hong Kong's social unrest in the 1960s. In this sense, the early anticolonial movement in Hong Kong was not an indigenous movement but had help from China.

Lo, alternatively, analyzed that while the postcolonial government opposed attaching Hong Kong identity to colonial legacies, it feared that developing a new Hong Kong identity based on the China-backed new governing system would hurt the interests of the middle class and elites and create social instability.[29] Consequently, the postcolonial government endeavored to maintain Hong Kong citizens' political neutrality so it could buy time and develop pro-establishment and patriotic forces while avoiding an alteration of the status quo. Some scholars expected a potential clash of Chinese and Hong Kong identities.[30] They noticed a gradual weakening of an identification with China and predicted the rise of localism, self-determination, direct elections, and even Hong Kong independence as the ultimate political goals.[31] In addition to changing political identities of Hongkongers in the post-Handover era, another study finds solid evidence of social prejudice against the Mainland Chinese that constitutes an important aspect of social identity of many Hong Kong people.[32]

Indigenization of Political Identity in Postcolonial Hong Kong

In this study, *political identity* is defined as an individual's sense of belonging to a political entity. Normally, this political identity is embodied by a geographic region and the governing body representing that region. In case the governing body is detached from the region, as in post-Handover Hong Kong, people may experience a political identity crisis and see cultural identity as a shelter where they can find emotional comfort. This is a process that can be described as "indigenization" of political identity.

This study will show that postcolonial Hong Kong has gone through a process of indigenization since its return to China by the United Kingdom in 1997—a process of returning to traditional Chinese culture as a symbol of political identity. By indigenization this study does not mean to imply primitiveness. Instead, it means the tendency of going back to the native culture.

---

[29] Lo 2015.
[30] Wong 1997.
[31] Lam 2018; Lo 2018; Ma 2018.
[32] Hong et al. 2004.

Studies of ethnic and national identities show that native culture and belief systems play an important role in shaping people's sense of community and political identity.[33] The state normally provides the foundation for political identity.[34] Cultural identity can be used as political identity if the state fails to do so, such as in postcolonial Hong Kong.

In a loose sense, indigenization overlaps with localization. This study, however, prefers the concept of indigenization over localization because indigenization focuses more on traditional culture and draws a clearer distinction from both colonialism and the Chinese political identity. Localism in post-Handover Hong Kong, on the other hand, does not draw such distinction, particularly from the territory's colonial past.

Hong Kong's postcolonial indigenization is formulated by several forces. First, it is shaped by the political vacuum left by the departure of the British colonists. Hong Kong was ruled by the UK for 150-plus years, and thus they were accustomed to thinking they were subjects of their colonial ruler. Once the colonial ruler was gone, there is a need to find a new collective identity. The colonial infrastructure may still be in place and functioning well, such as public services, but a sense of collective belonging was lost by the UK's departure, and thus the vacuum was created.

This political vacuum did not exist in some other postcolonial societies. In the cases of India and South Africa, for example, the colonists literally created the modern states and then lost them to the local elites. The local elites as new rulers continued with the same political systems and therefore the same political identity as their colonial rulers, such as in Indonesia, Malaysia, Singapore, and many others. In these societies, political power returned to the native people, yet the political system stayed the same. Admittedly, in many of these societies, there is a significant local adaptation of the colonial system, yet political institutions, such as political parties and elections, were mostly adopted by the local elites. Hong Kong was not that lucky, in the sense that the UK did not leave a functional political-institutional design for the local elites to adopt.

Second, indigenization was created by the need to resist being identified with their supposedly newly rich but unsophisticated new ruler. Hong Kong is one of those postcolonial societies (together with Macau) where the colonists did not build a modern state. When they left, they returned a piece of land that they "rented" some 150 years ago from its owner, who, at the time of regaining control of the territory, had never lived under colonial rule.

---

[33] Smith 1995 and 1998.
[34] Gellner 1983.

Photo 3.1 Protest slogan: Light up Hong Kong, arouse the public. Hong Kong Island. Photo by Wenfang Tang, 8/24/2019.

The new rulers, understandably, demanded Hong Kong people's new political identity. China is perceived as powerful, but it's nouveau riche (*tucaizhu*) and often acts without style (*xiangbalao*). Among many other things that Hongkongers are proud of comparing with the Mainlanders, Hong Kong has the best and most efficient public transit system, the best mixture between Eastern and the Western cultures, and a rare combination of natural environment and modern high rises, while in China although infrastructure was developed quickly, people are still much less exposed to the outside world. Mainland tourists in Hong Kong are often portrayed as loud, dirty, rude, and disorderly.[35]

Third, the One Country, Two Systems policy, at least for the first 23 years after Hong Kong's return to China in 1997 and before the National Security Law was passed on July 1, 2020, facilitated the feeling of political distance between Hong Kong and China, further strengthened the vacuum left by the UK in which indigenization of Hong Kong identity took place. The Two Systems idea and China's relative inability to establish its desired political socialization process in the first 23 years further encouraged Hongkongers to keep the two political systems separate. Many people may think the People's Republic of China (PRC) intervened a lot during this time,[36] yet by other standards the PRC tolerated many things that its leaders would never allow in China, such as the yearly parade on June 4 in memory of the "1989 Tiananmen massacre," and not mentioning the numerous, large-scale opposition movements and protests. This reluctant hands-off policy further encouraged the growing impact of the anti-China elements that wanted to keep Hong Kong away from Chinese influence.[37]

Next, indigenization was further encouraged by the availability of traditional culture. Luckily Hong Kong's native culture is very rich, highly developed, and well preserved. Such culture, unique in some respects, such as the spoken language, local diet, social norms, and so forth, overlaps with Chinese culture in many other ways, such as the written language, literature, philosophy, religious beliefs, traditional holidays, and so on. The difference between Hong Kong and China is that, in China, political identity is based on the Chinese state, while cultural identity in Hong Kong became a political identity due to the lack of other attractive alternatives.

Finally, some studies show that there has always been a tradition of indigenization in Hong Kong under British rule. For example, the 1967 riot and the contention of Indigenous villagers were attempts to resist British rule under the slogan of returning to traditional culture.[38] If this is true, indigenization is a continuity from the old rule to the new one. One question is the nature of indigenization. Under British rule, news reports show that such movement

---

[35] Cheung 2012; Li 2013 and 2014.
[36] Maizland and Albert 2021.
[37] Yan 2015.
[38] Chan 1998; Lo 2018.

had a strong backing from the PRC, and the British colonial government closed down the pro-PRC newspapers and arrested Chinese Communist Party sympathizers in its efforts to crack down on the 1967 riots.[39] In the postcolonial era, it remains to be seen if this indigenization process differs from that under colonial rule.

In this environment, being pushed away by the colonialists while trying to resist the pull from China, traditional culture is a natural psychological fallback.

Based on the above discussion, this chapter will test the following four hypotheses:

> *Hypothesis 1: Hong Kong residents are expected to express weak political identity with the Chinese state.*
> *Hypothesis 2: Hong Kong residents are expected to show lukewarm feelings toward their former colonial rulers.*
> *Hypothesis 3: Hong Kong residents are expected to show strong feelings toward Confucian-based East Asian identity and toward Chinese culture.*
> *Hypothesis 4: The reluctant laissez-faire policies in education, language, and media under the One Country, Two Systems are expected to further promote indigenization.*

Data and Measures of Political Identity

The empirical evidence for this study is drawn from the Hong Kong Political Culture Survey conducted in 2021 as described in Chapter 2. The survey contained many questions related to the respondents' political attitudes including political identity, policy satisfaction, political trust, social tolerance and social trust, religious values and behavior, law and order, political participation, and media consumption, as well as embedded survey experiments on social desirability and media effects.

This study will use the following questions from the above survey to test the respondents' political and ethnic identities:

1. *Cultural and political nationalisms.* Please tell us how much you agree with the following statements (agree strongly, agree, disagree, disagree strongly):

[39] FCCHK 2017; Webster 2021.

a. Chinese civilization has great vitality.
   b. Chinese culture is one of the most advanced in the world.
   c. I will support Chinese national teams in sports games.
   d. I like Chinese movies and TV shows.
   e. China's political system is superior to Western liberal democratic systems.
   f. Only the Chinese Communist Party is capable of leading China to be a world power.
2. *National images of selected countries and regions.* Please tell us your impressions of people from the following countries and regions (very good, good, bad, very bad): Singapore, Taiwan, the UK, Mainland China, the United States, and India.
3. *Political orientation.* Which of the following colors best represent your political view (blue=pro-establishment, green=neutral, yellow=pro-democracy): dark blue, blue, light blue, green, light yellow, yellow, and dark yellow.
4. *Ethnic identity.* Would you call yourself Hongkonger, Chinese, or Chinese Hongkonger?
5. *East-West value preference.* Please tell us which set of values is more important to you?[40]
   g. Freedom, democracy, human rights, and the rule of law.
   h. Benevolence, integrity, filial piety, and restraint.
   i. Both are important.
6. *Immigration intention.* In the next two years, do you plan to immigrate to Europe, North America, Japan, or Taiwan? (yes or no)

Pioneers of the study of Hong Kong identity during the transitional period suggested the above-mentioned as vital elements to map out Hong Kong identity in multiple dimensions such as Chinese civilization, cultural identity, national versus global values, political values,[41] and immigration intention.[42] For the sources of the above measures of political and ethnic identity, this study will analyze the effects of language, education, age, social class, birthplace, and media.

Language is measured by the respondents' ability to use English and Mandarin Chinese (or Putonghua—the common language). In the survey sample, 88% of the respondents' native language is Cantonese, 3% Mandarin, 1% English, and 7% other languages. Each language ability is an index of the

---
[40] Lau 2017.
[41] Lau 2017; Lau and Kuan 1988; Ma and Fung 2007.
[42] Lau 1997; Zheng and Wong 2002.

respondent's ability to listen, speak, read, and write in either English or Mandarin. Mandarin is expected to improve China identity, and English is expected to promote pro-West sentiment.

Education is measured from 0 (lowest) to 1 (highest), ranging from primary or below (0), lower secondary (0.25), upper secondary (0.5), sub-degree (0.75), and degree and above (1). The education sector in Hong Kong allegedly has been at the forefront of the anti-China social movements.[43] If this allegation is true, education is expected to promote pro-West and anti-China feelings.

To compare the difference between the colonial era and the postcolonial era, dividing the survey sample into two age groups, 39 and younger in one group, and 40 and older in another group is necessary. Age 16 is considered the year when one completes political socialization during which one's political attitudes and values are taught.[44] If one turned 16 in or before 1997, by the time of the survey in 2021, that colonial cohort should be 40 or older. The postcolonial cohort turned 16 in 1998 or later. Twenty-three years later, in 2020, that cohort should be 39 or younger. Given the PRC's reluctant hands-off policy in the postcolonial period, the postcolonial generation should be more anti-China than the older cohort.

Social class is measured by a question about the respondents' self-reported social status. It is divided into five categories, upper, upper middle, middle, lower middle, and lower classes. It is not immediately clear if the upper classes are more or less pro-China. There are reasons to believe that these people are expected to show their loyalty to China because their economic interests are more tied to the Mainland. Others would argue that these people are more exposed to Western values through their education and economic activities and therefore expected to be more pro-West.

Place of birth will be included in the analysis. It is expected that those who were born in Hong Kong will be more anti-China than the respondents who were born in the Mainland.

Finally, media effect is measured by the respondents' reported usage of two media outlets, *Apple Daily* and *Oriental Daily News*, ranging from never, monthly, weekly, several times a week, daily, and several times daily. These two newspapers are chosen for two reasons. First, they are known for their political orientations. *Apple Daily* is known for its anti-China view, and *Oriental Daily News* is considered pro-China.[45] Second, these are the top two most popular paid newspapers among the 19 media outlets included in the

---
[43] Lee 2021.
[44] Tang and Parish 2000.
[45] Yu 2014.

Hong Kong Political Culture Survey.[46] On a scale from 0% (least popular) to 100% (most popular), *Oriental Daily News* ranks at the top (22%) and *Apple Daily* is the second most popular at 19%. *Apple Daily* is expected to encourage anti-China sentiment and *Oriental Daily News* will have an opposite effect.

Appendices 3.1 and 3.2 show the coding schemes of the above variables and their summary statistics.

Levels of Political Identities in Hong Kong

This section will analyze the six measures of Hong Kong political identity described in the previous section, including (1) perceived identity with traditional Chinese culture and with the Chinese state, (2) preference for people from different countries and regions, (3) ideological orientation measured by political color, (4) perceived ethnicity, (5) preference for Eastern or Western values, and (6) intent to immigrate to the West. The next section will further examine the sources of these political identity measures.

Figure 3.1 shows the respondents' weighted assessment of the six items related to China, including Chinese civilization, Chinese culture, Chinese movies/TV shows, Chinese sports, Chinese political system, and Chinese Communist Party (CCP). The top two highest scores are for Chinese civilization (0.57) and Chinese culture (0.56), followed by the other four significantly lower scores of Chinese sports (0.45), Chinese movies (0.30), Chinese political system (0.30), and the CCP (0.26). A factor analysis groups the six items into two categories, the first two in one and the remaining four in another. The factor behind the first two items is related to traditional Chinese culture and the factor behind the four items in the second category is related to the Chinese state. As shown in Appendix 3.2, the weighted mean values are 0.57 for Chinese cultural identity or cultural nationalism (variable named as cultural nationalism), which is 20% higher than the identity to the Chinese state or political nationalism (0.33, variable named as political nationalism).

Figure 3.2 shows the Hong Kong respondents' feelings toward people from six countries and regions. The top two are Taiwan (0.78) and Singapore (0.75) followed by the United Kingdom (0.68) and the United States (0.63). At the bottom are China (0.50) and India (0.49).

This ranking does not seem to rely on the respondents' assessment of the level of political democracy in these countries and regions. For example, Singapore is by no means a model of Western liberal democracy. It is only

---

[46] If we also include free newspapers, the freely distributed *Headline* is the most popular (33%), followed by the second most popular *Oriental Daily News* (22%, paid), and the third most popular *Apple Daily* (19%, paid).

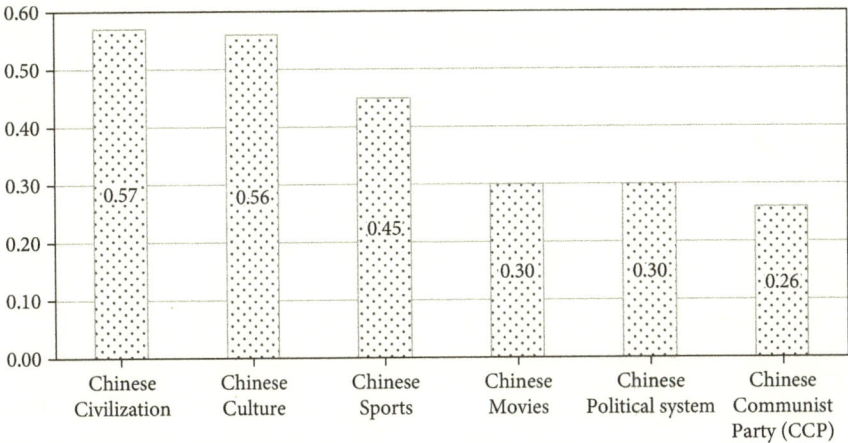

Figure 3.1 Hong Kong residents' feelings toward Chinese culture and the Chinese state (weighted by social desirability)

Main findings: This figure shows the respondents' weighted assessment of the six items related to China, including Chinese civilization, Chinese culture, Chinese movies/TV shows, Chinese sports, Chinese political system, and Chinese Communist Party (CCP). The top two highest scores are for Chinese civilization (0.57) and Chinese culture (0.56), followed by the other four significantly lower scores of Chinese sports (0.45), Chinese movies (0.30), Chinese political system (0.30), and the CCP (0.26).

Notes: The chart displays the level of support of six China-related items ranging from 0 to 1, where 1 indicates the highest level of support. Figures are rounded off to the nearest hundredths.

Source: Hong Kong Political Culture Survey 2021.

scored 48 out of 100 and received the status of "partly free" on the annual global report on political rights and civil liberties by the Freedom House.[47] Yet Singapore is preferred to Taiwan, which received a score of 94 and was labeled as "free" in the same Freedom House ranking. What the two share is the identification with East Asian Confucian tradition. India, which scored 66 as partly free, is ranked the lowest among the six selected countries and regions, together with China with a Freedom House score of only 9. Again, the gap in the alleged levels of democracy between the two countries did not matter. The United Kingdom and the United States, the two supposed models of democracy, were understandably ranked higher than China and India. Yet interestingly Hongkongers did not extend the same levels of welcome as they gave to their East Asian neighbors of Taiwan and Singapore.

[47] Freedom House 2021.

54 Proud and Angry

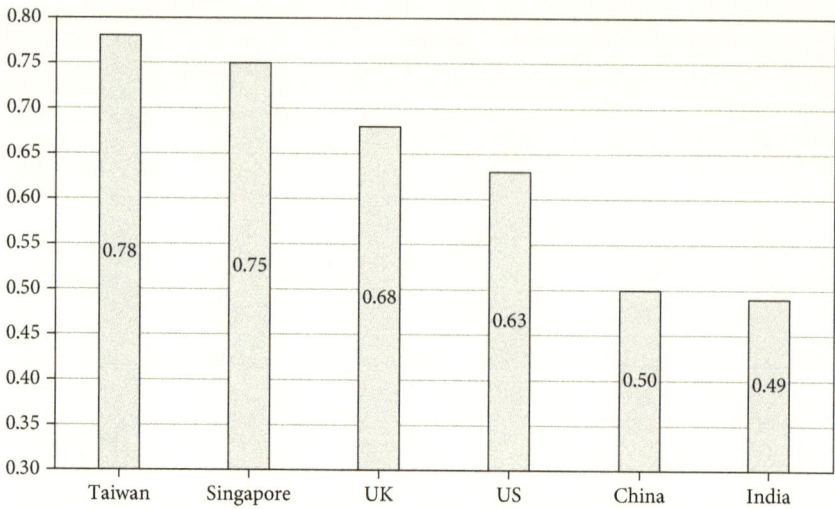

Figure 3.2 Hong Kong residents' feelings toward people from other countries and regions

Main findings: This figure shows the Hong Kong respondents' feelings toward people from six countries and regions. The top two are Taiwan (0.78) and Singapore (0.75) followed by the United Kingdom (0.68) and the United States (0.63). At the bottom are China (0.50) and India (0.49).

Notes: The chart shows the weighted impressions of people from six countries or regions with values ranging from 0 to 1. 1 indicates the best impression, and 0 means the worst. All differences are statistically significant at *p*<.001, except for the differences between Singapore and Taiwan, and between China and India. Figures are rounded off to the nearest hundredths.

Source: Hong Kong Political Culture Survey 2021.

Table 3.1 includes the remaining three measures of political identity: perceived ethnicity, preference for Eastern or Western values, and intention to immigrate to the West. When asked about their identification with an ethnic category, around 76% identified themselves as Hongkongers, 21% as Chinese Hongkongers or Chinese, and 3% as other. Local Hong Kong identity is the strongest, while the percentage of Chinese identity has fluctuated over time according to a local survey.[48] Even though the 21% of Chinese identity is significantly lower than local identity, it is still a sizable minority group.

For Eastern and Western values, a slight majority (56%) of the survey respondents picked Western liberal values; 44% thought Confucian values or both Western and Confucian values were important. Though Western values are more popular than Confucian values, a sizable minority are supportive of traditional Chinese culture.

---

[48] Hong Kong Public Opinion Research Institute 2021.

Indigenization of Political Identity 55

Photo 3.2 Taiwan became the biggest beneficiary of the Hong Kong protest. Tsai Yin-wen rode on the anti-China sentiment and easily won her presidential reelection in 2020. Tamkang University, Taiwan. Photo by Wenfang Tang, 12/22/2023.

The last item in Table 3.1 is the intention to immigrate to societies that are friendly to Western liberal values, such as Europe, North America, Japan, or Taiwan. Only about 18% of the survey respondents expressed their

Table 3.1 Three Selected Identity Measures (weighted by social desirability)

Perceived Ethnic Identity		Weighted%
	Hong Kong	76.25%
	Chinese	11.54%
	Chinese Hong Kong	9.16%
	Other	3.04%
East or West Values Preference		
	Western liberalism	56.16%
	Confucianism	7.72%
	Both are important	36.12%
Move to Europe, North America, Japan, or Taiwan		
	No	82.20%
	Yes	17.80%

The table indicates the weighted percentage of respondent's (1) ethnic identity represented by Hong Kong, Chinese, Chinese Hong Kong, or other; (2) preference for Eastern (benevolence, integrity, filial piety, and restraint), Western (freedom, democracy, human rights, and the rule of law), or both values; and (3) having a plan to immigrate to Europe, North America, Japan, or Taiwan.

Note: Percentages do not sum to 100% due to rounding.

Source: Hong Kong Political Culture Survey 2021.

willingness to immigrate to these societies in the next two years. This low percentage may be somewhat unexpected since Hong Kong is supposedly in a state of shock by the Hong Kong National Security Law, and many people who were active during the anti-China protests in the past are supposedly feeling scared and unsafe.[49]

In summary, the findings in this section show a cold attitude toward the Chinese state among Hong Kong residents. Their view of the Chinese state is significantly less favorable than their view of Chinese culture. Mainland Chinese are generally less preferred than other East Asians, particularly those from Singapore and Taiwan. The majority do not identify themselves as Chinese.

In the meantime, the sentiment toward the former colonists and their allies is not as warm as expected. For example, the UK and the US are not viewed the most favorably, and relatively few people are thinking about immigrating to the West.

Finally, there seems to be a strong preference for Hong Kong's self-identity, and such identity seems to be related to preference for traditional Chinese culture and Confucian values. For example, there is a very strong preference

---

[49] Needler 2020; Wazir 2021.

for Hong Kong's ethnic identity; strong support of traditional Chinese civilization; surprisingly strong preference for people from East Asian societies; and a large minority thought that Confucian values were at least just as important as Western liberal values. These findings point to a pattern of indigenization of political identity in postcolonial Hong Kong.

Sources of Political Identity

This section analyzes the sources of political identity. Specifically, it will examine how the respondents' language ability, education, age, social class, birthplace, and media consumption affect the above measures of political identity. To make the results easier to present, the six items in Figure 3.1 are regrouped into cultural identity and political identity (variables named as cultural nationalism and political nationalism); only China and the UK are selected for country preferences in Figure 3.2 (variables named as impression of Mainlanders and impression of British), representing old and new rulers; level of pro-establishment orientation is measured by political color coded from 0 to 1 scale (variable named as pro-establishment); ethnic identity is coded 1 as Chinese, 0.5 as both, and 0 as Hongkonger (variable named as Chinese identity); preference for Eastern or Western values are coded 1 as Eastern, 0.5 as both and 0 as Western (variable named as Eastern values); immigration intention is coded 1 and others as 0. Please see Appendices 3.1 and 3.2 for further details about these variables. To make sure the estimates of the above variables are unbiased, the survey respondents' geographic location is controlled by including the 72 electoral districts. The multilevel regression results are presented in Table 3.2.

In Table 3.2, Mandarin ability (variable named as Putonghua ability) promotes both Chinese culture and PRC identities (variables named as cultural nationalism and political nationalism, impression of Mainlanders, pro-establishment) but discourages pro-West feelings (variable named as impression of British). Since all the variables are coded on 0–1 scale (see Appendix 3.2), except education, the OLS coefficient for each independent variable has a range from −1 to 1, and it can be interrupted as a percentage change. In the case of Mandarin ability, increasing it from minimum (0) to maximum (1) will increase cultural identity by 14.8% and PRC identity by 18.5%. It will improve the image of Mainlanders by about 13.4% but worsen the image of the British by 15.7%. Mandarin ability also makes the respondents about 5.5% bluer or closer to pro-establishment and increases Eastern values by about 5.6%.

Table 3.2 Sources of Hong Kong Ethnic and Political Identity (multilevel OLS regression)

Variables	(1) Cultural nationalism	(2) Political nationalism	(3) Impression of Mainlanders	(4) Impression of British	(5) Pro-establishment	(6) Chinese identity	(7) Eastern values	(8) Immigrate intention
Putonghua ability	0.148***	0.185***	0.134***	−0.157***	0.055***	0.035	0.056***	−0.001
English ability	−0.087***	−0.092***	−0.072***	−0.022	−0.038***	−0.095***	−0.166***	0.125***
Edu	−0.013**	−0.035***	−0.014***	0.041***	−0.018***	−0.014*	−0.003	0.004
Post97	−0.143***	−0.146***	−0.095***	0.043	−0.084***	−0.133***	−0.140***	−0.075**
Post97#c.edu	0.024***	0.019***	0.011*	−0.009	0.006	0.020*	0.013	0.027***
Lower class (comparison)								
Lower middle class	0.019**	0.037***	0.017*	−0.035***	0.012*	−0.029**	0.037***	−0.012
Middle class	0.009	0.037***	0.011	−0.009	0.024***	−0.037**	0.045***	0.001
Upper middle class	−0.003	0.024	0.012	0.034	0.032**	−0.026	0.064**	0.106***
Upper class	−0.212***	−0.102	−0.074	0.060	−0.083	−0.053	−0.030	0.273***
Born HK (comparison)								
Born Mainland	0.019**	0.058***	0.059***	−0.009	0.045***	0.440***	0.073***	−0.031**
Born elsewhere	−0.071***	−0.097***	0.106***	0.013	0.030***	−0.120***	0.008	−0.076***
Apple Daily	−0.183***	−0.222***	−0.193***	0.110***	−0.189***	−0.191***	−0.258***	0.115***

Oriental Daily	0.056***	0.128***	0.072***	-0.085***	0.130***	0.167***	0.194***	-0.072***
Constant	0.690***	0.493***	0.601***	0.612***	0.520***	0.292***	0.444***	0.030**
Observations	3696	3605	3725	3725	3705	3517	3723	3726
Adj. R^2	0.202	0.419	0.255	0.098	0.368	0.450	0.238	0.114
Number of district council constituency areas	72	72	72	72	72	72	72	72

*** $p<0.01$, ** $p<0.05$, * $p<0.1$

This table shows that Mandarin ability (variable named as Putonghua ability) promotes both Chinese culture and PRC identities (variables named as cultural nationalism and political nationalism, impression of Mainlanders, pro-establishment) but discourages pro-West feelings (variable named as impression of British). Since all the variables are coded on 0–1 scale (see Appendix 3.2), except education, the OLS coefficient for each independent variable has a range from −1 to 1, and it can be interrupted as a percentage change. In the case of Mandarin ability, increasing it from minimum (0) to maximum (1) will increase cultural identity by 14.8% and PRC identity by 18.5%. It will improve the image of Mainlanders by about 13.4% but worsen the image of the British by 15.7%. Mandarin ability also makes the respondents about 5.5% bluer or closer to pro-establishment and increases Eastern values by about 5.6%.

Notes: See Appendices 3.1 and 3.2 for the definition of the variables and their summary statistics. Gender is controlled but not shown (women are more pro-UK less pro-establishment, with less Chinese ethnic identity but with more Eastern values and less intention to immigrate). OLS is used for categorical variables immigrate intention, Chinese identity, and Eastern values for easier comparisons with other coefficients. Logit regression was used, and the results were the same in significance levels and in their signs (− or +).

Source: Hong Kong Political Culture Survey 2021.

Mandarin-language education has been one of the controversial policies implemented by the postcolonial Hong Kong government. Before 1997, the British colonists promoted bilingual education of Cantonese and English while discouraging Mandarin or Putonghua.[50] After 1997, trilingual education in schools was first proposed by then Chief Executive Tung Chee Hwa in his 1997 policy address, aiming at proficient written English and Chinese and spoken Cantonese, English, and Putonghua for secondary school graduates,[51] as well as formulating Putonghua as an elective subject in the Hong Kong Certificate of Education Examinations by the year 2000. Since 1998, Putonghua has become one of the compulsory subjects at the primary and junior secondary levels,[52] and a nonmonetary supporting scheme was launched to make Putonghua a primary medium of instruction for Chinese-language courses in 40 schools by the Standing Committee on Language Education and Research between 2008 and 2013.[53]

Such initiatives encountered resistance by some local groups.[54] Currently, in Hong Kong's public examination—Hong Kong Diploma of Secondary Education Examination, or HKDSE—the core subjects include Chinese, English, math, liberal studies, and citizenship and social development. Putonghua has never been a core subject; students have the option to select Putonghua as a testing language in listening and integrated skill section of their Chinese-language examination.[55] Consequently, Mandarin was only recommended but never required in public exams and as a teaching medium in the first stage of postcolonial Hong Kong.[56] This resistance to Mandarin seems to contribute to the overall resistance to Chinese influence in the former colony.

Understandably, English-language ability plays the opposite role of Mandarin. Compared with non-English speakers, English speakers identify less with Chinese culture (variable named as cultural nationalism) by −8.7%, with Chinese state (variable named as political nationalism) by −9.2%, with Mainlanders (variable named as impression of Mainlanders) by −7.2%, with pro-establishment orientation (variable named as pro-establishment) by −3.8%, with Chinese ethnicity (variable named as Chinese identity) by −9.5%, and with Eastern values (variable named as Eastern values) by −16.6%

---

[50] Wen 2021.
[51] Tung 1997.
[52] CDC 2017; GHKSAR 2021b.ss
[53] SCOLAR 2018.
[54] Ng, Yi, and Lee 2017; Wen 2021.
[55] HKEAA 2021a and 2021b.
[56] HKEAA 2021a and 2021b.

Photo 3.3 Wall slogan: Protect Hong Kong and kick out the disease-carrying Mainland locusts. Hang Hau MRT station. Photo by Wenfang Tang, 1/20/2020.

and are more likely to encourage immigration to Western-friendly societies (immigrate intention) by about 12.5%.

Education is another controversial policy in postcolonial Hong Kong. Topics such as the Opium War, Hong Kong's colonial beginning, and the CCP's

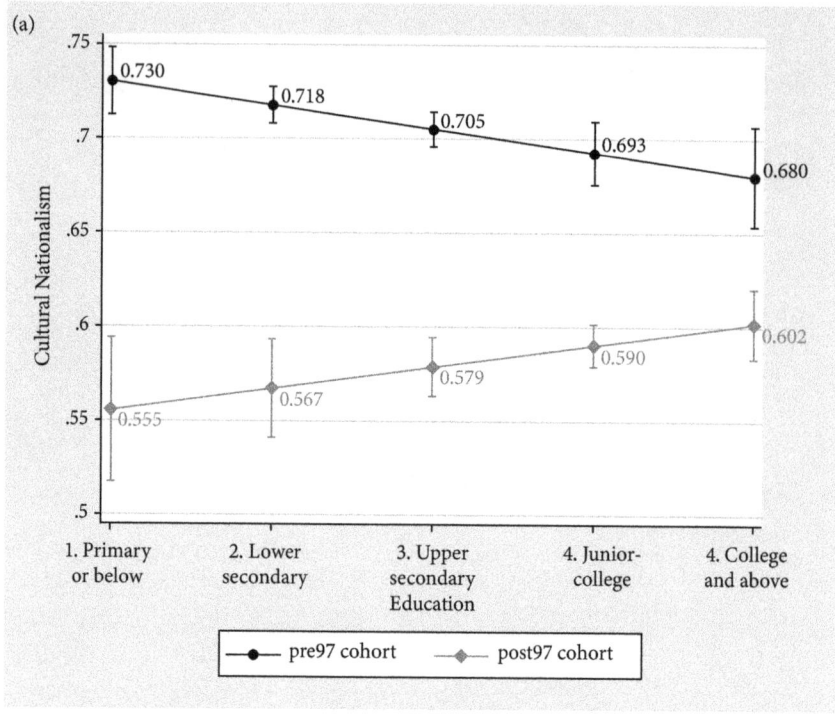
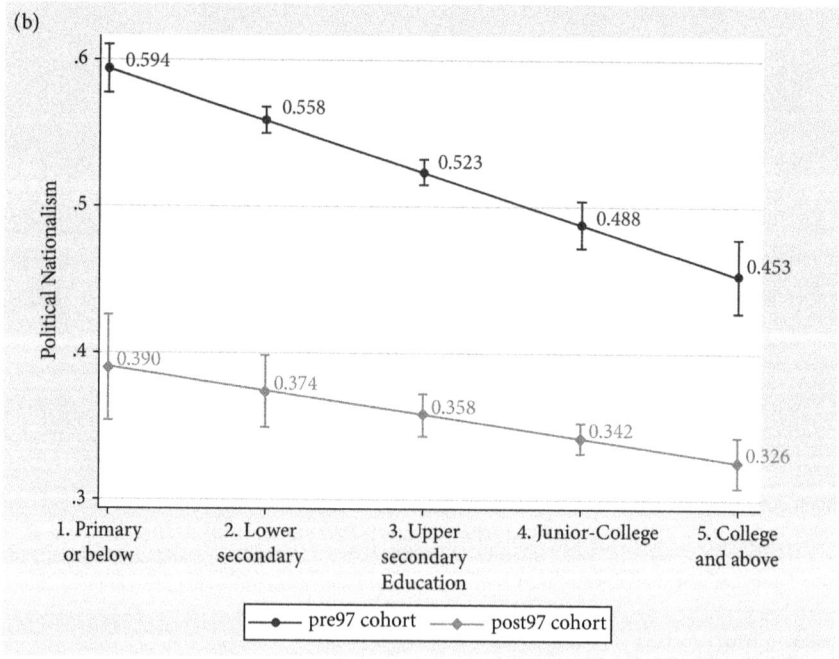

Figure 3.3

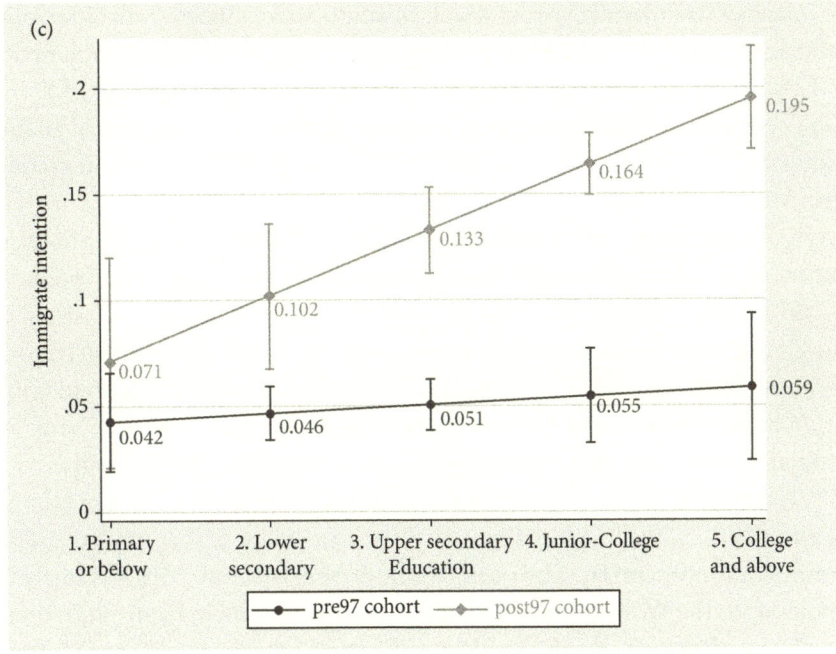

Figure 3.3 Two-way interaction between education and age on cultural nationalism (a), political nationalism (b), and immigration intention (c).
Main findings: In Figures 3.3a and 3.3b, when education improves from the lowest level (primary or below) to the highest level (college degree or above), both cultural nationalism and political nationalism decrease by 5% (0.730–0.680=0.05x100=5.0%, Figure 3.3a) and by 14.1% (0.594–0.453, Figure 3.3b) for the pre-1997 cohort, suggesting a consistent anti-tradition and anti-PRC association with education under the British colonial rule. For the post-1997 cohort, education plays the opposite role in promoting cultural nationalism and political nationalism. It promotes cultural nationalism by 4.7% (0.602–0.555, Figure 3.3a), but suppresses political nationalism by 6.4% (0.39–0.326, Figure 3.3b). In Figure 3.3c, education slightly increases the pre-1997 cohort's intention to immigrate to Western friendly societies (0.059–0.042=1.7%), but it does so by a much higher 12.4% (0.195–0.071, Figure 3.3c) among the post-1997 cohort.
Source: Hong Kong Political Culture Survey 2021.

victory over the Kuomintang (KMT) are resisted by the local teachers' groups from being taught in the common core education in postcolonial Hong Kong.[57] Consequently, as education moves from lower to higher levels, it plays a negative role by reducing Chinese cultural and state identities (cultural nationalism and political nationalism) by −1.3% and −3.5%, respectively, and

---

[57] Lam and Zhao 2017.

the image of Mainlanders by −1.4%. Education also reduces one's blue political color by about −1.8%. In the meantime, it makes the British look better by 4.1%. Some people may think the PRC had intervened enough in Hong Kong's education.[58] In contrast, the findings in this study based on available evidence show that education leads to alienation from, but not integration with, Mainland China.

Age shows a strong and consistent association on anti-China and pro-West sentiment. For the age group 39 and younger who completed their political socialization in postcolonial Hong Kong, it is predictably and consistently anti-China, anti-tradition, and pro-West. Compared with the colonial cohort, the postcolonial cohort is −14.3%, −14.6%, and −9.5% less likely to identify with Chinese culture, the Chinese state, and Mainland Chinese. The postcolonial cohort does not show a significant preference for the British, but 8.4% less blue, 13.3% less likely to think they belong to the Chinese ethnicity, and 14% less likely to identify with Confucian values. The only exception is immigration intention. The postcolonial cohort is about 7.5% less likely to immigrate to the Western-friendly societies. But as shown in Figure 3.3c, there are diverse directions of immigration intention when age cohort is jointly studied with education.

The above discussion treats the associations of the dependent variables with education and age separately. Sometimes examining their joint impact may yield clearer patterns of how they interact with each other. The interaction variable of Post97#c.edu integrates education and age on the measures of political identity. It shows that the negative association with education is significantly stronger for the postcolonial cohort than the pre-1997 cohort in cultural and PRC identities and for their intention to immigrate.

Figures 3.3a, 3.3b, and 3.3c are more intuitive ways to show the association of cultural nationalism, political nationalism, and immigration intention with the interaction of the education and age cohorts. In Figures 3.3a and 3.3b, when education improves from the lowest level (primary or below) to the highest level (college degree or above), both cultural nationalism and political nationalism decrease by 5% (0.730−0.680=0.05x100=5.0%, Figure 3.3a) and by 14.1% (0.594−0.453, Figure 3.3b) for the pre-1997 cohort, suggesting a consistent anti-tradition and anti-PRC association with education under the British colonial rule. For the post-1997 cohort, education plays the opposite role in promoting cultural nationalism and political nationalism. It promotes

---

[58] Chau 2020.

cultural nationalism by 4.7% (0.602–0.555, Figure 3.3a) but suppresses political nationalism by 6.4% (0.39–0.326, Figure 3.3b). In other words, in postcolonial Hong Kong, education is positively associated with both cultural identity and anti-PRC sentiment. In Figure 3.3c, education slightly increases the pre-1997 cohort's intention to immigrate to Western-friendly societies (0.059–0.042=1.7%), but it does so by a much higher 12.4% (0.195–0.071, Figure 3.3c) among the post-1997 cohort. These findings suggest that education experienced a very interesting shift, from suppressing both Chinese tradition and pro-China sentiment under British rule to promoting Chinese tradition but encouraging anti-China feelings in the post-1997 era. The shifting role of education from anti- to pro-tradition could be a reflection of the education sector's lost colonial mandate and its effort to search for a new focus while continuing to keep a distance from China. Consequently, education seems to have contributed to the indigenization of the post-Handover generation's political identity.

Social class also shows an interesting pattern. The top 1% very rich are significantly less pro-Chinese culture. This group is also less pro-PRC, more pro-UK, less blue and with less Chinese ethnic identity, less Eastern values but more intention to immigrate than the lower classes. Even if some of the regression coefficients are not statistically significant, their values are high enough to notice (model 4, Table 3.2). The lower middle classes stand out as the least pro-UK among the five social classes, perhaps due to the colonial memory of powerlessness. Though the top 5% upper middle class seems to show more pro-establishment sentiment by being more blue or pro-establishment, this group is also interestingly more likely to move to the West than the other lower classes. One possibility is that this is their survival strategy. They want to show their support for the regime to protect their vested interests in Hong Kong while safeguarding themselves by getting ready to leave if things go wrong. This seems to be an opportunistic approach.

Place of birth demonstrates a consistent pattern. Compared with those born in Hong Kong, those born in the Mainland reported stronger sentiments toward Chinese culture, the Chinese state, Mainlanders, blue color (pro-establishment), Chinese ethnicity, and Confucian values, and they are less likely to immigrate. These are all expected.

For media consumption, *Apple Daily* and *Oriental Daily News* created opposite results. The former encouraged anti-PRC and anti-Chinese culture feelings consistently across all measures. *Oriental Daily News*, on the other hand, is exactly the opposite. These are again expected, given the known political stands of the two papers. What is interesting, is the different degrees of influence between the two top-circulated newspapers. For every single measure of political identity, the negative association with *Apple Daily* is stronger than *Oriental Daily News*'s positive association, and the correlation coefficients of *Apple Daily* are the highest among almost all the independent variables in Table 3.2. It is understandable why the Hong Kong government closed *Apple Daily* given its powerful influence in negatively shaping public opinion in postcolonial Hong Kong.[59] Chapter 6 will further discuss the role of media in Hong Kong.

To summarize, the above findings show the consequences of stage one of Hong Kong's return to China in which China was unable to interfere with Hong Kong's colonial social infrastructure left by the UK, particularly in language policy, education, postcolonial cohort's political socialization, and the media sector.

Robustness Check

This final section will conduct a further check on the reliability of the media estimate in Table 3.2. *Apple Daily*, as shown in Table 3.2, played a strong and negative role in promoting pro-China sentiment in Hong Kong. Is such an estimate real? Could it be possible that people develop anti-China feelings first, and that makes them read *Apple Daily* more often? In other words, could the causal direction from *Apple Daily* to anti-China attitude be in reverse?

How to confirm the causal impact of *Apple Daily* in anti-China sentiment? One option is to use an instrumental variable.[60] The instrumental variable (Z) is a variable that is related to X (*Apple Daily*) but not to Y (anti-China feeling). If X causes Y to change through Z, then the causality from X to Y can be further confirmed. One variable in the survey that can serve as an instrumental variable is the closure of *Apple Daily*'s hardcopy edition on June 24, 2021, halfway through our survey. It is a 0–1 variable (after *Apple Daily* closure) for before (coded 0) and after (coded 1) the paper's closure. In examining the correlations (not shown), after *Apple Daily* closure is strongly correlated with the consumption of *Apple Daily* but not with the eight dependent variables in Table 3.2, thus it is qualified to serve as an instrumental variable.

Table 3.3 presents the results of the two-stage instrumental variable regression. In the first stage (models 1 and 4), *Apple Daily*'s readership significantly dropped after the closure of its paper edition (after *Apple Daily* closure). Consequently, its negative correlation coefficients (cultural nationalism and political nationalism) are also reduced in models 2 and 5 in Table 3.3, as

---

[59] Chen, Cui, and Leng 2021.
[60] Pokropek 2016.

Table 3.3 Robustness Check (two-stage IV regression)

VARIABLES	(1) Apple Daily	(2) Cultural nationalism	(3) Cultural nationalism	(4) Apple Daily	(5) Political nationalism	(6) Political nationalism
Oriental Daily	−0.048***	0.062***	0.058***	−0.050***	0.137***	0.133***
After Apple Daily closure	−0.147***			−0.149***		
Apple Daily		−0.114**	−0.184***		−0.156***	−0.221***
Constant	0.213***	0.681***	0.691***	0.215***	0.507***	0.517***
Observations	3,696	3,696	3,696	3,605	3,605	3,605
R^2	0.200	0.211	0.219	0.201	0.425	0.431

*** $p<0.01$, ** $p<0.05$, * $p<0.1$

This table presents the results of the two-stage instrumental variable regression. In the first stage (models 1 and 4), *Apple Daily*'s readership significantly dropped after the closure of its paper edition (after *Apple Daily* closure). Consequently, its negative correlation coefficients cultural nationalism and political nationalism are also reduced in models 2 and 5, as compared to *Apple Daily*'s coefficients in models 3 and 6 that are almost the same as in Table 3.2 without using predicted value of *Apple Daily* by the instrumental variable to estimate the OLS model. This causal chain from the instrumental variable to X then to Y suggests that the correlation direction is from *Apple Daily* to the anti-China sentiment while rejecting the possibility of reversing the direction of the correlation.

Notes: Results controlled for socioeconomic factors, including language abilities (Putonghua and English), age cohort, education, gender, and birthplace. See Appendix 3.3 for the full models with control variables.

Source: Hong Kong Political Culture Survey 2021.

compared to *Apple Daily*'s coefficients in models 3 and 6 that are almost the same as in Table 3.2 without using predicted value of *Apple Daily* by the instrumental variable to estimate the OLS model. This causal chain from the instrumental variable to X then to Y suggests that the correlation direction is from *Apple Daily* to the anti-China sentiment while rejecting the possibility of reversing the direction of the correlation.

Conclusions

In the beginning section, this chapter describes the various theories of postcolonial identity, ranging from continued colonial legacy to a new decolonized identity, as well as the constructivist view of the interaction between the old and the new in identity formation. In Hong Kong's unique postcolonial political vacuum, this study suggests that political identity is formed neither by the colonial legacy nor by the new ruler's ideology. Instead, Hongkongers are going back to their cultural roots and converting such cultural identity into a political one.

The empirical evidence presented in this chapter mostly supports the hypotheses developed earlier. It shows an overall cold feeling toward the Chinese state and Mainland Chinese people (hypothesis 1). The findings also present a somewhat indifferent feeling toward the West, particularly toward the territory's former colonial rulers (hypothesis 2). In this vacuum left by the old and new rulers, Hong Kong residents are looking to restore traditional culture for their political identity in a process that can be described as indigenization (hypothesis 3). China's reluctant laissez-faire policies further encouraged the trend of indigenization (hypothesis 4).

Hong Kong's experience with indigenization of political identity suggests that the One Country, Two System policy will not work well if there is not a unified political identity in the "One Country" part of the institutional design. It is easy to talk about it as a clever design; the implementation of "One Country" runs into problems in many branches of Hong Kong society, education, legal system, media, and even the official language policy, resulting in the failure of a pro-China identity. The Hong Kong National Security Law of 2020 requires mandatory political identity and loyalty. In another 20 years or so, it will be time to re-examine political identity in phase 2 of postcolonial Hong Kong.

Finally, this chapter contributes to the existing studies on "local identity."[61] It further clarifies the meaning of local identity by separating traditional cultural identity from colonial identity and Chinese state identity. It shows how people can fall back to their cultural identity in a political vacuum under One Country, Two Systems. In this political vacuum, political anxiety was created by the departure of the colonists and the inability of China as the territory's new ruler to establish its own effective governance. To cope with this political anxiety, indigenization of political identity emerged. To what extent this trend will continue depends on how quickly China can establish its own political reputation among the territory's residents.

---

[61] Fung 2001; Steinhardt, Li, and Jiang 2018; Veg 2017.

4
Political Trust Under One Country, Two Systems

Introduction

July 1, 1997, Hong Kong was in the spotlight on the world stage when the British flag was lowered and the Chinese flag was raised. The event symbolized the end of the 156-year rule by the British Empire and the rise of communist China as a new "empire." Yet Hong Kong's return to Chinese rule could not have happened in a more politically "incorrect" moment in history. The last decade of the 20th century was a time when the Western world was celebrating the triumph of liberal democracy and market capitalism after the collapse of communism in the Soviet bloc. It could not be more anticlimactic and more ironic when the Chinese communist government took control of Hong Kong, which was a crown jewel of market capitalism. When some patriotic Hongkongers praised their new ruler, Western politicians and many other Hongkongers were biting their tongue and could not get over the bitter taste of Hong Kong's return to China, an event that did not seem to make sense in history. Such animosity planted deep-rooted distrust in the minds of some people in Hong Kong and in the Western liberal democratic world.

This chapter will draw data from the 2021 Hong Kong Political Culture Survey and show how this distrust developed and how it is distributed between the central and local governments, as well as among different institutions, officials, and policies. Before analyzing the survey data, it is necessary to provide readers with a background discussion of Hong Kong's political landscape in the postcolonial era.

The Evolving Political Landscape in Postcolonial Hong Kong

Hong Kong's political system is difficult to categorize in a standard comparative politics textbook. It carries elements of both liberal democratic and authoritarian systems left by the British and under the new institutional arrangement created by China under the One Country, Two Systems policy. This hybrid system that mixes oil and water has created tensions and controversies in the past quarter century since Hong Kong's Handover.

The Basic Law and the Chris Patten Controversies

The Basic Law of the Hong Kong Special Administrative Region (HKSAR) of the People's Republic of China was jointly drafted in 1990 by China and the British-backed Hong Kong representatives and promulgated in 1997 upon Hong Kong's return to China. As the de facto constitution of Hong Kong, the Basic Law defines Hong Kong's postcolonial political structure, which will be discussed below. Perhaps the best-known and the most controversial aspect of the Basic Law is its promise to keep Hong Kong's "capitalist system and its way of life" unchanged for 50 years. While the Basic Law declares China's sovereignty over Hong Kong, it recognizes Hong Kong's self-governance and grants the HKSAR a high degree of autonomy.[1]

One of the controversies surrounding the Basic Law is the so-called electoral reform initiated by the colony's last British governor Chris Patten. In the Basic Law, China and the UK agreed that the members of Hong Kong's Legislative Council, or Legco, would be elected by a Beijing-backed electoral council called the functional constituencies. In 1995, two years before Hong Kong's Handover to China, Patten unilaterally changed the rule of the game by bypassing the functional constituencies and allowing direct elections of the Legco members by popular vote. The elected Legco members' term was four years according to the original rule of the Basic Law, which meant the directly elected members would serve beyond Hong Kong's Handover in 1997 and could potentially play an uncooperative role under Chinese rule in post-1997 Hong Kong.

Patten's behavior intensified the conflict between China and the West over Hong Kong, which lasts until today. Supporters of Patten justified his action as revenge against China's crackdown on the 1989 Tiananmen protests, which the Western liberal world criticized because they sanctioned the protests.[2] China was unsurprisingly furious about Patten's betrayal of not keeping the mutual agreement of indirect elections through an electoral council in the

---

[1] GHKSAR 2021a.
[2] Amies 2009; Liu 2019.

Basic Law. In 1997 after the Handover, China replaced the directly elected Legislative Council with a Provisional Legislative Council until the next Legco election in 1998, which was held under the previously agreed rules specified in the Basic Law.

Patten's electoral reform deeply divided postcolonial Hong Kong.[3] Those who were suspicious of China became even more distrustful as they thought Patten sparked hope of a democracy, but it was crushed by China's authoritarian rule.[4] Others who felt closer to China became more hostile to the West and to the pro-Western forces in Hong Kong. They saw Patten's move as opportunist, unethical, and hypocritical because the British never promoted direct elections in their 150-plus years' rule in the colony.[5]

Article 23 and the National Security Law Controversies

Article 23 of the Basic Law is an untied knot that created major political instability in post-Handover Hong Kong. According to Article 23, Hong Kong should "enact laws on its own" concerning security issues related to treason, secession, sedition, and subversion against the central government in Beijing and against the HKSAR government and its political system of One Country, Two Systems. In 2003, six years after the Handover, the HKSAR government attempted to pass this law in the Legislative Council, but massive demonstrations on the streets erupted. The protesters were told that the law, if passed, would mean the end of Hong Kong's autonomy from China.[6] After realizing that it would not get enough votes in the Legco, the HKSAR government had to withdraw the bill.[7]

The anti-China forces in Hong Kong were encouraged by the perceived success of the 2003 protests. They continued to build anti-China momentum in 2014 during the Umbrella movement by resisting Beijing's effort to prescreen the candidates for the chief executive election to be held in 2017. The Umbrella movement ended after the protesters occupied the key areas of the city in Admiralty, Causeway Bay, and Mong Kok for two and half months, but without any compromise from Beijing. The Umbrella protesters argued that prescreening was an effort by Beijing to take total control and that it was a violation of free and competitive elections.[8] Others felt that it was the loss

---

[3] Ip 2020; Sing 2004.
[4] Mo and Zhou 2018.
[5] Wang 2021; Yee 2020.
[6] Chinoy 2003.
[7] Tong 2018.
[8] Bush 2014; Steven 2014.

of an opportunity to have the first universal suffrage in Hong Kong's chief executive election, even if it was limited.[9]

The anti-China sentiment in Hong Kong culminated in 2019 during the anti-extradition movement, which led to Beijing's running out of patience and passing and enforcing the National Security Law (NSL) in Hong Kong. The movement was triggered by a murder case committed by a Hong Kong tourist who killed his girlfriend in a hotel in Taiwan and escaped back to Hong Kong.[10] The Taiwanese court could not bring the fugitive back for trial because there was no extradition agreement between the two regions. The HKSAR government initiated an extradition bill, including not only Hong Kong, Taiwan, and Macau but also Mainland China. Fearing that if the bill were passed, Hong Kong residents could lose their legal protection and be arrested by the legal authorities in the Mainland,[11] massive protests erupted in the spring of 2019 and continued for almost a year into the spring of 2020.

China faced two choices in handling the increasingly violent anti-extradition protests in Hong Kong. One, it could send troops across the border and put down the violent protests by force, as it did during the 1989 Tiananmen crackdown. This option could be effective, but it would run into major condemnation by Western forces that were already actively supporting the anti-extradition protests.[12] Learning the lessons of Western boycotts against China in the aftermath of the 1989 Tiananmen protests, Beijing decided not to use force but to take the second option—the legal route.

To Beijing's benefit, the Basic Law left an opportunity to take legal action against the anti-extradition protests. This legal opportunity is in Article 18 of the Basic Law, which states that China can include a Chinese national law in Annex III of the Basic Law and make it applicable to Hong Kong when Beijing believes that its national security and national integrity are threatened. Previously, the national laws included in Annex III were related to issues such as requiring the use of the Chinese national anthem and national flag in Hong Kong. On July 1, 2020, the National People's Congress of China enacted the Hong Kong National Security Law (NSL) and inserted it in Annex III of the Basic Law.[13] From that time on, any radical anti-China and/or anti-HKSAR government behavior could be punished under treason, secession, sedition, and subversion. For some people, the NSL is simply a return of the colonial

---

[9] Greenberg 2015; Leung 2014.
[10] Sui 2019.
[11] Cheung 2019; Lum and Lam 2019.
[12] Lau and Delaney 2019.
[13] NPC 2020.

Photo 4.1 The total number of protesters reached an estimated 2 million people. Central, Hong Kong Island. Photo by Wenfang Tang, 7/1/2019.

era anti-sedition laws that were introduced in the early 20th century under British rule.[14]

The Hong Kong National Security Law of 2020 was immediately condemned by the US, the UK, and their followers in the Western liberal world.[15] Yet China seems to have emerged as a winner in this round of the fight for several reasons. The most obvious is the almost overnight crackdown of the anti-China protests and the restoration of political control and social order. Second, China was able to stop the political unrest without shedding a single drop of blood, therefore avoiding harsher and longer lasting Western political and economic sanctions unlike after the Tiananmen crackdown in 1989. Finally, by relying on Article 18 and Annex III, China was finally able to end the legal stalemate and paved the way for the eventual passage of Hong Kong's local security law in March 2024 as required in Article 23.[16] The remaining question, however, is whether China can win the hearts and minds of the public in Hong Kong in the post-NSL era. This is the question addressed in this chapter.

The Chief Executive Controversies

Hong Kong's young postcolonial political system has three branches, the executive, the legislative, and the judicial. Each branch is still evolving with its own built-in political tensions.

The executive branch is led by the chief executive, who is indirectly elected every five years by the Election Committee of 1,500 members evenly distributed in five sectors, including industrial and commercial, professional, grassroots, HKSAR and district legislators, and, finally, HKSAR deputies to the National People's Congress, Chinese People's Political Consultative Committee, and other national organizations.[17]

The elected chief executive (CE) may not serve more than two consecutive terms. There were five CEs in the first 25 years from 1997 to 2022: Tung Chee-hwa (1997–2005), Sir Donald Tsang (2005–2012), Leung Chun-ying (2012–2017), Carrie Lam (2017–2022), and John Lee Ka-chiu (2022–).

Tung Chee-hwa started his first term when the 1997 Asian financial crisis was occurring, which prevented him from realizing his goals, such as public housing construction. Tung resigned during his second term in 2005,

---

[14] Lai and Chan 2022; Torode and Pomfret 2022.
[15] Gopalakrishnan and Doyle 2021; Norman and Marson 2020.
[16] NPC 2020. See Article 7 of the Hong Kong National Security Law, Hong Kong Free Press. (HKFP), March 19, 2024.
[17] GHKSAR 2021b.

two years after his failed attempt to pass the national security law as specified in Article 23 of the Basic Law, which triggered massive public protests in 2003. Tung's resignation was also related to public dissatisfaction with his handling of SARS and corruption scandals surrounding his government officials.

Tung's successor Donald Tsang came into office in 2005 with the promise of universal suffrage for the CE and Legco elections. Tsang's tenure was marked by partial success in political reform. He managed to negotiate the agreement between Beijing and the pro-Western groups, or the pan-Democrats, to agree with limited reform in the 2012 CE election by introducing more directly elected district legislators in the Legco and in the Election Committee. Beijing conditionally agreed to implement universal suffrage in the 2017 CE election if the candidates could be pre-screened. Tsang resigned in 2012 during his second term due to a corruption scandal.

The third CE, Mr. Leung Chun-ying, continued to promote political reform when he entered office in 2012. Leung's effort faced a major problem when Beijing announced in 2014 that candidates for the CE election in 2017 would be nominated by a majority of a Beijing-controlled nomination committee. This news triggered another round of street protests and later became the Umbrella movement. The anti-China forces refused to accept Beijing's proposal, and the 2017 CE election continued to be an indirect election by the Election Committee without universal suffrage. As discussed above, some people say that the pan-Democrats missed an opportunity to have limited universal suffrage,[18] while others condemned China's unwillingness to compromise.[19]

The fourth CE, Carrie Lam, was the first female CE in Hong Kong and came into office in 2017. She experienced arguably the most turbulent time in Hong Kong's already turbulent postcolonial history. First was the anti-extradition movement in 2019, then the Covid-19 pandemic, and later the political purges of the anti-China and pro-West forces after the passage of the National Security Law in 2020.

Under her government, Beijing was able to revamp the election rules by strengthening the pro-China voices in the Election Committee (further discussed below). Universal suffrage was put aside indefinitely.

Carrie Lam completed her five-year term in 2022 and decided not to run for reelection. John Lee Ka-chiu, the police chief of Hong Kong loyal to Beijing, became the fifth CE.

---

[18] Lo 2021.
[19] Zeng 2015.

Photo 4.2 Poster against Chief Executive Carrie Lam. Hong Kong University of Science and Technology, Clear Water Bay. Photo by Wenfang Tang, 7/21/2019.

The Legislative Council Controversies

The Legislative Council, or the Legco, is the legislative branch of Hong Kong's political system. Since the election law was revised in 2021, the Legco contains 90 members serving five-year terms: 20 are directly elected from 10 electoral districts, 30 are elected by the traditional functional constituencies or occupational groups, and 40 are elected from the 1,500-member Election Committee. Before 2021, this rule was able to guarantee that pro-China candidates maintained their majority in the Legco since the Handover.[20]

However, during the 2019 anti-extradition movement, the pro-China control of the Legco faced a serious challenge. Riding on the momentum of the anti-China protests, the anti-establishment candidates grabbed 90% of the 452 district legislative council seats.[21] Encouraged by the landslide victory in the district elections, the real ambition of the anti-China groups was to gain a majority in the Legco election scheduled for the following year in 2020.[22]

To break the opposition's political momentum, Beijing decided to postpone the 7th Session Legco election until 2021 and revised the election rules.[23] By enlarging the size of the Legco from 70 to 90, the most important change implemented was the addition of the 40 members elected by the Beijing-controlled 1,500-member Election Committee. Meanwhile, the number of directly elected members from the 10 districts was reduced from 35 to 20. The purpose of such change was to minimize the uncontrollable elements and their influence while maintaining about the same number of 30 Legco members elected from the mostly pro-Beijing functional constituencies. To further limit the opposition's influence, Beijing also announced that only "patriots" were allowed to run. Such policies effectively eliminated the anti-China candidates from campaigning.

Consequently, voter turnout was only a little over 30%, and the pro-China candidates dominated the 7th Session of the Legco. Many think that the low-turnout rate was a sign of sliding support for Beijing.[24] Others, however, argue that the level of China support has not dropped. The low voter turnout is simply a reflection of the elimination of the non-patriotic candidates, and nonparticipation is due to the lack of choices among their supporters.[25] The turnout rate would be very similar to the previous elections had the anti-China candidates been allowed to run.

---

[20] Wikipedia 2023; Wong 2019.
[21] Graham-Harrison 2019.
[22] Davidson 2020; Soo 2020.
[23] Chau 2021.
[24] Yang 2021.
[25] Chan 2022; Gunia 2021; Strumpf and Yu 2021.

The Judiciary and Law Enforcement Controversies

Hong Kong's judicial structure has been mostly left unchanged in the post-Hanover era. It is organized hierarchically by the Court of Final Appeal at the top, followed by the High Court, district courts, and the magistrates' courts. Judges of the courts are appointed by the chief executive. Only Hong Kong permanent residents can serve as the chief judges of the Court of Final Appeal and the High Court.

Similar to the executive and legislative branches, Hong Kong's judicial system has been controversial since the Handover. At the center of controversy is judicial independence. Article 85 of the Basic Law states that members of the judiciary "shall exercise judicial power independently, free from any interference," and they "shall be immune from legal action" when performing their judicial functions. The anti-China groups see this article as a mechanism to guarantee checks and balances and separation of power, as well as prevent Beijing's interference in Hong Kong's judicial process.[26] China, on the other hand, rejects such ideas. It argues that Hong Kong is not a sovereign state, and it reports to Beijing through its officials in the executive branch. Hong Kong's courts should work under the framework of the Basic Law. Those who advocate judicial independence should not be allowed because they actually want judicial dominance in Hong Kong's political system so that they can overwrite China's sovereignty over Hong Kong.[27]

The second and related controversy about Hong Kong's judicial system is its elements left from the colonial era, namely the existence of foreign judges, or nonpermanent overseas judges from the British common law jurisdictions. This system left the former colonists with significant influence in the legal system in post-Handover Hong Kong, particularly in the Court of Final Appeal, which is filled mostly by non-local judges at the time of this writing.[28] Supporters of the system argue that such an arrangement can serve as a guarantee to prevent Beijing's control of Hong Kong.[29] Critiques say that such a system with the majority of judges in the Court of Final Appeal as foreigners with the title of British "lords" can hardly be independent from colonial rule when making their decisions. During the anti-extradition protests in 2019, the courts were frequently criticized for applying light or no sentences on those who committed violent anti-China actions.[30] In the post–National Security

---

[26] Pepper 2022.
[27] Global Times 2020; Xinhua News Agency 2020.
[28] Hong Kong Court of Final Appeal 2021; Judiciary of HKSAR 2021.
[29] Hui 2020.
[30] Kwok 2019.

Law era, these foreign judges are facing increasing pressure to resign.[31] In the meantime, the Court of Final Appeal, led by Chief Justice Andrew Cheung, continued to play a deviant role. For example, on March 6, 2025, it overturned the convictions of three members of an anti-Beijing group that organized an annual candlelight vigil to mark China's 1989 Tiananmen Square protest, arguing that the government prosecutors had obscured key facts.[32]

The third controversy surrounding Hong Kong's legal system is about the role of law enforcement. Hong Kong's law enforcement agencies have been caught in an awkward position during the numerous anti-Beijing protests since the Handover. They need to perform their duty of maintaining social order and show their loyalty to Beijing, but in the meantime, they have to face public anger and resentment toward China, and many of the protesters are probably their friends, neighbors, or even family members. During the anti-extradition movement in 2019, the police forces were divided—some upheld their professional responsibility of maintaining order,[33] and others showed more sympathy toward the protesters.[34] The public was equally divided between supporting the police crackdown on street violence[35] and aiding the protesters against police violence.[36]

In sum, in the 23 years between the Handover in 1997 and the National Security Law in 2020, although there were moments of calmness and short-lived goodwill toward China, Hong Kong was a society that was torn by political tension, conflict, and constant anti-China protests. In the remaining pages, this chapter will show how the Hong Kong public reacted to the political changes by examining their political trust and satisfaction with various government policies. Before showing the public opinion survey findings, the reader may benefit from a brief discussion on what political trust is about and how it is generated in different political systems.

Political Trust in Democratic and Authoritarian Societies

Political trust in this study is broadly defined as public support of the political system, the government, its officials, and policies. Political trust is a lubricant

---

[31] Cheung, Lam, and Lau 2020; Zhen 2020.
[32] Hong Kong's top court quashes convictions of pro-democracy Tiananmen group, March 6, 2025, *Reuters*, https://www.voanews.com/a/hong-kong-s-top-court-quashes-convictions-of-pro-democracy-tiananmen-group/8000733.html.
[33] Ives 2019; Hong Kong Police Force 2019.
[34] Yu 2019.
[35] Leung 2019.
[36] Leung and Lee 2019; Mahtani et al. 2019.

between the state and society.[37] It is desirable political capital that any government needs because it ensures the smooth functioning of the state as well as political stability in a society.[38]

In liberal democratic societies, governments gain public political trust through elections. By permitting political parties to compete with each other in periodical elections and by public acceptance of majority rule, liberal democratic governments enjoy the legitimacy of the commonly agreed procedure, or procedural justice.[39] Accordingly, election-based governments should enjoy strong public trust and regime legitimacy.[40]

The liberal democratic system worked well during the Cold War from the end of the World War II to the collapse of the Soviet bloc in the early 1990s. Regime support for and public political trust in democracy were high.[41] In recent years, however, political trust in liberal democracies has declined noticeably. For example, trust in political institutions has been consistently below 50% since the late 1990s and early 2000s in democratic societies such as the US, France, South Korea, India, Germany, the UK, Mexico, and Japan.[42]

Several reasons contribute to the decline of political trust in democratic societies. First, some key values, such as social and political diversity and pluralism, led to fragmentation of society and the government, intensified partisan fighting, and lowered government decision-making effectiveness. Second, competitive elections make politicians and political parties hyper-responsive to public opinion, but only during election seasons. In the time between elections, they enjoy relative job security and don't feel the need to respond to the voters, particularly to those who vote for the opposition parties. Consequently, constant partisan fighting, ineffectiveness in decision-making, and the low level of responsiveness to public demand may have caused the decline in political trust in these societies.[43]

In non-liberal democracies, political trust is less about so-called procedural justice and more about substantive justice, to borrow the distinction between the two approaches in legal studies.[44] In these societies, leadership succession is based on negotiation and consensus between various political groups within the ruling party, and no party competition is permitted. Yet even in these societies, it would be naive to believe that the government

---

[37] Fukuyama 1995.
[38] Easton 1965; Leonardi, Raffaella, and Putnam 1993.
[39] Schumpeter 1942.
[40] Almond and Verba 1963; Finifter 1970.
[41] Diamond 2008; Fukuyama 1992; Huntington 1993b.
[42] Yang and Tang 2010.
[43] Citrin and Luks 2001; Crozier, Huntington, and Watanuki 1975; Jaffer, Knaudt, and Morris 2014; Tang 2021; Rainie, Keeter, and Perrin 2019.
[44] Schaefer 2007; Stancil 2017.

is so repressive that it can ignore public opinion. In fact, governments in non-electoral societies need to be more responsive to public opinion than in electoral societies precisely because of the lack of direct elections.

Without competitive elections, these governments cannot show their legitimacy by the percentage of vote they receive. Instead, they need to respond to public demand more frequently than in electoral societies. For example, in authoritarian China, government responsiveness is much higher than in other electoral societies.[45] A higher rate of responsiveness, in turn, leads to more public satisfaction and political trust. This tendency has become more noticeable in recent years in China, for example, which has been consistently found to have one of the highest levels of political trust in the world.[46] In a 2022 study by the Edelman Trust Barometer, China enjoyed the highest level of political trust among 28 selected countries, and many of them were electoral societies.[47] This gap was likely created by the Chinese government's coordinated handling of Covid-19 during the initial stage of the pandemic.

As a postcolonial society with a hybrid political system that has been strongly influenced by both Western liberal tradition and China's One Country, Two System framework, would Hong Kong follow the liberal democratic pattern of low trust or the Chinese model of high trust?

Measuring Political Trust in Hong Kong

The 2021 Hong Kong Political Culture Survey was conducted at a perfect time. Since the passage of the Hong Kong National Security Law in 2020, the political climate has rapidly changed, and the anti-China forces have been pushed off the political stage. As Hong Kong faces a new political reality that will feature further Chinese domination, it is important to record the public sentiment at Hong Kong's historic juncture between the first 23 years of political vacuum created by the One Country, Two Systems framework (see Chapter 3 on political identity) and the post-NSL era since 2021. In this sense, the Hong Kong Political Culture Survey can provide an accurate picture of the public sentiment in this turning point of Hong Kong's postcolonial history.

The 2021 survey asked many questions about the respondents' trust in political institutions, government officials, and political figures, as well as people's satisfaction with government policies. Since these are politically sensitive questions, the respondents may feel political pressure and social desirability.

---

[45] Tang 2016.
[46] Dickson 2016; Pew Research Center 2008; Shi 2008; Tang 2016.
[47] Edelman 2022.

They may provide what they think are politically correct answers. In the post-NSL era, being politically correct means the respondents may tone down their anti-China feelings in their answers, therefore underreporting their distrust of China. To solve this problem of social desirability, this chapter will again rely on the statistical weighting technique developed in Chapter 2. This technique will provide a more accurate measurement of public opinion in Hong Kong. The interested reader should review the discussion of list experiments and the statistical weighting method based on the activator variable discussed in Chapter 2.

Institutional Trust: National Level

The first set of questions in the 2021 survey was about public trust of political institutions both at the national level and in Hong Kong. The institutions at the national level include the Chinese Communist Party (CCP), the Chinese government (NATGOV), the National People's Congress (NPC), the Chinese courts (NATCOURT), the PRC representatives in Hong Kong (PRCREP), the Chinese media (NATMEDIA), and the People's Liberation Army stationed in Hong Kong (PLA).

The 2021 survey results are presented in Figure 4.1, which shows the support percentage of political institutions before and after weighting for social desirability. On the surface before weighting, the levels of institutional trust seem not too bad. Though trust in the CCP and in the Chinese media are relatively low at 40% and 36%, the levels of trust are at or slightly over 50% for the other five institutions before weighting for social desirability.

When the results are corrected, or weighted, for social desirability, the true levels of institutional trust are significantly lowered. On average, the corrected level of trust is barely above 30%, ranging from the lowest at 23% for Chinese media to the highest at 34% for the PLA stationed in Hong Kong (Figure 4.1).

Are these results of political trust in national institutions too low? It depends on whom you ask. The answer is definitely "yes" if you ask China, where political trust is consistently high at around 70%–80% in public opinion surveys.[48] While social desirability may not be a factor according to some studies,[49] the lack of political competition between the CCP and other political parties may be the reason for such a high level of political trust in China. Yet the Chinese public would not have "voted" for the CCP if its own performance was not satisfactory according to public assessment.

---

[48] Dickson 2021; Tang 2018.
[49] Tang 2016.

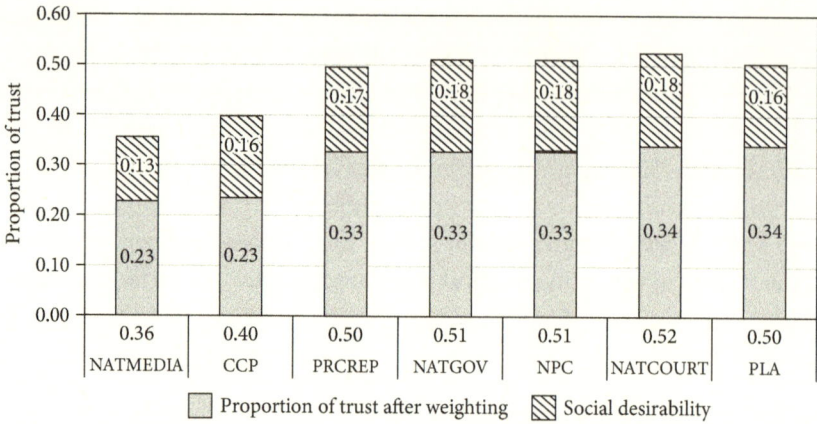

Figure 4.1 Institutional trust in China before and after weighting
Main findings: This figure shows the political trust of political institutions at the national level, including the Chinese Communist Party (CCP), the Chinese government (NATGOV), the National People's Congress (NPC), the Chinese courts (NATCOURT), the PRC representatives in Hong Kong (PRCREP), the Chinese media (NATMEDIA), and the People's Liberation Army stationed in Hong Kong (PLA). Before weighting for social desirability, the levels of trust are at or slightly over 50% for five institutions, though trust in the CCP and in the Chinese media are relatively low at 40% and 36%. When the results are weighted for social desirability, the true levels of institutional trust are significantly lowered. On average, the corrected level of trust is barely above 30%, ranging from the lowest at 23% for Chinese media to the highest at 34% for the PLA.

Note: The numbers below the bars represent unweighted percentages. For example, for NATMEDIA, the unweighted support is 36% but only 23% after weighting for social desirability (13%).

Source: Hong Kong Political Culture Survey 2021.

On the other hand, Hong Kong's levels of political trust in national institutions seem quite normal if compared to other liberal democracies where party competition divides the public vote and lowers public political support for the ruling political party and the incumbent government. For example, in the World Values Surveys, trust in political institutions in liberal democratic societies are significantly lower than in China[50] and comparable to Hong Kong. The low political trust in liberal democracies is likely a consequence of people's disappointment amid constant in-house partisan fights and the lack of government attention to issues related to people's everyday livelihood.[51]

[50] Yang and Tang 2010.
[51] Norris 2011.

Institutional Trust: Local Level

The 2021 survey also asked the respondents about their trust in seven local political institutions. These institutions include Hong Kong police (HKPOLICE), Hong Kong's current political system (HKPOLSYSTEM), the SAR government (SARGOV), Hong Kong Legislative Council (HKLEGCO), Hong Kong's district councils (HKSUBLEGCO), Hong Kong media (HKMEDIA), and Hong Kong's courts (HKCOURTS).

Figure 4.2 presents the levels of political trust in the above seven local institutions before and after correcting for social desirability. Without correcting for social desirability, the levels of trust are relatively high, ranging from the lowest 49% for Hong Kong police to the highest 64% for Hong Kong courts.

The role of social desirability is interesting. Unlike trusting Chinese national institutions that showed a uniform pattern of reporting more trust than the respondents really felt, there is more variation in social desirability of trusting local institutions. Social desirability effect is more noticeable in trusting Hong Kong police, Hong Kong's political system, the SAR government, and the Legco. For these institutions, at least 10% of the survey respondents lied about their trust by hiding their distrust. This is similar to trusting Chinese national institutions in Figure 4.1.

For Hong Kong district councils, Hong Kong media, and Hong Kong courts, the survey respondents were more honest about expressing their true levels of trust. Only about 7% overreported their trust in courts, and only a negligible 2%–3% did so for district councils and for Hong Kong media. For these items, statistical weighting did not change the results significantly, suggesting that people did not feel much political pressure and the need to be politically correct when they answered these questions (Figure 4.2).

The real levels of trust in local institutions after correcting for social desirability are also interestingly different from that of national institutions. Overall, they are significantly higher than for national institutions. The least trusted local institution is Hong Kong police (30%, Figure 4.2), which is still higher than the least trusted institution in the Mainland (23%, Figure 4.1, NATMEDIA). Trust in Hong Kong's Legislative Council (43%, Figure 4.2) is higher than trust in the National People's Congress (33%, Figure 4.1). Similarly, trust in Hong Kong courts (58%, Figure 4.2) is much higher than trust in Chinese courts (34%, Figure 4.1). Trust in Hong Kong media is 56% (Figure 4.2), more than doubling the 23% trust in Chinese media (Figure 4.1). Trust in the SAR government (38%, Figure 4.2) is almost at the same low level of trust in the national government in Beijing (33%, Figure 4.1), which may be a

Photo 4.3 A poster referring to "the local police force as CCP officials and mafia." Central, Hong Kong Island. Photo by Wenfang Tang, 8/24/2019.

reflection of Hongkongers' belief that unlike other local institutions, the SAR government follows Beijing's orders too closely.

Between different local institutions, trust is significantly higher for local media, local courts, and local district councils than for local police, SAR

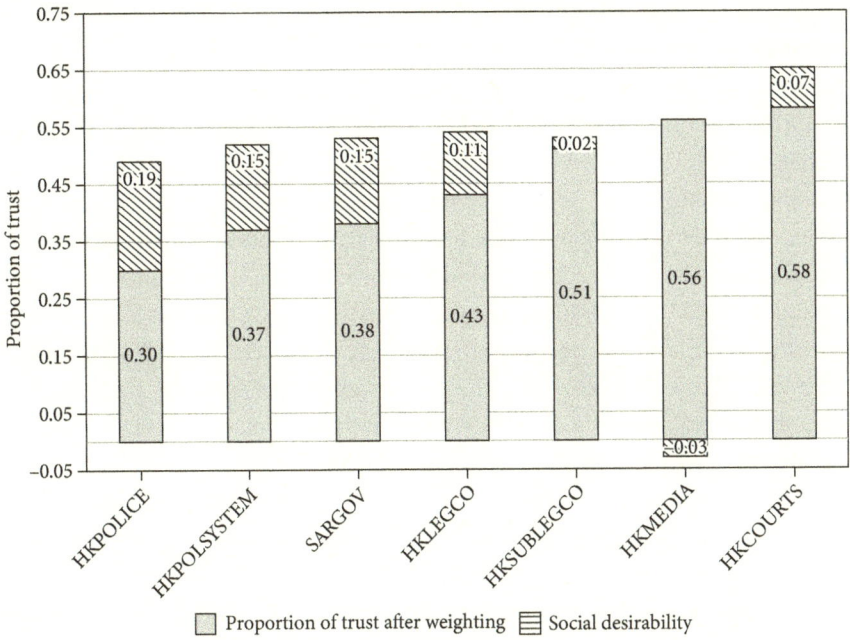

Figure 4.2 Institutional trust in Hong Kong before and after weighting
Main findings: This figure shows the political trust of political institutions at the local level, including Hong Kong police (HKPOLICE), Hong Kong's current political system (HKPOLSYSTEM), the SAR government (SARGOV), Hong Kong Legislative Council (HKLEGCO), Hong Kong's district councils (HKSUBLEGCO), Hong Kong media (HKMEDIA), and Hong Kong's courts (HKCOURTS). Without correcting for social desirability, the levels of trust are relatively high, ranging from the lowest 49% for Hong Kong police to the highest 64% for Hong Kong courts. After weighting for social desirability, at least 10% of the survey respondents lied about their trust by hiding their distrust in Hong Kong police, Hong Kong's political system, the SAR government, and the Legco.
Source: Hong Kong Political Culture Survey 2021.

government, the Legco, and the local political system represented by One Country, Two Systems. It seems that the pattern is related to how much control there is from China. At the time of 2021 survey, local media, local courts, and the district councils were more trustworthy perhaps because they were perceived as under less control from Beijing.

The gap between low trust in national institutions and high trust in local institutions is worth further attention. In surveys conducted in Mainland China, there is also a gap of trust between national and local governments, but the pattern is reversed. Trust in local governments is lower than in the central government.[52] This is because the central government often makes the local governments responsible for any wrongdoing and for venting public dissatisfaction such as in handling the Covid-19 pandemic.[53] On the other hand, Hong Kong seems more similar to some election-driven liberal democracies, where trust in local governments is higher than in the national governments.[54] The relatively high trust in Hong Kong's local political institutions is perhaps a reflection of Hongkongers' belief in the relative autonomy of the SAR under the framework of One Country, Two Systems. As Beijing gains more control in Hong Kong's local institutions in the post-NSL era, trust in local institutions may decline. It will be interesting to watch if trust in Beijing will improve under Beijing's new policy initiatives such as public housing construction, preferential trade policies, and the infrastructure development in the Greater Bay Area of Shenzhen, Hong Kong, and Macau.[55]

Another dimension of institutional trust is change over time. The Asian Barometer Surveys (ABS) contain data on institutional trust in selected Asian societies. Figure 4.3 shows how trust in key political institutions, including Hong Kong courts, SAR government, Hong Kong Legislative Council, Hong Kong civil service, and Hong Kong police, changed over time in Hong Kong over four waves of the ABS conducted in 2001, 2007, 2012, and 2016. It also shows such trust in Hong Kong compared to other Asian neighbors in 2016. Institutional trust in Hong Kong experienced a low point in 2001 after the Asian financial crisis and when SARS hit the former colony around then. In the meantime, Hongkongers were probably suspicious of China's intention to pass the national security legislation required by Article 23 of the Basic Law that the then-CE Tung Chee-hwa tried and failed to pass later in 2003, two years after the 2001 ABS survey. Political trust bounced back between 2007 and 2012 when Hong Kong's relationship with the Mainland was relatively smooth. Major events around this period include the large number of Mainland tourists in Hong Kong and their economic benefits for the local economy, the Wenchuan earthquake when China received large amounts of donations from Hong Kong, and the 2008 Beijing Olympics that boosted China's international image. It returned to another low point in 2016, two years after the Umbrella movement in 2014 that failed to resist Beijing's effort to prescreen the candidates for the CE elections.

Compared to other Asian societies, Hong Kong's political trust was not that low even at its lowest point in 2016. Korea, Taiwan, Mongolia, and Japan all

---

[52] Tang 2016.
[53] Kuo 2020; Liu 2022; Zheng 2022.
[54] O'Leary, Welle, and Agarwal 2021; Pew Research Center 2020.
[55] HKPORI 2021.

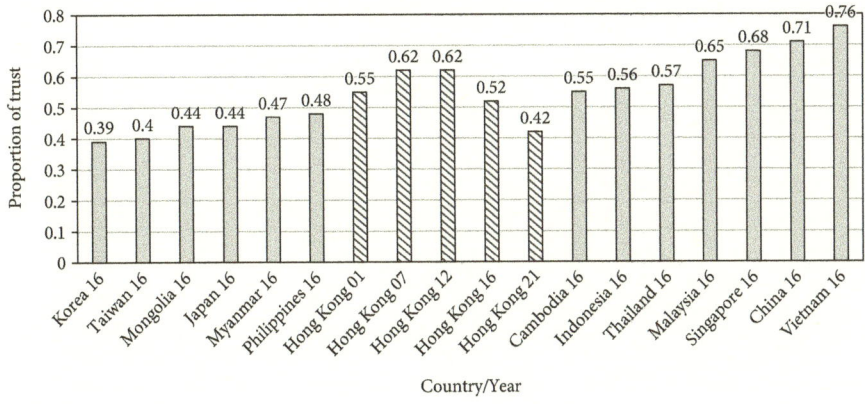

Figure 4.3 Comparing level of trust in key institutions of Asian countries in 2016 and Hong Kong's change over time

Main findings: This figure shows trust in key political institutions, including Hong Kong courts, SAR government, Hong Kong Legislative Council, Hong Kong civil service, and Hong Kong police, has changed over time in Hong Kong over four waves of the ABS surveys conducted in 2001, 2007, 2012 and 2016. It also shows such trust in Hong Kong compared to other Asian neighbors in 2016.

Notes: Data for Hong Kong are drawn from the four waves of the ABS in 2001, 2007, 2012, 2016 and from the 2021 Hong Kong Political Culture Survey. The 2021 Hong Kong trust level is the average of the four institutions including policy, courts, Legco, and SAR government from Figure 4.2, while controlling for social desirability. Social desirability may not have been a problem in Hong Kong before the passage of the National Security Law in 2020. Data for other countries and regions are based on the fourth-wave ABS surveys in 2016.

Source: Asian Barometer Surveys Wave1–Wave4 (http://www.asianbarometer.org/) and Hong Kong Political Culture Survey 2021.

had lower levels of institutional trust than Hong Kong in 2016's fourth wave of the ABS surveys. One caution is that trust in other societies is about national institutions, but it's measured at the local level in Hong Kong. As shown in Figure 4.1, Hongkongers' trust in national institutions in the post-NSL era is low at 20%–30%.

Trust of Officials and Dissidents

The 2021 survey asked the respondents about their trust of government officials. In Figure 4.4, after controlling for social desirability effects, trust in central government officials and in Beijing officials stationed in Hong Kong was the lowest. Among local officials, trust in the SAR government officials and Legco members was lower than in the district councilors and judges.

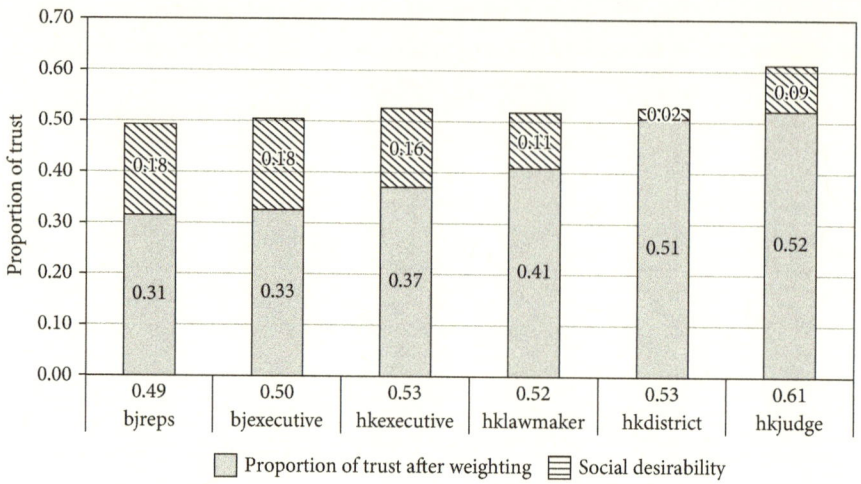

Figure 4.4 Proportion of trust in government officials before and after weighting
Main findings: After controlling for social desirability effects, trust in central government officials and in Beijing officials stationed in Hong Kong were the lowest. Among local officials, trust of SAR government officials and Legco members were lower than district councilors and judges.
Source: Hong Kong Political Culture Survey 2021.

This pattern is very similar to the results about institutional trust presented in Figures 4.1 and 4.2.

The 2021 survey also asked the respondents to evaluate four chief executives, Tung Chee-hwa, Donald Tsang Yam-kuen, Leung Chun-ying, and Carrie Lam Cheng Yuet-ngor, and six well-known political activists or political dissidents, including Anson Chan Fang On-sang who is a former high-ranking official from the colonial era; Martin Lee Chu-ming who is a lawyer and veteran political activist; Albert Ho Chun-yan who is a former Legco member and an opposition party leader; Benny Tai Yiu-ting who was an associate professor at the law school at the University of Hong Kong; Jimmy Lai Chee-ying who is a businessman and the owner of *Apple Daily*, the most famous anti-China newspaper in Hong Kong; and Joshua Wong Chi-fung who is a student activist and later turned into a political dissident. All of these dissidents were behind the numerous protests and anti-China activities in the post-Handover era since 1997. At the time of this writing, five of the six dissidents except for Anson Chan were convicted and jailed for violation of the NSL.

In Figure 4.5, while controlling for social desirability, assessment of CEs declined over time from Tung (41%), Tsang (40%), Leung (21%), to Lam

(19%), and evaluations of the dissidents were all slightly above 50%. These opposition leaders, riding on the political momentum of the anti-China sentiment during the anti-extradition movement in 2019, may very likely have won the Legco election originally scheduled for September 2020 had China not passed the NSL, put the dissidents on trial, and postponed the Legco election until a year later. The low evaluation of the incumbent CE Lam and her predecessor Leung, who is also outspoken against the opposition movement, is a reflection of the anti-China sentiment in Hong Kong's public opinion at the time of the 2021 survey.

The attentive reader may observe two opposite directions of social desirability. That is, the survey respondents overreported their support for both Beijing-backed chief executives and the anti-Beijing dissidents. This may be caused by the possibility of people under political pressure from both sides. On the one hand, they feel the pressure of the NSL and overreport their support for the Beijing-backed CEs. On the other hand, they also felt a moral obligation to overreport their support for the dissidents. These opposite tendencies of social desirability are indeed detected in the weighted list experiment results in Chapter 2.

Policy Satisfaction

Finally, the respondents to the 2021 survey were asked about their satisfaction with a list of public policies related to social, economic, and political issues. Overall, people were more satisfied with social and economic policies than political issues. Among the social and economic policies, the highest levels of satisfaction were for gender equality, educational opportunity, and the environment, followed by welfare policy and anti-Covid measures. The least satisfied include social equality, job opportunity, and home prices. The last three items also witnessed the most deterioration in the past two years from the time of the survey (Figure 4.6).

For political policies in Figure 4.7, the levels of satisfaction are much lower, ranging from mid-20% to high 30%. The only items that enjoyed slightly over 30% satisfaction are government integrity (38%), social order (37%), rule of law (32%), and One Country, Two Systems (30%). It was all below 30% for freedom of speech (27%), governance (27%), National Security Law (26%), and law enforcement (25%). All of these policies experienced more than 50% deterioration in the past two years from the time of the survey.

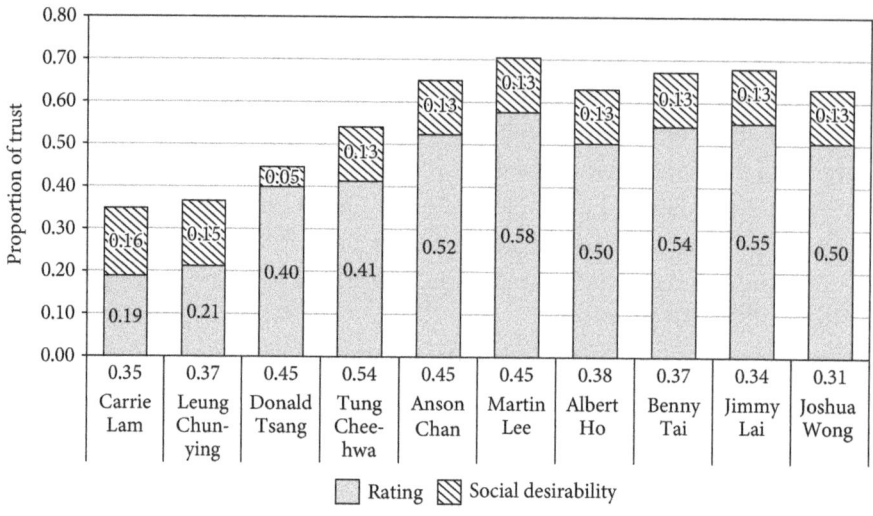

Figure 4.5 Rating of Hong Kong chief executives and political activists before and after weighting

Main findings: This figure shows respondents' trust of key political figures in Hong Kong before and after the weighting of social desirability. The political figures are the four CEs, Tung Chee-hwa, Donald Tsang Yam-kuen, Leung Chun-ying, and Carrie Lam Cheng Yuet-ngor; and six well-known political activists or political dissidents, including Anson Chan Fang On-sang who is a former high-ranking official from the colonial era; Martin Lee Chu-ming who is a lawyer and veteran political activist; Albert Ho Chun-yan who is a former Legco member and an opposition party leader; Benny Tai Yiu-ting who was an associate professor at the law school at the University of Hong Kong; Jimmy Lai Chee-ying who is a businessman and the owner of *Apple Daily*, the most famous anti-China newspaper in Hong Kong; and Joshua Wong Chi-fung who is a student activist and later turned into a political dissident. All of these dissidents were behind the numerous protests and anti-China activities in the post-Handover era since 1997. While controlling for social desirability, assessment of CEs declined over time from Tung (41%), Tsang (40%), Leung (21%), to Lam (19%), and evaluations of the dissidents were all slightly above 50%.

Source: Hong Kong Political Culture Survey 2021.

Sources of Political Trust and Policy Satisfaction

The final section will further examine the sources of political trust and policy satisfaction. To make it easier for the reader, it will simplify the analysis by focusing on only four variables, namely, trust in national political institutions (cntrust), trust in Hong Kong political institutions (hksystrust), satisfaction with socioeconomic policies (satsoc), and satisfaction with political policies (satpol).

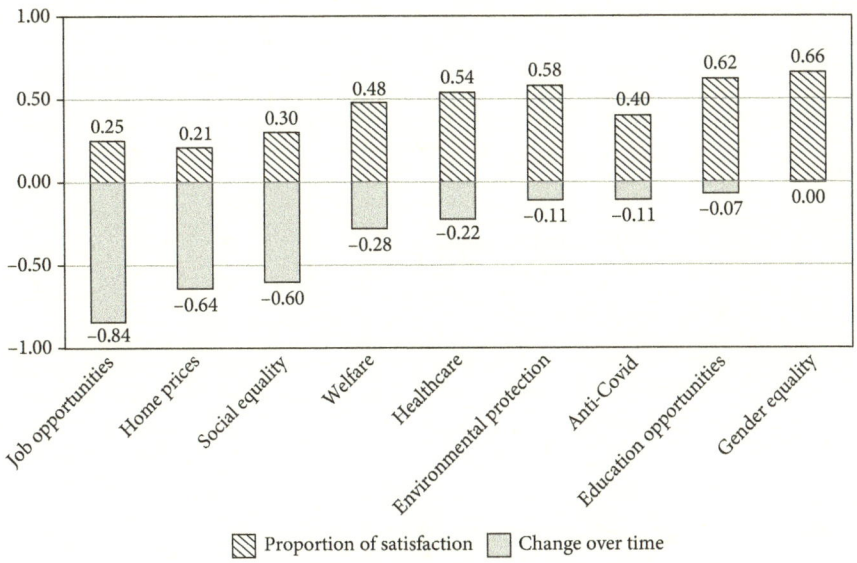

Figure 4.6 Social policy satisfaction and its change over time, 9 weighted areas
Main findings: This figure shows respondents' satisfaction with a list of public policies related to social, economic, and political issues. Overall, people were more satisfied with social and economic policies than political issues. Among the social and economic policies, the highest levels of satisfaction were for gender equality, educational opportunity, and the environment, followed by welfare policy and anti-Covid measures. The lowest satisfaction levels were social equality, job opportunities, and home prices.
Source: Hong Kong Political Culture Survey 2021.

Dependent Variables

Trust in national institutions is a factor index of the seven institutions in Figure 4.1, including Chinese media, Chinese Communist Party, Chinese government, Chinese People's Congress, Supreme People's Court, Chinese government offices in Hong Kong, and the People's Liberation Army stationed in Hong Kong.

Trust in local institutions is the second factor index of the five institutions in Figure 4.2, including Hong Kong police, Hong Kong's political system, the SAR government, the Legislative Council, and Hong Kong courts.

Satisfaction with socioeconomic policies is another factor index of the nine policy items in Figure 4.6, including home prices, job opportunities, social equality, anti-Covid policy, social welfare, healthcare, environment, education, and gender equality.

94 Proud and Angry

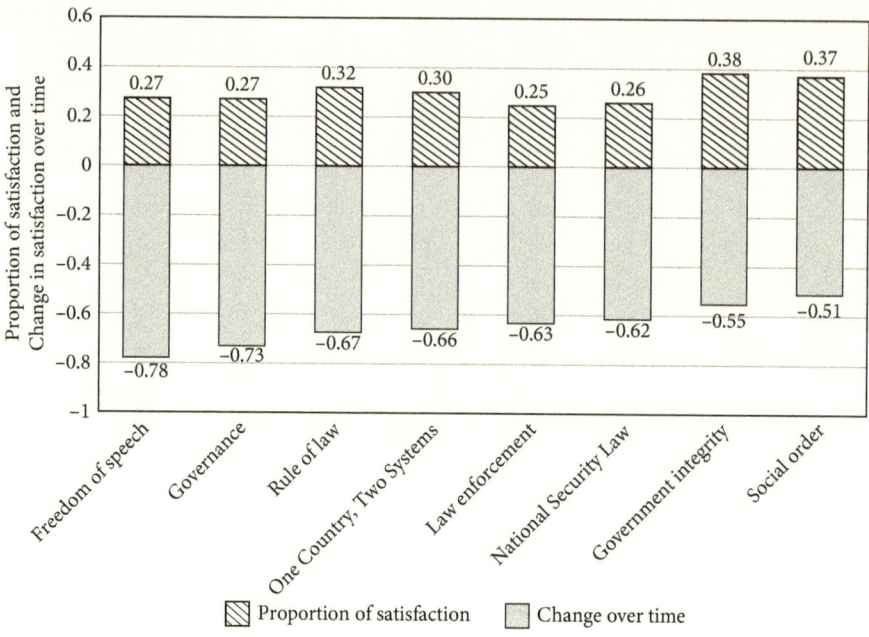

Figure 4.7 Political policy satisfaction and its change over time, 8 weighted areas
Main Findings: The figure shows respondents' satisfaction with different political policies and change in satisfaction levels. It shows that overall levels of satisfaction are much lower, ranging from mid-20% to high 30%. The only items that enjoyed slightly over 30% satisfaction were government integrity (38%), social order (37%), rule of law (32%), and One Country, Two Systems (30%). It was all below 30% for freedom of speech (27%), governance (27%), National Security Law (26%), and law enforcement (25%). All of these policies experienced more than 50% deterioration in the past two years from the time of the survey.
Source: Hong Kong Political Culture Survey 2021.

Satisfaction with political policies is the fourth factor index of the eight items in Figure 4.7, including law enforcement, National Security Law, governance, freedom of speech, One Country, Two Systems, rule of law, social stability, and government integrity.

The four factor indices are converted into 0–1 scale so the multivariate regression coefficients can be interpreted as percentage changes. Their coding schemes and summary statistics and related variables for construction are listed in Appendices 4.1a, 4.1b, and 4.1c.

Interested readers can find more detailed regression analysis about each institution, each policy, and each political figure and dissident in Appendices 4.2–4.5.

Independent Variables (Sources)

For the sources of or the reasons for political trust and policy satisfaction, this section will show the effects of the following independent variables: age, education, gender, religiosity, marital status, social class, ethnic identity, political color, Mandarin ability, media, and region.

Age is coded into four groups: (1) 16–24 years; (2) 25–44 years; (3) 45–64 years; and (4) 65 years or above.

Education is also coded into five groups: (1) primary and below (0); (2) lower secondary (0.25); (3) upper secondary (0.5); (4) sub-degree (0.75); (5) degree or above (1).

Gender (variable named as female) by two categories: 0=male and 1=female.

Religiosity is a measure of one's intensity of religious belief. It is a factor index derived from the following questions in the Hong Kong Political Culture Survey 2021: Aside from weddings and funerals, how often do you participate in religious activities (0=never; 2=only in the religious festivals; 3=few times a year; 4=once a month; 5=once a week; 6=few times a week); Have you ever done any of the following: a. Palm reading by yourself, use a computer or Tarot for fortune telling by yourself; b. Finding a fortune teller to tell your fortune; c. Drawing a fortune stick, evaluating Feng Shui; and, Do you agree with the following statements: a. The soul survives after death; b. Selecting an auspicious date for the joyous occasion, funeral, celebration on opening a business or home relocation; c. It is good to be worshipped by posterity after death; d. More religious people mean higher social stability; e. An individual should have his/her own religious beliefs. The factor index of religiosity based on these questions ranges from 0 (none) to 1 (maximum).

Marital status is coded as 1=married and 0=single.

Social class is a variable of five levels of self-perceived social class, including upper, upper middle, middle, lower middle, and lower. Missing values are imputed using multiple imputations with an ordered logistic regression, which accounts for age, education level, occupation economic activity status, household income per capita, housing property ownership, and type of house.

Ethnic identity a categorical variable of four self-perceived ethnic identity which includes (1) Hongkonger; (2) Chinese; (3) Chinese Hongkonger; and (4) others.

Political color (variable named as yellow=1) is the respondents' reported political leaning between pro-establishment (blue) and anti-establishment (yellow). It ranges between blue (0), light blue (0.25), green (0.5), light yellow (0.75), and yellow (1).

Media effect is measured by respondents' reported usage, including online and hardcopy, of two media outlets of the city, *Apple Daily* and *Oriental Daily*, ranging from never, monthly, weekly, several times a week, daily, and several times daily.

Putonghua ability is a factor index of four questions about Mandarin speaking, listening, reading, and writing, ranging from 0 (none) to 1 (native speaker). The mean value in the sample is 0.49.

Region includes the 18 districts in Hong Kong, namely, Central and Western, Wan Chai, Eastern, Southern, Yau Tsim Mong, Sham Shui Po, Kowloon City, Wong Tai Sin, Kwun Tong, Kwai Tsing, Tsuen Wan, Tuen Mun, Yuen Long, North, Tai Po, Sha Tin, and Sai Kung, Islands.

Appendix 4.1c shows the statistical details of the above dependent and independent variables.

Table 4.1 presents the results of multilevel OLS regression coefficients, which can be interpreted as the impact of the above independent variables, measured as percentage change, on the four dependent variables related to political trust and policy satisfaction.

Age

Age shows a significant effect on the trust index of local political institutions but not on national political institutions or the two policy satisfaction indices. The two older age groups (45–64 and 65+) were significantly more trusting in local political institutions than the two younger age groups (16–24 and 25–44). One possible explanation about the difference between the older and younger groups is that the older generations had more memory of the colonial era and were able to make comparisons between the two systems before and after the Handover. The other possibility is that the younger generations went through post-Handover, anti-China political socialization that taught them to distrust the political institutions under One Country, Two Systems.

Education

Education shows a strong and negative effect. Those with senior high school education and above expressed significantly less trust in national institutions and less satisfaction with political policies than the two lowest levels of education. The reader is reminded of the similar negative effect of education on political identity in Chapter 3. The highest education group with

Table 4.1 Sources of Political Trust and Policy Satisfaction (multilevel OLS regression)

VARIABLES	(1) cntrust	(2) hksystrust	(3) satsoc	(4) satpol
Age4				
4. >65 (comparison)				
1. 16–24	−0.012	−0.043***	0.001	0.020
2. 25–44	−0.013	−0.023**	−0.008	0.005
3. 45–64	0.002	−0.010	−0.007	0.000
Education				
1. Primary or below (comparison)				
2. Lower secondary	−0.011	0.019**	−0.001	−0.011
3. Upper secondary	−0.021**	0.012	−0.002	−0.018*
4. Sub-degree	−0.037***	0.002	−0.005	−0.034***
5. Degree or above	−0.040***	0.006	0.017*	−0.026**
female	0.012**	0.024***	0.004	0.001
religiosity	0.018	−0.013	0.003	0.065***
married	0.002	−0.002	0.006	0.034***
Class				
1. Lower (comparison)				
2. Lower middle	0.027***	0.003	0.028***	0.038***
3. Middle	0.026***	0.010	0.022***	0.023***
4. Upper middle	0.028*	0.036***	0.012	−0.004
5. Upper	−0.034	0.113**	−0.002	−0.145***
Ethnic identity				
1. Hongkonger (Comparison)				
2. Chinese	0.107***	0.078***	0.034***	0.089***
3. Chinese Hongkonger	0.085***	0.073***	0.037***	0.062***
4. Others	0.080***	0.079***	0.059***	0.138***
yellow01	−0.741***	−0.590***	−0.255***	−0.584***
putonghua	0.082***	−0.020**	0.004	0.087***
appledaily	−0.153***	−0.094***	−0.037***	−0.107***
orientdaily	0.002	0.007	0.012*	0.062***
District level				
dcbornml_2016	0.722***	0.585***	0.494***	0.482***
dchighhin_2016	0.199***	0.182***	0.091*	0.190***
dcmedianage	0.010**	0.006	0.008***	0.015***
dcpop	−0.003	−0.015	−0.044***	−0.056***
dcpopdensity2	−0.002***	−0.001***	−0.001***	−0.001
elderlyresidence2	−0.023**	−0.021***	−0.028***	−0.025***
erdensity2	0.147**	0.125**	0.072*	0.111**

continued

Table 4.1 *continued*

VARIABLES	(1) cntrust	(2) hksystrust	(3) satsoc	(4) satpol
vote2019y	−0.374*	−0.449**	−0.327**	−0.239
Constant	0.370**	0.661***	0.415***	−0.014
Observations	3,567	3,647	3,639	3,607
Number of groups	18	18	18	18

* $p<0.1$, ** $p<0.05$, *** $p<0.01$

Eight variables are identified to represent the demographic characteristics of the 18 districts in Hong Kong, including (1) the proportion of Mainland-born residents in each district, (2) the percentage of high-income households in each district, (3) median district age, (4) total district population, (5) district population density, (6) number of government-subsidized elderly care centers in each district, (7) the density of the government-subsidized elderly care centers in each district, and (8) percentage of anti-establishment votes in the 2019 District Council election.

Notes: 18 district-level variables are the proportion of Mainland-born population (dcbornml_2016), the proportion of high-income household (dchighhin_2016), the median age (dcmedianage), population (dcpop), population density in thousand people per km² (dcpopdensity2), the number of subsidized home for elderly in thousand (elderlyresidence2), the density of subsidized home for elderly in thousand per km² (erdensity2), and the proportion of vote garnered by the anti-establishment camp in 2019 election by 18 districts (vote2019y). (See Appendix 4.6 for the detailed definition of variables and their summary statistics.)

Sources: Hong Kong Political Culture Survey 2021; 2016 Population By-Census and Mid-2020 Population Estimate Report by the Census and Statistics Department; and Finance Committee Agenda of the Legco.

college and more education was slightly more satisfied with social and economic policies than the four lower levels. This could be a reflection that the most educated were probably more aware of social policies related to postmodern values such as gender equality and environmentalism, both were part of the index of socioeconomic policy satisfaction.

Gender, Religiosity, and Marital Status

Women showed more institutional trust at both national and local levels. Religiosity and being married played positive roles in promoting satisfaction with the political changes in the post-NSLera. These findings could be the consequences of the respondents' desire for political stability.

Social Class

Social class shows an inverted-U shape. Overall, both the lowest and highest classes demonstrated the least trust and satisfaction across the board. The middle classes, including lower middle, middle, and upper middle classes, were more trusting and satisfied. The unhappiness among the lower classes may reflect the increasing income gap in Hong Kong society. The upper classes, on the other hand, benefited very little from government subsidies for the poor and saw the new political changes in Hong Kong as a threat from the Mainland. One exception to this inverted-U pattern is local political trust. The two highest classes, upper middle and upper, were more trusting than the three lower level classes. One possibility may be their stronger belief in One Country, Two Systems that benefited the upper classes.

Ethnic Identity and Political Color

Both ethnic identity and political leaning produced uniform and strong effects on all the dependent variables. Those who identified themselves as Hongkongers only as compared with Chinese, Hong Kong Chinese, and other ethnicity, and those who expressed their political leaning as yellow, or anti-establishment, were less trusting of national and local institutions and were also less satisfied with socioeconomic and political policies. These findings are expected and not surprising.

Mandarin

Mandarin ability increased one's trust in national institutions and in satisfaction with the political changes in the post-NSL periods. In the meantime, it seems to discourage one's trust in local institutions that are run by Cantonese-speaking local officials. The language gap could be a source of the psychological gap of the Mandarin-speaking survey respondents with local political institutions.

Media

Media plays different roles between the two media outlets included in the analysis. As expected, *Apple Daily*, the popular anti-China paper, led to across-the-board negative reactions to institutional trust and policy satisfaction. On the other hand, *Oriental News*, the supposedly pro-establishment paper, only showed a relatively weak and positive effect on satisfaction with socioeconomic and political policies but played no role in promoting political trust at national or local levels. The contrast is surprising, with *Apple Daily* being a much stronger force in generating political distrust and policy dissatisfaction.

District-Level Variables

As mentioned above, eight variables are identified to represent the demographic characteristics of the 18 districts in Hong Kong, including (1) the proportion of Mainland-born residents in each district (dcbornml_2016), (2) the percentage of high-income households in each district (dchighhin_2016), (3) median district age (dcmedianage), (4) total district population (dcpop), (5) district population density (dcpopdensity2), (6) number of government-subsidized elderly care centers in each district (elderlyresidence), (7) the density of the government-subsidized elderly care centers in each district (erdensity2), and (8) percentage of anti-establishment votes in the 2019 District Council election (vote2019y) (see Appendix 4.6 for further details of these variables and their sources).

Districts with higher proportions of Mainland-born residents, higher percentages of high-income families, and higher levels of median age expressed higher levels of political trust and policy satisfactions at both national and local levels. Rich districts may have stronger economic ties with the Mainland. Districts with higher median age may be more likely to welcome China's presence due to their desire for more social stability.

Districts with larger populations showed more dissatisfaction with both socioeconomic and political policies, while higher population density led to more political distrust at both central and local levels as well as more dissatisfaction with socioeconomic policies. One possible explanation is that population and population density may lead to higher housing prices, more pollution, and shortages in jobs and public services, which causes greater public dissatisfaction.

Higher density of government-subsidized elderly care centers, which can be seen as an indicator of easier access to social services, created more political trust and policy satisfaction at both local and national levels. On the other hand, the total number of the government-subsidized elderly centers failed to generate political trust and policy satisfaction. It suggests that the total number may reflect a shortage of social services in large districts, while density may bring more accessibility and is a better measure of public service provision.

Finally, as expected, districts with more anti-establishment votes were less trusting of central and local governments and less satisfied with both socioeconomic and political policies.

Overall, as shown in Table 4.1, the sources of political trust and policy satisfaction can be summarized as from political socialization, demographic traits, and access to government services. Postcolonial anti-China political socialization, as measured by age, education, exposure to anti-China media, political color, anti-establishment voting, locally born with less Mandarin-language ability all contributed to political distrust and policy dissatisfaction. For demographic factors, those groups that are more conservative and desire more social stability, such as the middle classes, married, those with more religious belief, and districts with higher household income showed more political trust and policy satisfaction. Finally, accessibility to public services, as reflected in the density of elderly care facilities, promoted more government trust and policy satisfaction.

Summary and Discussions

Hong Kong in the first 23 years after the Handover witnessed political tension, conflict, and controversies that divided the postcolonial society and caused political turmoil and constant social unrests. Consequently, political trust at the national level declined, while trust in local political institutions remained relatively high, particularly in those institutions less controlled by Beijing. The distrust of Beijing has been worsened by the introduction of the NSL. Similarly, satisfaction with recent political policy changes also plunged. Though satisfaction with social and economic policies was relatively high, access to housing, income gaps, and a shortage of jobs remained sources of public dissatisfaction. The lack of political trust in and satisfaction with Beijing can be contributed to the failure of political socialization. The middle class and those who were more concerned about their everyday livelihood seemed to show more trust and satisfaction with the Beijing government and were less likely to support anti-China sentiment.

One interesting finding in this chapter is the gap between what people say in public opinion surveys and what they really think. On the surface, public opinion is relatively supportive of the Beijing government. After correcting for social desirability by statistical weighting, however, the true sentiment is significantly more negative about China than what people show publicly. This tendency to hide one's opinion may be a result of the political pressure after the NSL. It may also be a habit leftover from the colonial era when the subjects of the colony were accustomed to feeling alienated and detached from the establishment[56]—as when Dizayi recapitulated the experience of the colonized wearing "white masks" to cope with the West.[57] In any case, the strong effect of social desirability is a warning to researchers and policymakers before they determine the true levels of public sentiment and make relevant policies.

It is true that China succeeded in changing Hong Kong's political institutions almost overnight by introducing the NSL and other measures of political and social reforms. It will take much more effort and time to change Hongkongers' hearts and minds and win their political support and trust.

---

[56] Hofstede 1980, 2001, and 2011, Hofstede, Hofstede, and Minkov 2010; Triandis et al. 2001.
[57] Dizayi 2019.

5
Political Contention

Introduction

In 2019, the largest anti-China protests broke out in Hong Kong's history. An estimated 2 million people went to the streets.[1] That is one-third of the adult population in Hong Kong.[2] The protests continued until a year later when China imposed the Hong Kong National Security Law on July 1, 2020. Almost overnight, the streets in Hong Kong became surreally quiet without a single protester. How would Hong Kong residents vent their political dissatisfaction and distrust discussed in Chapters 3 and 4 in the post–National Security Law era? This chapter will address this question by drawing data from the Hong Kong Political Culture Survey conducted in the summer of 2021.

This chapter will first discuss the trajectory of local political activism in the post-Handover period and how it evolved from targeting local policy issues to a social movement with obvious anti-China sentiments. It then reviews the existing theories of social movements and discusses how these theories can be applied to Hong Kong. Finally, the chapter will show the survey findings of Hongkongers' political behavior in problem-solving in the post–National Security Law era.

Political Participation in Post-British Hong Kong

The landscape of political activism in Hong Kong changed drastically after the Handover. In the British colonial era, Hong Kong people were depicted as apolitical, materialistic, and concerned with only individual and family interests.[3] This profile of Hong Kong people, however, has undergone tremendous changes since Hong Kong returned to China and became one of its special

---

[1] BBC 2019.
[2] According to the 2021 Hong Kong Population Census, a total of 6 million residents were in the 16–80 age group. See *Table E2021A: 2021 population census*, https://www.censtatd.gov.hk/en/EIndexbySubject.html?scode=600&pcode=D5212101#section1
[3] Ku and Pun 2006; Lau 1984.

administrative regions (SAR; the other example is Macau). The Chinese government did not expect that granting more autonomy to Hong Kong would push the local society away from China instead of bringing it closer. Yet, with more political opportunities and more power to govern itself, Hong Kong society became more engaged in the local policymaking process and, more importantly, in fighting for full democracy. After about six years of silent adaptation of the local society to the post-Handover political circumstances, a massive demonstration suddenly broke out in the summer of 2003 when around 500,000 people protested on the streets against the local government's proposed legislation of the National Security Law (see below for further discussion).

The local government suspended the legislative proposal immediately under the pressure of mass protests. This move encouraged the local community to become more involved in politics, as they saw in this movement the power of collective action. The post-2003 years saw a surge in political activism in Hong Kong. Almost every three to four years there was a major public event with citywide and even international attention. Each of these landmark events brought new and often younger activists into the public spotlight. Table 5.1 summarizes these events in Hong Kong's postcolonial era.

July 1st Mass Demonstration

The first major showdown between Hong Kong residents and the Beijing-backed Hong Kong government after the Handover began in 2003, when Chief Executive Tung Chee-hwa attempted to pass the Hong Kong National Security bill in the Legislative Council, which was required in the Basic Law, the constitutional document of the territory (see Chapter 4). Fearing that such legislation would strengthen Beijing's control over Hong Kong, the anti-China groups organized massive anti-China public protests on July 1, 2003, the seventh anniversary of the Handover, with an estimated crowd of half a million participants. Tung later had to withdraw the bill and suspend the legislation. Encouraged by the victory, the rally became an annual event} as a symbol of resisting Chinese rule until it was banned in 2020 under the National Security Law. Compared with other major protests in Hong Kong, the annual July 1st rally is perceived as a movement platform for political moderates, as it calls for protesting in a "peaceful, self-constrained and nonviolent" way (和理非). This form of protest was later criticized by young Hongkongers as being too conservative and was then

Table 5.1 Major Public Events in Post-British Hong Kong

Year	Protest event	Scale	Main participants	Demands	Outcome
2003	July 1st mass demonstrations	≈ 500,000	Middle-class group	Protesting the Basic Law Article 23	Positive (Legislation suspended in 2003, and the annual rally continued until the implementation of NSL in 2020)
2006–2007	The heritage preservation movement	<1,000	Young Hongkongers in their 20s and 30s (people born in the 1970s and 1980s)	Protesting the demolition of the Star Pier and the Queen's Ferry Pier	Negative (Both piers were demolished)
2009–2010	The anti-high-speed railway movement	≈ 2,000	Young Hongkongers in their 20s and 30s (people born in the 1970s and 1980s)	Protesting the construction of the Guangzhou-Shenzhen-Hong Kong express railway	Negative (Railway constructed, but controversy remained)
2012	The anti-national education movement	5000–10,000	High-school students (people born in the 1990s)	Protesting national education reform	Positive (The proposed reform was suspended)
2014	The Umbrella movement	≈ 200,000	Young Hongkongers in their 20s (people born in the 1990s and even 2000s)	Demanding direct election of chief executive	Negative (China agreed to direct election, but candidates must be approved by Beijing. Protesters refused the proposal, and no reform on direct election of chief executive)
2019	The anti-extradition law amendment movement	≈ 2 million	Teenage Hongkongers (people born in the 2000s)	Protesting the extradition bill; later demanding direct election of chief executive	Partly (The bill was withdrawn, but no concession by Beijing on direct election of chief executive)

boycotted by them.⁴ The size of July 1st rally shrank drastically from the year 2015 and continued to decrease in the following years until the breakout of the biggest protest in postcolonial Hong Kong in the summer of 2019.⁵

Heritage Preservation Movements

Months-long protests from 2006 to 2007 to preserve two old piers—the Star Ferry Pier and the Queen's Ferry Pier—by a group of young Hongkongers provoked heated public discussion on the emerging local identity defended by the young generation.⁶ Different from the July 1st mass demonstration, the preservation movement never managed to mobilize such a sizable population to participate, yet it attracted citywide public attention. Commentators and scholars view this movement as groundbreaking, as the main participants were mostly young people who were almost absent in previous social movements.⁷ When the young men and women occupied the demolition site of the Star Ferry Pier and later the Queen's Ferry Pier, it was a milestone in the social movements in postcolonial Hong Kong. These movements were the first attempt by these youngsters to engage in collective action and to practice their own forms of protests, i.e., occupying the sites and using performing arts as a form of protest. During the protests, the activists loosely organized a mobilization group called Local Action. They exercised deliberative democracy within the group to discuss protest and recruitment tactics.⁸ The key members of the group later became the leaders and core activists of the anti-Guangzhou-Shenzhen-Hong Kong-express-railway movements in 2009.

Protesting the Cross-Border High-Speed Rail Project

The July 1st rally, the heritage preservation movements, and other social movements of different scales in the first decade of Hong Kong's postcolonial era created great momentum for political activism in the local society. During this process, the young generation was widely mobilized and actively engaged in local politics. While the older generation of activists turned to

⁴ Lin 2019a and 2019b.
⁵ On.cc 2018.
⁶ Cou 2007; Ma 2008.
⁷ Ku 2012; Ting 2013.
⁸ Ku 2012.

party politics, the newly emerged young activists became the main power of local social movements. Two years after the initial practices of the heritage protection movements, they were able to organize a much larger and more influential movement in 2009.

In 2009, the local government planned to construct a high-speed rail connecting Hong Kong with the rest of China's high-speed rail network. The former activists of the heritage preservation movements publicly opposed this project, accusing it of being too developmentalist and hegemonic because this costly railway would mainly serve the interests of business groups but not the general public, especially the poor. During the public consultation and legislative debate stage, the activists managed to mobilize thousands of young Hongkongers, most of whom were college students, to protest on the streets for days against the government plan. The physical confrontation between angry young protesters and the police shocked the local society, triggering a wide discussion on the *radicalization* of the post-80s (referring particularly to the movement participants, many of whom were born in the 1980s). The protests eventually dimmed out after the Legislative Council passed the government's proposal, but the controversy surrounding the project remained. The frustrated young men and women gradually realized that the fundamental "sin" was in the constitutional structure of Hong Kong's political system in that only half of the seats in the Legislative Council were directly elected. (Although, in the later phase of the protests, the demand for universal suffrage and full democracy had already appeared in the protest scenes.[9]) To some extent, this movement acted as a watershed moment in Hong Kong's social movements from targeting mainly local policy issues to more fundamental political demands.

Anti-National Education Reform Protest

The next battleground between Beijing and the former British colony was in national education. In 2012, 15 years after the Handover, the SAR government attempted to introduce a national education curriculum in Hong Kong's primary and secondary schools. The core of the curriculum reform was to promote patriotism and support for the Chinese Communist Party (CCP). This was a key measure by Beijing to establish a sense of citizenship with China in a former colony where people were accustomed to feeling that they were the subjects of the British Empire. Such education reform was perceived

---

[9] Xia 2016.

by students and parents as a propaganda and brainwashing measure by Beijing.[10] Soon after the chief executive announced the reform plan, thousands of high school and college students marched in the streets and protested outside the central government complex of HKSAR for days. The young crowd refused to leave unless the government withdrew the plan. Adults were mobilized by these student protesters, and several rallies took place simultaneously when the students were sitting outside the building. In September 2012, after more than one month of social protests, Chief Executive Leung Chun-ying announced the temporary suspension of the proposed national education reform. His compromise was regarded as a huge success of the Hongkongers in defending its political autonomy from being jeopardized by the CCP's propaganda. One of the notable features of this movement was the advent of even younger protesters—teenage high school students born in the 1990s. The leading figure of this movement, Joshua Wong Chi-fung, later became one of the leaders of the 2014 Umbrella movement and a world-known advocate of democracy movements in Hong Kong.

The Umbrella Movement

One of the key demands of the anti-China forces in Hong Kong after the Handover was the direct election of the chief executive (CE) by popular vote rather than indirectly by the Beijing-controlled Election Committee. As discussed in detail in Chapter 4, Beijing conditionally agreed in 2012 to hold direct elections of the CE in 2017. As the election approached, Beijing announced a condition in 2014 that the candidates must be prescreened by a nomination committee that was to be appointed by Beijing. The anti-China forces perceived this measure as Beijing's manipulation of the election and organized massive protests with an estimated crowd of over 100,000 participants. Protesters held an umbrella to protect themselves from police pepper spray, so the protest was also labeled as the Umbrella movement.[11] Unwilling to cross the red line, Beijing did not yield this time, as it did two years prior during the anti-national education protest in 2012. The anti-China forces refused to accept Beijing's nomination proposal, and the CE election was carried out in 2017 in the same indirect procedure as stated in the Basic Law.

Soon after its breakout, the international media put the Umbrella movement in the spotlight. Its attractiveness to the foreign media is conceivable. First, it was by then the longest-lasting if not the largest social movement

[10] Lau 2021; Tang 2012.
[11] Molloy 2014.

for full democracy in post-Handover Hong Kong. The whole event lasted for almost three months when the protestors occupied the main roads in downtown for 79 days.[12] People's anger with China's control over the local demand for democratization was expressed directly and strongly.[13] Second, it was also by then the most confrontational movement after Hong Kong's return to China. During the initial days of the protests, the Hong Kong police fired dozens of tear gas canisters at the protesters, which was very rare in the social movements in postcolonial Hong Kong. Finally, one of the signatures of the Umbrella movement was the leading role played by young Hongkongers throughout the entire three-month-long process. Although initiated by three middle-aged activists, this movement in effect started as a student movement.[14] College students and high school students were deeply involved throughout. Despite the inevitable failure of the movement, the young people's political activism was enlightened and motivated. This led to young people's stronger commitment in later movements, especially the most drastic events in 2019.

The Anti-Extradition Bill Movement

The final and the largest showdown by the anti-China pan-democrats took place 20 years after the Handover, in 2019. The triggering event was the SAR government's attempt to pass extradition legislation that would allow exchange and trial of criminals between Hong Kong, Macao, Taiwan, and Mainland China (see Chapter 4). The pan-Democrats convinced the Hong Kong public to believe that such legislation would allow Beijing to arrest and punish Hong Kong anti-China political activists. Starting in June 2019, they mobilized a series of protests through social media with more than 2 million participants.[15] As the protests escalated, young people became the main force and drove the movements toward violence. The SAR government withdrew the bill in September, but the protesters refused to back down. Instead, they made four more demands in addition to canceling the extradition bill, including the investigation of alleged police brutality, retracting the labeling of protesters as rioters, amnesty for arrested protesters, and direct elections of the CE as well as the members of the Legislative Council. These conditions, particularly direct elections, hit a nerve and pushed Beijing into a corner. The

---

[12] Cai 2017.
[13] Arranz and Lam 2019; Leung 2019.
[14] Congressional Research Service 2014.
[15] Davis and Kellogg 2019; Frosina 2021.

Photo 5.1 The closed Hang Hau MRT station entrance after being destroyed by the protesters. Sai Kung District. Photo by Wenfang Tang, 10/10/2019.

street demonstrations lasted violently for months and were only slowed down by the Covid pandemic in early 2020. After watching the protests anxiously for more than a year, Beijing finally took a decisive step by enacting the Hong Kong National Security Law (see Chapter 4).

In short, anti-China protests became daily life events during the first 23 years of the Handover. What are the deeper reasons for these social movements?

Theories of Social Protests

Hong Kong's social protests can be explained by theories of social movements, including rational choice, relative deprivation, resource mobilization, and political opportunity.

According to theories of rational choice, individuals participate in social movements because they believe that the benefit of such participation is greater than the cost; when the benefit is selective only for those who participate; and people are capable of processing complex information in calculating their benefits by taking shortcuts based on their preexisting political orientations.[16] In the case of Hong Kong, the costs and benefits of individuals participating in protests are two sides of the same coin. The mainstream literature suggests that Hong Kong people's political activism is more likely to be triggered by their perception of the costs of "non-action" than by the benefits they can derive directly from collective action.[17]

For Hongkongers, the benefit of participating in social protests is to resist the perceived Chinese threat to their comfortable lifestyle and social autonomy. Rational choice theories are helpful in explaining some social movements, particularly those with clear objectives and a good chance of winning, such as the anti-civic education protests, but they are less useful in explaining those movements that do not have clearly defined goals and that have little chance of winning, such as the later stage of the anti-extradition movement.

Another theory of social movement is relative deprivation.[18] According to this theory, structural changes in a society may cause people to feel a relative deterioration in their social and political status, even when their lifestyle and social status remain the same. When the feeling of relative deterioration intensifies, people may rise to resist the structural change. The theory of relative deprivation can be applied to explain Hong Kong's social movements. The transition from British rule to Chinese rule created a structural change. The new Chinese ruler was perceived as inferior to the former British ruler in terms of economic development, political system, and social order (see Chapter 3).[19] Hongkongers feel a relative deterioration of their social status under a new and inferior ruler, which led to their resistance to the new structural change.[20]

Both theories of rational choice and relative deprivation are about individual-level concerns. They pay less attention to macro-level factors that shape individual behavior, particularly rational choice theory. Instead, cultural explanation focuses on societal factors that motivate social movement.[21] According to cultural theory, a society (or a group) is "framed" by its own distinctive cultural characteristics, such as history, language, ethnicity, and so on. Cultural framing forms a common identity that serves as a powerful force for political mobilization. When such identity faces external threats, people may join social protests to defend their common identity. In the case of Hong Kong, the political vacuum in the post-Handover era under One Country, Two Systems facilitated the creation of a self-identity (see Chapter 3).

---

[16] Coleman 2000; Lichbach 1995; Olson 2003.
[17] E.g., Cheng 2014.
[18] Brinton 1965; Fanon and Philcox 2004; Gurr 2016; Smelser 2013.
[19] Chan 1998; FCCHK 2017; Lo 2018; Webster 2021.
[20] Cai 2017: 17–31.
[21] Benford and Snow 2000; Foran 1994; Polletta and Jasper 2001.

China was framed as a common enemy that might threaten this self-identity. Anti-China protests are a natural solution to protect Hongkongers' identity.

The final set of popular theories of social movement are resource mobilization and political opportunities.[22] Political opportunities for social movements are created during state breakdown or elite conflict. When state political authority or political elites holding state power are vacant or weak, social movements are more likely to succeed. In the meantime, social movements are only possible if resources can be mobilized, such as material resources, media, and existing social and political networks such as labor unions, ethnic networks, religious organizations, and so forth. Such creation of political opportunities and brewing social movements can be manipulated by external powers.[23] In the case of Hong Kong, political opportunities were created in the political vacuum after the British left but before the CCP could fully establish itself as the state power. Under One Country, Two Systems, Hong Kong has its own legal system, which has provided the local people with much more freedom of assembly, of speech, and of the press and publication than Mainlanders.[24] Traditional and new media outlets served as social resources and actively participated in mobilizing public participation in social protests.

Compared with Beijing, Americans were better students in applying resource mobilization theories to Hong Kong. Beijing believed that Hong Kong would be easy to manage by controlling and co-opting its business elites,[25] but it severely underestimated the anti-China sentiment in Hong Kong society and how such sentiment could make Hong Kong "go out of control." In the meantime, the UK and US governments, as well as their followers, actively cultivated this anti-China sentiment and mobilized Hong Kong's social resources. For example, during the 2019 anti-extradition protests, an American diplomat, Julie Eadeh, was photographed in a luxury Hong Kong hotel in a meeting with protest organizers and political activists on August 6.[26] The US government strongly condemned the China-controlled media for publishing the photo as interference with US government officials "normal work" and a violation of the diplomat's privacy.[27] One can only imagine what the "normal work" was and the purpose of the meeting.

In summary, four sets of theories are discussed in this section, including rational choice, relative deprivation, cultural identity and political

---

[22] McAdam 1999; McCarthy and Zald 1977; Goldstone 2023; Skocpol 1979 and 1997; Tocqueville 1835.
[23] Perry, Ekiert, and Yan 2020.
[24] Lo 2001.
[25] Lee, Yuen, et al. 2019.
[26] Hao 2019.
[27] AFP 2019; Brunnstrom 2019; Higgins 2019.

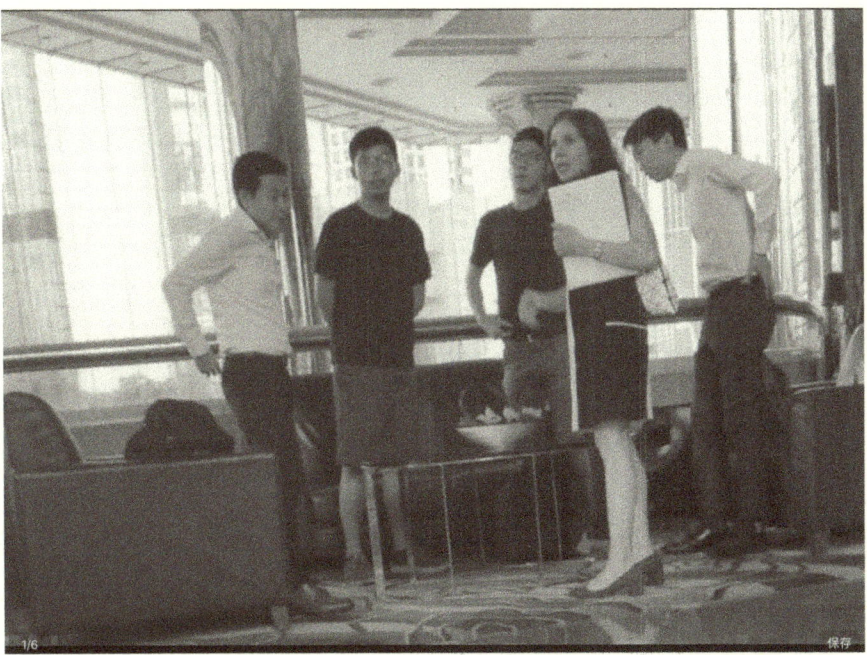

Photo 5.2 Protest leaders Pang Ka-ho (*far left*), Wong Chi-fong (*second from left*), Nathan Law (*second from right*), and Zhang Kunyang (*far right*) meeting with Julie Eadeh (*front*), suspected political chief at the US Consulate General in Hong Kong, in the lobby of the Golden Bell Marriott Hotel in Hong Kong. Published by *Ta Kung Pao*, 8/8/2019.
Source: https://www.takungpao.com/news/232109/2019/0808/333028.html

opportunities and resource mobilization. Each of these theories can provide some insight in understanding the reasons for the social protests in Hong Kong.

Channels of Political Action

The 2020 National Security Law (NSL) played the role of natural experiment in studying political participation in Hong Kong. On the surface, the NSL put an emergency brake on protest behavior almost immediately. Yet given the high levels of political distrust and policy dissatisfaction with Beijing that were discussed in Chapter 4, how would Hongkongers express such negative feelings in the post-NSL era? Did the NSL play the role of political deterrent as expected? The 2021 Hong Kong Political Culture Survey was conducted a year after the NSL, and it was an ideal time to address this question by examining the survey respondents' patterns of political action under political deterrence.

The core questions related to political behavior in the survey are about the respondents' likely political action when facing political dissatisfaction: What would be your most likely action if you think government policies are unreasonable or when you feel being mistreated by the government, such as welfare policy, housing policy, or police action in law enforcement?[28] Please pick one of the following actions:

1. Visit government bureaus/officials.
2. Express dissatisfaction through media or the internet.
3. Ask for help from members of the Legislative Council or district legislative council.
4. Express dissatisfaction through peaceful or violent protest.
5. Express dissatisfaction through my vote in elections.
6. Ask for help from political parties.
7. Express dissatisfaction through legal channels.
8. I would do nothing.

The respondents were asked to pick a second action from the above list if their first action did not solve the problem, then the third action if the first two actions were not effective.

Figure 5.1 shows the respondents' eight political actions as their first, second, and third choices. The most interesting contrast is between "visiting government" and "protest." Visiting government is the most popular first option among the survey respondents, as 40% of them picked this channel as their first choice, but it dropped quickly to 18% as second choice and 8% as third choice. In contrast, only 4% picked "protest" as their first choice, but 9% picked it as the second choice, and an alarming 30% picked it as the third choice. This contrast suggests that people would ask government for help at first and resort to protest if government failed to solve their problems. The NSL seems to play the role of deterrent only on the surface, and protest continued to be seen as the most effective means for problem-solving in the initial stage of the post-NSL era.

[28] 有時候政府嘅政策定得唔合理，或者啲人喺同政府部門來往時會遇到唔公正嘅對待，例如在社會福利政策、警察執法、房屋政策等方面。如果您認為政府嘅政策唔合理，或者被不公正咁對待，您首先會做啲咩？ (限制一個項目) (1)透過選票表達不滿; (2)告上法庭(如司法覆核); (3)通過媒體或互聯網表達不滿; (4)直接向政府有關部門反映; (5)向立法會議員或區議員求助; (6)向政黨求助; (7)參加和平抗爭(包括示威、請願、罷工等等); (8)使用暴力手段; (9)咩都唔做，忍咗佢. Note: (7) and (8) are combined because of small percentages.

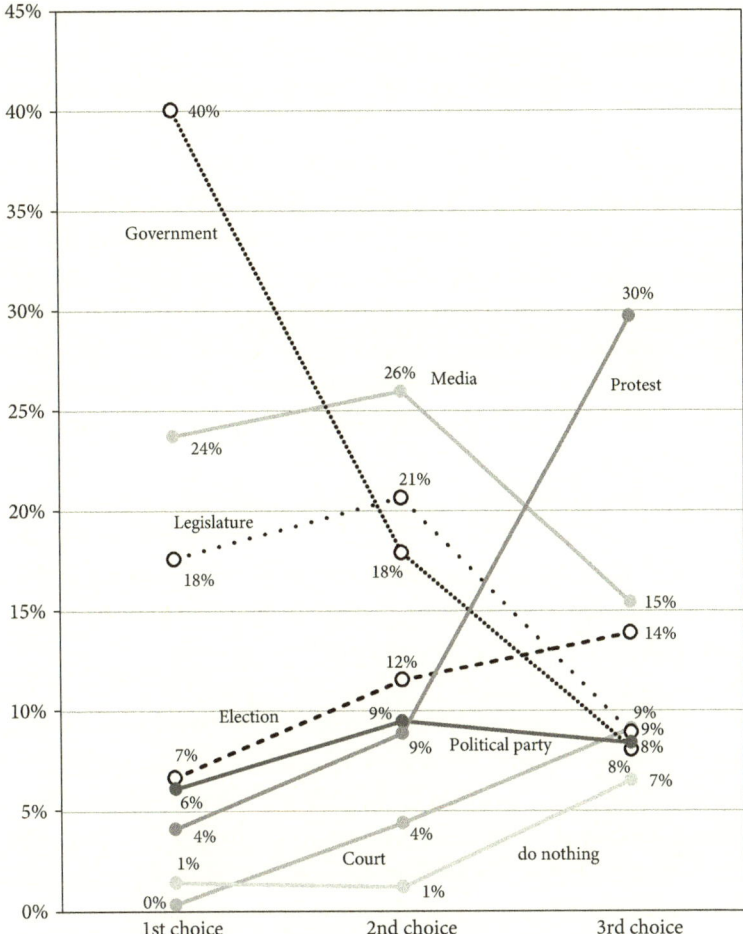

Figure 5.1 Problem-solving channels: 1st, 2nd, and 3rd choices (% weighted by social desirability)

Main Findings: The figure shows respondents' eight political actions as their first, second, and third choices after taking into consideration social desirability effects. The most interesting contrast is between "visiting government" and "protest." Visiting government is the most popular first option as 40% of them picked this, but it dropped quickly to 18% as second choice and 8% as third choice. In contrast, only 4% picked "protest" as their first choice, but 9% picked it as the second choice, and an alarming 30% picked it as the third choice.
Source: Hong Kong Political Culture Survey 2021.

Another category worth noting is "do nothing." Only about 1% chose "do nothing" as their first and second options, and only 7% would do nothing if the first and second options did not work. These numbers suggest that over 90% of the survey respondents would do *something* to solve their problems with the government. There seems to be a very high level of political activism in the post-NSL era.

Media is popular as first (24%) and second (26%) choices, but a significantly smaller number of the respondents would rely on media as the last resort (15%). Similarly, legislature is initially and secondly popular at 18% and 21% but drops to 9% as the third choice. The initial popularity of these channels is probably a reflection of the media's role in promoting political opposition before the NSL and the landslide victory by the opposition during the 2019 district council elections. The survey respondents seemed to expect that both media and legislature would play a less important role in the post-NSL period.

Finally, election, political party, and court experience an upward gain, as more people would rely on them as the last resort (election: 14%, political party: 8%, and court: 9%) than as the first (7%, 6%, and 0%) and second choices (12%, 9% and 4%). Nevertheless, these channels are less sought after compared with the other channels, as shown in Figure 5.1.

Boycotting is another political behavior that is related to protest. The Hong Kong Political Culture Survey asked the respondents two questions related to boycotting: I would support a business if it holds the same political view as mine; I would boycott a business if it holds a different political view from mine. The respondents were asked to answer strongly disagree, disagree, agree, and strongly agree. The two questions are highly correlated and are combined into a single factor index because both measure the respondents' level of political tolerance or their willingness to boycott businesses with different political stands.

Overall, about 51% (weighted) of the respondents expressed their willingness to boycott. This tendency is the most obvious among the anti-China group. As shown in Figure 5.2, an overwhelming majority of the anti-China (yellow) respondents (70%) were willing to boycott, but only 39% pro-China (blue) and 30% politically neutral (green) respondents would do the same thing. This gap indicates a much higher level of political intolerance and hostility in the anti-China group.

Another indicator of political action is voting. The anti-China forces staged a landslide victory in the 2019 district council elections. The anti-China groups intended to ride on the coattails of this victory and win the majority in the next Legislative Council election to be held in 2021. Had the election law stayed unchanged as before 2021, the anti-China opposition may have had a real chance of winning the majority in Legco because the old rule

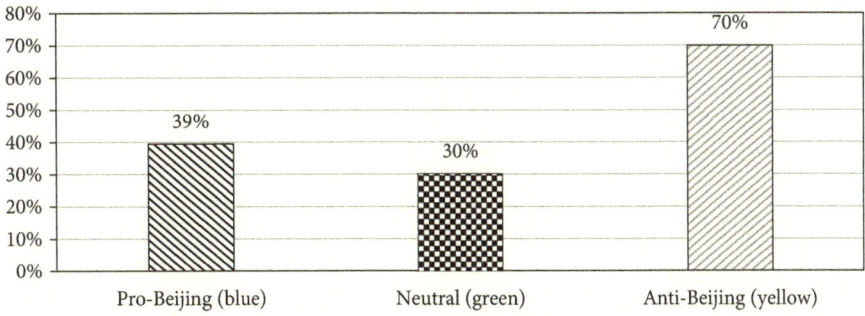

Figure 5.2 "Will not do business if political view is different" by political leaning (weighted %)

Main Findings: The figure shows the combined results of respondents' attitude toward boycotting a business that holds the same political view with the respondent and a different political view. All the results have calculated the social desirability effects. Overall, about 51% of respondents expressed their willingness to boycott. This tendency is the most obvious among the anti-China group. An overwhelming majority of the anti-China (yellow) respondents (70%) were willing to boycott, but only 39% pro-China (blue) and 30% politically neutral (green) respondents would do the same thing. This gap indicates a much higher level of political intolerance and hostility in the anti-China group.

Source: Hong Kong Political Culture Survey 2021.

allowed half of the members to be elected by the Beijing-controlled functional constituencies and the other half directly elected from the districts that were more autonomous. Seeing the danger of losing control of Legco, Beijing announced a plan to revise the rule by reducing the proportion of directly elected members and by increasing the number of indirectly elected legislators (see Chapter 4).

In the Hong Kong Political Culture Survey, the respondents were asked if they voted in the 2019 district elections and if they would vote in the upcoming Legco election in 2021. In Table 5.2, it shows that about 74% of the survey respondents voted in the 2019 district elections and 26% did not.[29] In the same survey, only about 50% answered that they planned to vote in the next Legco election, and the other half said no. Among the 74% who voted in 2019, as many as 42% said they would not vote in the next Legco election. By the time the Legco election was held in 2021, according to official statistics only

---

[29] This is very close to the 71% voter turnout in the official count. See *Voter turnout rate*, 2019, District Council Elections, HK.gov, https://www.elections.gov.hk/dc2019/eng/turnout.html

Table 5.2 Voted in 2019 and Plan to Vote in 2021 (weighted %)

Vote2019	Vote2021 No	Vote2021 Yes	Total
No	73.62	26.38	100
	38.81	13.97	26.42
Yes	41.68	58.32	100
	61.19	86.03	73.58
Total	50.12	49.88	100
	100	100	100

Respondents' voting behavior in the 2019 district elections and 2021 Legislative Council election. About 74% of the survey respondents voted in the 2019 district elections and 26% did not. Only about 50% answered that they planned to vote in the next Legco election and the other half said no. Among the 74% who voted in 2019, as many as 42% said they would not vote in the next Legco election.

Note: 2019 was district council elections, and 2021 was Legislative Council election.

Source: Hong Kong Political Culture Survey 2021.

30% of all eligible voters cast their vote.[30] This is an indication that 20%–40% of the voters boycotted the Legco election in 2021.

In summary, the most surprising finding in this section is the strong tendency to protest among Hong Kong residents. It may not be surprising had the survey been conducted before the NSL and during the peak of the anti-extradition movement. Under the newly imposed political deterrent, the survey respondents still showed a very high level of political activism; they would initially address the government for problem-solving, but they would not hesitate to engage in protest as the last resort. In the meantime, the anti-China forces expressed a strong sense of political intolerance by boycotting pro-China businesses and Beijing-sponsored elections. The National Security Law does not seem to be deterring political opposition, at least not at the time of this writing.

Sources of Political Action

To better understand Hongkongers' political behavior, it will be helpful to examine the sources of different types of political action in Figures 5.1 and 5.2. Specifically, this section will show how policy dissatisfaction, political

---

[30] See *Voter turnout rate*, 2021, Legislative Council Election, HK.gov, https://www.elections.gov.hk/legco2021/eng/turnout.html

orientation (or political color), media consumption, and age can impact the respondents' political actions.

As described in Figure 5.1, the survey respondents were asked if and how they would take political actions if they felt mistreated by the government. These action channels include government, protest, legislature, media, election, political parties, and courts. The respondents' first choice of action is coded as 3, second choice is coded as 2, and the third choice is coded 1. For example, the respondent is coded 3 if she/he picks government as the first choice, 2 as the second choice, 1 as the third choice, and 0 if government is not picked by this respondent. The respondent can pick the same action for all three choices and get a score of 6. For each type of political action, the score can range anywhere from 0 to 6. These action variables are converted into 0–1 scales by dividing each variable by 6. The advantage of the 0–1 scale is that the average of each variable can be interpreted as a percentage. For example, the average for media is 0.187, which means the popularity of media among the respondents is around 18.7%.

For boycott behavior (Figure 5.2), the respondents were asked if they would do business only with people holding the same political views and if they would never do business with people whose views were different from theirs. The two questions are highly correlated and combined into a factor index labeled boycott and converted into a 0–1 scale.

Policy dissatisfaction is further divided into two factor indices: dissatisfaction with social policies and with political policies (see Chapter 4). Social policies include housing prices, job opportunities, income equality, anti-Covid policy, welfare policy, healthcare, environment, education, and gender equality. Political policies consist of law enforcement, National Security Law, freedom of speech, governance, One Country, Two Systems policy, rule of law, social order, and government corruption. The two policy factor indices are converted into 0–1 scales.

Political leaning (yellow5) is a 0–1 variable. Zero is coded as deep blue (strongly pro-China), 0.25 as light blue (pro-China), 0.5 as neutral, 0.75 as light yellow (anti-China), and 1 as deep yellow (strongly anti-China).

Apple Daily is a popular newspaper in Hong Kong. Its readership can range from never (0), monthly (0.2), weekly (0.4), several times a week (0.6), daily (0.8), and several times daily (1).

The respondents are divided into four age groups, 16–24, 25–44, 45–64, and 65 and older.

In the OLS regression analysis in Table 5.3, political behaviors serve as the dependent variables, and the independent variables include dissatisfaction with social and political policies, political leaning, frequency of *Apply Daily* readership, and age. Other variables are controlled but not shown, including education, gender, religious denomination, religiosity, social class, marital status, and the 18 districts. The full models are presented in Appendix 5.1, and the summary statistics are shown in Appendix 5.2.

In Table 5.3, dissatisfaction with social policies and political policies encourages people to express their unhappiness through protest, local legislature, media, election but avoid government and court, which are seen as less accessible and less effective in changing undesirable policies.

Boycott is more related to political policy dissatisfaction but not to social policy dissatisfaction. Political policies are more connected to Beijing, and social policies are more likely made at the local level. This difference suggests that boycotting is perhaps more directed against Mainland China and Mainland Chinese businesses. In the same token, political parties seem to attract those with more localized social policy dissatisfaction, but they are not seen as capable of reducing political policy dissatisfaction.

The anti-China people (yellow) are more likely to protest, boycott, and use media to express their opinions but avoid other channels, particularly government, legislature, elections, and court.

Readers of the anti-China newspaper *Apple Daily* are expectedly encouraged to protest and to boycott. They are also more likely to rely on political parties and the court while avoiding government, legislature, and the media.

Compared with the older age groups, the youngest group (16–24) is significantly more prone to protest, boycott, and use media but less likely to go through the institutional channels of government offices and the legislature.

Overall, political dissatisfaction, anti-China political orientation, anti-China media, and the youngest age group tend to engage in more radical political action such as protest and boycott. These factors also lead people to avoid problem-solving through institutional channels, particularly the government.

Summary and Discussions

This chapter examines Hong Kong residents' political participation in the post–National Security Law era. It opens by describing the escalation of the anti-China social movements in post-Handover Hong Kong from 1997 to 2020. It attempts to explain Hong Kong's social protests by discussing the

Table 5.3 Sources of Political Action (OLS)

VARIABLES	(1) actgov	(2) actprotest	(3) boycott	(4) actleg	(5) actmedia	(6) actvote	(7) actparty	(8) actcourt
disatsoc	-0.064*	0.038**	-0.081*	0.019	0.082**	0.000	0.064**	-0.049***
disatpol	-0.134***	0.039***	0.148***	0.189***	-0.030	0.077***	-0.122***	-0.002
yellow5 0–1	-0.038***	0.065***	0.123***	-0.143***	0.141***	-0.025*	0.018	-0.021***
appledaily0–1	-0.044***	0.050***	0.194***	-0.036***	-0.041***	0.009	0.017*	0.055***
16–24 (comparison)								
25–44	0.057***	-0.022***	-0.055***	0.051***	-0.065***	0.008	0.005	-0.003
45–64	0.042**	-0.031***	-0.092***	0.097***	-0.107***	0.004	0.002	0.005
>65	0.042**	-0.035***	-0.112***	0.115***	-0.152***	0.014	0.013	0.011
constant	0.589***	0.007	0.223**	-0.043	0.192***	0.079	0.070	0.039
Adj R^2	0.093	0.191	0.249	0.088	0.126	0.032	0.053	0.077
N	3,365	3,365	3,371	3,365	3,365	3,365	3,365	3,365

* $p<0.10$**, $p<0.05$, ***, $p<0.01$

Shows OLS regression analysis of various independent variables on political behavior. Main results include the following: (1) Dissatisfaction with social policies and political policies encourages people to express their unhappiness through protest, local legislature, media, and/or elections but avoid government and court, which are seen as less accessible and less effective in changing undesirable policies. (2) Boycott is more related to political policy dissatisfaction but not to social policy dissatisfaction. (3) Anti-China people are more likely to protest, boycott, and use media to express their opinions but avoid other channels, particularly government, legislature, elections, and court. (4) Readers of the anti-China newspaper *Apple Daily* are unsurprisingly encouraged to protest and to boycott. They are also more likely to rely on political parties and the court, while avoiding government, legislature, and the media. (5) Compared with the older age groups, the youngest group (16–24) is significantly more prone to protest, boycott, and use media but less likely to go through the institutional channels of government offices and the legislature.

Note: Education, gender, religion, religiosity, social class, marital status, and districts are controlled but not shown (see Appendix 5.1).

Source: 2021 Hong Kong Political Culture Survey.

Photo 5.3 An elderly protester wearing a poster supporting young protesters. Hong Kong Island. Photo by Wenfang Tang, 8/24/2019.

merits and limitations of four theories of social movement, namely rational choice, relative deprivation, political culture and political opportunity, and resource mobilization. It shows how Hongkongers saw the relative deterioration of their social and economic status under Chinese rule. The political

Photo 5.4 A protester's last effort at continuing the social movement by distributing flyers after the passage of the National Security Law. Hong Kong Island. Photo by Wenfang Tang, 12/25/2021.

vacuum left by the departure of the British colonists and the inability of China to establish its control under the One Country, Two Systems framework encouraged Hongkongers to develop their own political identity; it created the political opportunity for the anti-China forces to confront any Chinese attempt to establish political and social control and to mobilize social and political resources for launching repeated anti-China social protests.

One research question that this chapter attempts to address is the impact of the National Security Law on Hong Kong residents' political participation. The empirical analysis based on the Hong Kong Political Culture Survey shows an interesting pattern. Initially, the NSL seemed to play a deterrent role. The survey respondents were willing to discuss their dissatisfaction by visiting government offices and reducing their protest behavior. Yet this peaceful action was short-lived. As many as 30% of the survey respondents would join protests again if the government failed to respond to their needs. The effectiveness of the NSL as a deterrent to political confrontation is temporary and remains on the surface. Political tension still exists, and it can explode again if the government fails to reduce such tension.

The cautious and pessimistic reader may not agree with the existence of the potential to protest because the National Security Law effectively cleared the protestors from the streets almost overnight. It is true that protests may not be seen on the streets for a while. Yet our findings still show the tendency to protest. One possibility is in the wording of the survey question: Is protest the most effective way to solve your problem if you feel unfairly treated by the government or government policies? The respondents may be simply responding to the question literally, not necessarily feeling they themselves had to take the action. This possibility also makes sense of why there are no protests, but people still have the potential to do so. Such potential may be released if triggered by the right events.

Tracing the sources of political participation, this chapter shows that policy dissatisfaction, anti-China political orientation, the anti-China media, and the young generation are the factors that encourage political actions through non-institutional channels, such as protest, boycott, and unofficial news media outlets.

The National Security Law was an effective, quick solution to clear the protesters from the streets in Hong Kong. Yet as shown in this chapter, its effect was temporary, and it does not fix the psychological cracks between Beijing and Hongkongers. For the reasons mentioned in this book, these political cracks were created over the past quarter century since the Handover. It will probably take as many years to fill these cracks and re-establish Hongkongers' political identity with the Chinese state. It will take at least another cycle of political socialization to create a new Chinese political orientation, depending on China's successful efforts not only to make new laws and pass legislation but also to clean up the media environment, change the school curriculum to include patriotic materials, promote Mandarin-language education, eliminate Western control of Hong Kong's legal system, and improve the SAR government's responsiveness to public opinion.

6
The "Apple-Lization" of Hong Kong Media

Introduction

Political culture does not emerge from a vacuum. It is partially produced and distributed by mass media (Chapter 1) and consumed by the public.[1] Many studies have proved that the mass media in Hong Kong played a crucial role in shaping people's political attitudes and influencing their political behaviors.[2] Despite the rise of digital media, newspapers and TV were still the dominant news sources in Hong Kong in the first 23 years after the Handover.[3] Previous chapters have pointed out that press media acted as one crucial factor influencing the political culture in post-Handover Hong Kong. Furthermore, newspapers of different political stances, particularly their attitudes toward China, played opposing roles in shaping individuals' political identity, political trust, and political behavior. Among them, *Apple Daily* stood out as the leading anti-China press. Its ability to cultivate Hong Kong people's negative feelings about and even resentments toward China was much greater than the ability of pro-establishment newspapers to promote people's positive affection for China (see Chapters 3, 4, and 5).

This chapter attempts to examine the reasons that made *Apple Daily* so effective in influencing public opinion in Hong Kong. First, it will conduct text analysis of 119,136 articles related to the Chinese Communist Party (CCP) published by two opposing newspapers: *Apple Daily* on the far right and *Wen Wei Po* on the far left, and identify the topic keywords. The findings in this section suggest that *Apple Daily* was able to promote anti-China sentiment partly because of its ability to relate its reporting to local interests and blame local problems on the CCP, while the pro-establishment papers were busy propagating the central government's political slogans.

---

[1] Street 1994.
[2] E.g., Lee and Chan 2008; Xia and Shen 2018.
[3] Ma, Wai-ket et al. *News and social media use behavior survey 2015* (in Chinese: 新闻与社交媒体使用行为调查 2015). Media Digest, https://app3.rthk.hk/mediadigest/content.php?aid=2029.

Proud and Angry. Wenfang Tang and Ying Xia, Oxford University Press. © Oxford University Press (2025).
DOI: 10.1093/9780197831588.003.0006

The second section shows the ideological stances of the 10 major newspapers in Hong Kong by examining 539,381 articles published by these 10 newspapers between 2002 and 2020. The results suggest a general trend of moving toward the far right, or "Apple-lization," among the major local papers.

The final section uses the 2021 Hong Kong Political Culture Survey data and examines the survey respondents' preferences of the 10 papers. One surprising finding is that the largest group of readers of all these papers except one was politically "yellow," or anti-establishment. It suggests that in a highly competitive media market, these papers had to rely on *Apple Daily*'s tactics to attract a greater audience; even some of these papers were conventionally believed to be pro-establishment.

Media Environment in Hong Kong

Before comparing the political orientations of *Apple Daily* and *Wen Wei Po*, it is necessary to provide some background information for those readers unfamiliar with Hong Kong's media environment and briefly discuss the existing studies on Hong Kong's media freedom (in the next section).

The news media market in Hong Kong is lively and competitive. In this city of 7.25 million people, there are 90 registered newspapers, including around 60 Chinese-language dailies (as of January 2024).[4] Of the 60-some Chinese-language newspapers currently registered, 10 are widely known in Hong Kong, and all of them have a long history of operation dating back to the colonial era before 1997. These 10 newspapers include, by the sequence of their founding date, *Sing Tao Daily*, *Ta Kung Pao*, *Sing Pao*, *Oriental Daily*, *Wen Wei Pao*, *Hong Kong Commercial Daily*, *Ming Pao*, *Hong Kong Economic Journal*, *Hong Kong Economic Times*, and *Apple Daily* (see Appendix 6.1 for further details).

Seven of them, including *Sing Tao Daily*, *Sing Pao*, *Oriental Daily*, *Ming Pao*, *Hong Kong Economic Journal*, *Hong Kong Economic Times*, and *Apple Daily* are owned by private newspaper groups. All of them but *Hong Kong Economic Journal* are listed on the stock market.[5] The remaining three,

---

[4] List of registered newspapers: https://www.ofnaa.gov.hk/filemanager/ofnaa/sc/content_1401/List_of_Registered_Newspapers_SC.pdf.

[5] Various surveys have been done by different research groups to measure the popularity of Hong Kong newspapers. For example, a survey done by Nielsen group from 2006 to 2007 found that the most popular three newspapers were *Oriental Daily*, *Apple Daily*, and *Ming Pao*, with a readership share of 32.8%, 24.2%, and 7.3% respectively. Other newspapers with more than 1% readership are by popularity sequence *Sing Tao Daily*, *Hong Kong Economic Times*, *Sing Pao*, and *Hong Kong Economic Journal*. Another popularity

namely, the *Hong Kong Commercial Daily*, *Ta Kung Pao*, and *Wen Wei Po*, are supported by China and serve as the propaganda mouthpieces of the CCP in Hong Kong.

The existing legislation governing the operation of the news media in Hong Kong only regulates the registration process of newspapers and hardly imposes any restrictions on the content of newspapers. Companies or individuals, whether local or overseas, can start a newspaper without having to pay a deposit or account for their political and economic background. All they need to do is to provide the basic information of the proprietor, printer, publisher, or editor and pay a registration fee of HK$1,140.[6] As long as a newspaper is legally registered, it is free to report news and publish editorials according to the interests of its target audience. The only explicit provision of the local law is that newspaper articles may not print and disseminate "obscene and indecent" materials.[7]

The British colonizers lifted most media control regulations before Hong Kong's return to China, including regulations allowing the government to penalize media outlets that published false news and news harmful to the public order.[8] The local government after the Handover did not impose pre-publication censorship or a formal editorial policy. Compared to their Mainland counterparts, Hong Kong's press media have enjoyed a higher degree of freedom for most of the post-Handover period. According to Statista, the average press freedom index of Hong Kong from 2014 to 2021 was around 71/100, while that of Mainland China was only around 24/100 during the same period. Higher scores refer to higher levels of press freedom.[9]

---

survey was done in 2019 by the Center for Communication and Public Opinion Survey of the Chinese University of Hong Kong. According to this survey, *Apple Daily*, *Oriental Daily*, and *Ming Pao* remained the most popular newspapers, but *Apply Daily* surpassed *Oriental Daily* and became the paper with the largest readership. Other less popular newspapers are also similar to those of 12 years ago. They include *Sing Tao Daily*, *Hong Kong Economic Times*, *and Hong Kong Economic Journal*. Overall, the two readership surveys share similar results of the most popular print media in Hong Kong. By contrast, three pro-China newspapers, *Wen Wei Po*, *Ta Kung Pao*, and *Hong Kong Commercial Daily* are all absent from the ranking, meaning that none of them reached the 1% readership threshold.

[6] Hong Kong Legislation Chapter 268, Registration of Local Newspapers Ordinance; and Chapter 268B, Newspapers Registration and Distribution Regulations. See Hong Kong e-Legislation database, https://www.elegislation.gov.hk.

[7] Hong Kong Legislation Chapter 390, Control of Obscene and Indecent Articles Ordinance. See Hong Kong e-Legislation database, https://www.elegislation.gov.hk.

[8] In 1987, the colonial government amended the Control of Publications Consolidation Ordinance to remove most of the provisions regulating the press and retained only one provision relating to fake news, which was transferred to the Public Order Ordinance. In the following year, the colonial government amended the Public Order Ordinance to repeal the provision regulating fake news. Since then, Hong Kong has not added any important legislation to regulate the press industry.

[9] See Press Freedom Index in Hong Kong from 2014 to 2023 by Statista, https://www.statista.com/statistics/1246005/hong-kong-press-freedom-index, and Press Freedom Index in China from 2014 to 2023 by Statista, https://www.statista.com/statistics/1117177/china-press-freedom-index.

British colonial rule of Hong Kong separated this region from China's Mainland for more than 150 years. The lack of communication between these two regions, plus two entirely different political systems, eventually led to two sharply different language and narrative systems. While Hong Kong kept the usage of traditional Chinese language and heavily incorporated local Cantonese and English into its local narrative system, the Chinese Mainland since CCP's rule has thoroughly replaced traditional Chinese language and local dialects with simplified Chinese characters. The different language systems are reflected in the narratives of the media systems in the two regions. Media in Hong Kong more frequently use narratives that are less formal, combining colloquial Cantonese and some localized English terms, while its counterpart, the Mainland newspapers, overwhelmingly use formal simplified Chinese-language narrative, rarely involving any colloquial or dialectic expression.

Existing Studies on Media Freedom in Hong Kong

In this lightly regulated media market with predominantly private ownership, media companies are profit driven. They compete fiercely to attract readers and advertisement revenue. The easiest way to grab the viewers' attention is through tabloid journalism and celebrity gossip.[10] Studies have shown that viewers in a market environment become consumers who have little patience for objective reporting after a busy working day. They are more likely to watch and read negative and opinionated news, namely political scandals, conspiracies, crimes, and natural disasters. This "dumbing down" tendency shapes media behavior and makes media outlets compete to publish negative news and opinionated op-eds.[11]

However, many existing studies on Hong Kong media have concluded that press freedom in Hong Kong has been seriously undermined after the Handover under China's increasing political control.[12] The main evidence provided by these studies is that the CCP has co-opted many media owners, granting them prominent political titles and thus giving them access to enormous political and economic resources.[13] For instance, in 2016, Chinese internet giant Alibaba acquired *South China Morning Post*, an English-language newspaper that had been one of the most influential in Hong Kong since

---

[10] Otto, Glogger, and Boukes 2016.
[11] Campbell 2004.
[12] E.g., Fung 2007; Lee 2018.
[13] Frisch, Belair-Gagnon, and Agur 2018.

British colonial rule. According to the Hong Kong Journalists Association (HKJA), as of 2016, 31% of Hong Kong's mainstream media was in the hands of Mainland companies. What is more, 80% of Hong Kong's media owners received appointments or awards from the Mainland and pro-establishment groups.[14] Among them, the owners of two major Chinese-language media, *Oriental Daily* and *Sing Tao Daily*, are members of the Chinese People's Political Consultative Conference (CPPCC), which is the CCP's main body for co-opting non-party elites in the Greater China region.[15]

According to this literature, changes in media ownership and the CCP's political co-optation tactics have led to widespread self-censorship in the local media.[16] In the name of professional objectivism, the reporting stance of local newspapers shifted toward neutral and even pro-China. *Apple Daily* became the only press that remained critical of China.[17] Moreover, in order not to offend the Chinese government during the sensitive period of the local democracy movement, the mainstream editorials of local newspapers shifted their focus to criticizing the protests rather than supporting them.[18]

The consensus of the existing studies on Hong Kong's media after reunification seems to show that, with the exception of *Apple Daily*, the local media have turned collectively to political conservatism, and the main reason behind this is Beijing's political influence. This argument, however, contradicts the market orientation of most privately owned newspapers as discussed above. It also fails to explain why *Apple Daily* survived Beijing's political pressure and became a popular newspaper among Hong Kong readers. If most other newspapers had indeed distanced themselves from the most popular *Apple Daily*, how had they responded to market demand and survived in the competitive media market? These outstanding issues suggest that existing studies may not have fully and accurately reflected media development in Hong Kong after the Handover.

Media Narratives of CCP: Evidence from *Apple Daily* and *Wen Wei Po*

So, why is *Apple Daily* so successful but *Wen Wei Po* so unsuccessful in attracting public attention? In this section, we search for some tentative answers to

---

[14] Hong Kong Journalists Association 2016.
[15] Lee 2018.
[16] Lee and Chan 2009.
[17] Fung 2007.
[18] Lee and Lin 2006; Kwong 2015.

these questions by analyzing the texts of 119,136 articles published between 2002 and 2020 by the two papers on the CCP.

Identify Topic Keywords of the Two Newspapers

To analyze such a large volume of text data, we used the text analysis method. To be more specific, we applied Latent Dirichlet allocation topic model to extract topic keywords from all articles of each of the two papers on a yearly basis. We then selected the top-10 most frequently used annual topic keywords when they wrote about the CCP. Below we take the topic keywords of five selected years to illustrate how the two papers differ completely in content narrative on the CCP. The full list of the 19 years analyzed is presented in Appendix 6.2.

The years we selected are 2003, 2008, 2012, 2014, and 2019. The main reason for choosing these years is that in each of the years except for 2008, there had been a major political event taking place in Hong Kong. As illustrated in Chapter 5, in 2003, it was the first large-scale protest since 1997. In 2012, it was the protest against national education reform. In 2014, it was the 79-day-long Occupy movement for full democracy. And in 2019, it was the seven-month-long anti-extradition-bill movement.

The year 2008 is the exception in that there was no controversial political event happening in Hong Kong. However, two big events happened in China in that year. It was the year that China for the first time since its founding hosted the Olympic Games. It was such a huge moment that a strong nationalist sentiment appeared in Hong Kong.[19] Another important but sad event also happened in this year. An inland city in China, named Wenchuan, was hit by a devastating earthquake that cost the lives of approximately 69,000 local residents.[20] This tragedy aroused great sympathy among many Hongkongers, and many of them went to Wenchuan voluntarily to help with the rescue and reconstruction work.

Narrative of Apple Daily

Table 6.1 presents the yearly topic keywords of the two papers in the selected years when reporting on the CCP. Overall, the two newspapers use

---

[19] Many public opinion surveys show that around 2008 the national identity of Hong Kong people reached a historical height after Hong Kong's return to China.
[20] World Heritage Convention 2008.

The "Apple-Lization" of Hong Kong Media   131

Table 6.1 Top-10 Topic Keywords Used by *Apple Daily* and *Wen Wei Po* in Selected Years

Year	Apple Daily	Wen Wei Po
2003	June 4th, Uncle Tung, Article 23, Bush, hide, Aha-Tung, local CCP(*tu gong*), Zhao Ziyang, July 1st, protest on the street (*shangjie*)	CPPCC (Chinese People's Political Consultative Conference, *renmin zhengxie*), spacecraft, the Ninth Conference, Bush, opportunity, Li Zongren, Tibetan, Yu Youren, Hui minority, Li Kenong
2008	June 4th, police, Bush, Hujia, the Hu-Wen regime, repression, pan-democrats, Chengxiang, democrats, Zhaoziyang	industry, construction, Guangdong-Hong Kong, promote, Guangdong-Hong Kong-Macau, service industry, Shishi, cartoons and comics, Taiwan and the Mainland (*haixia liang'an*), Haining
2012	June 4th, Li Wangyang, brain-washing, Leung Chun-ying, National Education Reform, Tang Ying-yen, march, Chief Executive, the government, protest on the street	construction, promote, socialism, innovation, economy-and-society, *xiaokang* society, implement, improve, our country, anti-corruption
2014	June 4th, pan-Democrats, Hongkongers, the government, resistance, the establishment, suppress (*da ya*), march, vote, repression (*zhen ya*)	construction, cadres, inspection, promote, North Korea, party integrity, Central Commission for Discipline Inspection, our country, party committee, get to know
2019	Call for action, go to vote, 11.24, kick off, free Hong Kong (*guangfu hongkong*), June 4th, resistance, anti-extradition-law, one-hundred days, summer of freedom	development, construction, socialism, promote, Guangdong-Hong Kong-Macau, innovation, Greater Bay Area, improve, with Chinese characteristics, governance

The table presents the yearly topic keywords of two papers in the selected years when reporting on the CCP. Overall, the two newspapers use entirely different topic systems related to the CCP. In a nutshell, topic keywords reflecting Hong Kong local politics appear in *Apple Daily*'s reports of all the selected years while completely absent from those of *Wen Wei Po*.

Note: Underlined words are all related to heated social or political events in that year.

entirely different topic systems related to the CCP. In a nutshell, topic keywords reflecting Hong Kong local politics appear in *Apple Daily*'s reports of all the selected years while completely absent from those of *Wen Wei Po*.

To take *Apple Daily*'s topic keywords for instance, the words in underline in Table 6.1 are all related to heated social or political events in each year. Among the others, one political event that had been constantly linked by *Apple Daily* to the CCP's repression of democracy movement is the June 4th urban protests in Beijing in 1989. Every year after the reunification, Hongkongers organized peaceful demonstrations on June 4th to commemorate the protest victims.

Without exception, this event was the focus of *Apple Daily* every year when it took place. The term "June 4th" appeared every year from 2002 to 2020 in the sets of topic keywords used by *Apple Daily* when it condemned the CCP for the crackdown of student activists and reminded Hongkongers to keep fighting for democracy.

In addition to the June 4th vigil, other annual topic keywords of *Apple Daily* mainly reflect major local events in the corresponding year. For example, the event of 2003 was the massive demonstration against the local administration's proposal to legislate Article 23 of the Basic Law of Hong Kong. The underlined words in Table 6.1, Uncle Tung (dongshu, 董叔) and Aha-Tung (a-dong, 阿董), are both local expressions of Tung Chee-Hwa, the chief executive of Hong Kong who launched the legislation procedure of Article 23. When Tung's administration announced the proposal to legislate Article 23, the local society was quickly mobilized by a widely spreading fear that this legislation might devastate civil and political freedom in Hong Kong. This fear, along with other discontents, eventually drove thousands of Hongkongers to the street on July 1st, which was the date to celebrate Hong Kong's handover to China. The other two topic keywords found in *Apple Daily*'s reports reflecting this event are "July 1st" and "protest on the street" (shangjie, 上街).

In 2012, 2014, and 2019, there were respectively the anti-national education reform protests, the Umbrella movement, and the anti-extradition bill protests. The topic keywords of *Apple Daily* of these three years correspondingly reflected the aforementioned social movement events. In 2012, the underlined keywords "brain-washing," "Leung Chun-ying," "national education reform," "Chief Executive," and "protest on the street" all refer to the protest against Chief Executive Leung Chun-ying's attempt to launch national education reform. In 2019, similarly, topic keywords such as "anti-extradition-law," "resistance," "one-hundred days," "free Hong Kong," and "summer of freedom" all point to the months-long protests against the extradition law. Another important political event of this year was the 2019 District Council Election, which was held on November 24. The remaining topic keywords including "call for action," "go to vote," "11.24" and "kick off" all refer to this election.

Below are two excerpts of articles from *Apple Daily*, showing how the narratives intentionally relate the two local political incidents to the CCP's repression of Hong Kong's democracy movements.

Example 1 A commentary article by Li Ping, published in the August 6, 2019, edition of *Apple Daily*, accused the chief executive, Ms. Carrie Lam Cheng Yuet-ngor of being loyal to the CCP's order to suppress Hong Kong people's actions for democracy. It states:

> Carrie Lam, as the Chief Executive, can hardly absolve herself of the blame. The CCP regards the national emblem in West Point as sacrosanct. They turned a blind eye to the mobs' attack on the public, triggering city-wide anger against the regime. "Carrie Lam Stepping Down," among the five major demands of the previous protests, has now evolved into the demand for full democracy in Hong Kong. The slogan "Free Hong Kong, Revolution Now" has reappeared and is gradually gaining wide acceptance.

The original Chinese version of this excerpt:

> 林郑身为特首都难辞其咎。中共港共视西环的国徽神圣不可侵犯，对无差别攻击市民的恐袭凶手只个别拘捕、控以非法集结，终于激发跨行业、跨年龄的全城抗争，五大诉求中的林郑下台已变成要求双普选"光复香港、时代革命"的口号重现并渐渐广为接受。

Example 2 During the 2019 District Council Election campaign, *Apple Daily* set up a special session, both online and in the paper, to do political advertisements for the pan-Democrat candidates. In this session, it states:

> The anti-extradition-law movements have been going on for more than five months, ranging from struggles within the Legislative Council to protests on the streets. Now the contention has extended to the District Council Election.... Some people use the phrase "Hong Kong People, fighting!" to pretend to support the people of Hong Kong, but they are actually part of the pro-establishment camp. They have been looking up to the Chinese Communist Party and acting as the dictator's "agents" in Hong Kong. These "agents" have blurred faces and can easily confuse the public. 11.24 District Election is around the corner. Apple Daily has specially produced the website "Free Hong Kong, the 2019 District Election," so that you can find out the real stance of certain candidates, and whether they can truly represent you and speak for the public in the District Councils, instead of continuing to be a "rubber stamp."

The original Chinese version of this excerpt:

> 历时逾5个月的反送中运动，由议会内抗争到议会外，多月的街头活动后，抗争平台再延伸到区议会...有人一句"香港人加油"，图撇清与亲建制团体的关系，这些仰极权鼻息、中共在港"代理人"，面膜模糊得容易让人混淆。11.24区选在即，《苹果》制作"2019区选光复香港"专题网站，让你了解候选人的真正取态，他能否真正代表到你，于区议会中为市民发声，而不是继续论文"橡皮图章"。

The quoted texts represent a typical narrative of many articles published by *Apple Daily*. The underlying logic of this narrative is that the fundamental reason for the stagnation of democracy in Hong Kong was the suppression by the CCP. The Hong Kong government and the pro-establishment political groups had never acted in the interests of the people of Hong Kong but only followed the orders of Beijing to slow down the democratization process. In other words, the real obstacle to the development of democracy in Hong Kong was the CCP. When the Hong Kong people were fighting for full democracy, they were fighting against the party and its local agents in Hong Kong.

Narrative of Wen Wei Po

In stark contrast, the topic keywords of *Wen Wei Po* over the 19 years under study have nothing to do with Hong Kong's local politics but the latest developments of the CCP and its central government. The reportage either introduced major political events of the party or propagated newly announced policies of the party's central government. Most of the information on the party was development oriented, and "development" itself was one of the mainstream propaganda themes in the Mainland. Below are three narrative lines used by *Wen Wei Po* based on our analysis of the topic keywords of each year.

1. *The party's important political meetings that relate to the interest of Hongkongers.* For instance, between 2003 and 2005, "Chinese People's Political Consultative Conference (CPPCC)" consistently appeared in *Wen Wei Po*'s list of topic keywords. This organ is led by the party to exercise its united front strategy and co-opt non-party-member elites from various social constituencies. Hong Kong's elite group is an important target of the party's united front. Every five years, the party appoints more than 2,000 new members to the National Committee of the CPPCC, of whom about 124 are from Hong Kong. Those who are qualified to serve as the members of the National Committee of the CPPCC should be politically loyal to the rule of the party and have sufficiently distinguished themselves in their respective professions. From the high frequency of the reports on CPPCC, it can be inferred that *Wen Wei Po* attempted to use the CPPCC as an important link between the party and Hong Kong society. However, this link only connects to a small number of elites in the local society rather than the general public.
2. *Central government's policy on regional cooperation and development between Hong Kong and its neighboring Mainland region, Guangdong Province.* From the policy around 2004 emphasizing the co-development of the Pan-Pearl-River-Delta region (泛珠三角) with

Hong Kong as the leader to the official announcement of the central government in 2019 to construct the Greater Bay Area of Guangdong-Hong Kong-Macau (粤港澳大湾区) as a national strategy. Central government's policy dynamics regarding the development of Hong Kong constitute another obvious narrative line.

3. *Major national polices and campaigns.* Since Xi Jinping became the general secretary of the CCP in 2012, there has been an obvious shift in *Wen Wei Po*'s narrative style. Prior to 2012, coverage of the CCP was relatively decentralized and focused primarily on regional economic development issues. In contrast, coverage from 2012 onward focused primarily on the party's main work during the year. As the complete list of topic keywords in the Appendix shows, from 2012 through 2016, coverage of the party largely focused on the aggressive anti-corruption campaign launched by Xi Jinping after he became the general secretary. Terms such as "the Central Discipline Inspection Commission" (中央纪委), "improve party conduct and ensure clean government" (党风廉政), and "comprehensive and strict governance of the party" (从严治党) are all relevant to the anti-corruption campaign. In addition to this, reports in recent years have focused on other important work of the CCP, such as fighting poverty (脱贫), technological innovation (科技创新), and enhancing modernization with Chinese characteristics (中国式现代化).

Of all the above three narratives of *Wen Wei Po*, none was relevant to the local issues that Hongkongers are familiar with. Even when a social movement occurred that drew the attention of the whole city, *Wen Wei Po* hardly commented on it, focusing instead on reporting the glorious story of the party and the country.

As shown in the findings of this section, *Apple Daily* skillfully used localized narratives to cultivate an always negative and sometimes evil image of the CCP into the minds of Hongkongers. In contrast, although *Wen Wei Po* attempted to transfer positive information of the CCP and its policies regarding Hong Kong society, it failed to localize the stories to a population with only a vague knowledge of the party and the Chinese nation. On this point, *Apple Daily* played a vital role in the overall anti-nation-building project in this former colonial city. It has been successful in pushing the local society away from the Chinese nation.

In short, as shown by the above analysis, *Apple Daily* seems to be very good at telling "bad" stories, while *Wen Wei Po* seems to be very bad at telling "good" stories.

Measuring Media Slant of Major Newspapers

What about the other major papers in Hong Kong? How can we know if the other papers are pressed to move to the left or right?

As mentioned above, existing studies have concluded that the Hong Kong media were becoming more and more conservative, avoiding critical reporting or commenting on sensitive issues related to the CCP. In this section, we attempt to retest this conventional conclusion with new evidence.

We measure the political slant of different newspapers using empirical materials similar to that of existing studies but with a much larger quantity and with different analytical methods. To be specific, we collected 539,381 unique articles on the CCP published by 10 major newspapers between the years 2002 and 2020.[21] The 10 newspapers include *Apple Daily, Oriental Daily, Ming Pao, Sing Tao Daily, Hong Kong Economic Times, Hong Kong Economic Journal, Sing Pao, Hong Kong Commercial Daily, Ta Kung Pao,* and *Wen Wei Po* (Appendix 6.1).

It is widely recognized, as mentioned, that *Apple Daily* and *Wen Wei Po* represent the right and the left ends of the political spectrum of the local media respectively. We therefore use these two newspapers as two benchmarks for measuring the political stances of other newspapers. Our approach is to measure the similarity of a news outlet's language to that of *Apple Daily* and *Wen Wei Po* respectively. The "similarity" score of two newspapers is obtained by calculating the cosine similarity of two corpuses of texts. This method was first developed by economists in the 2010s to measure the political slant of newspapers in the US.[22] Following their way of processing the text data, we calculated the annual cosine similarity scores of the language used by each of the eight newspapers with *Apple Daily* and *Wen Wei Po* respectively.

Figure 6.1 shows the yearly changes of media slant of Hong Kong's eight major newspapers from 2002 to 2020, as compared to the two polars *Apple Daily* and *Wen Wei Po*. Positive values on the *y*-axis indicate that the newspaper's ideological stance is closer to that of *Apple Daily*, while negative values suggest a closer stance to that of *Wen Wei Po*. Several overall trends can be observed from Figure 6.1.

---

[21] To do this, we first searched for articles related to the CCP reported by the 10 newspapers from an e-news database named "wisenews." We used seven different keywords that are often used by local newspapers to refer to the CCP, and they are *zhongguo gongchandang* (中国共产党), *zhonggong* (中共), *gongchandang* (共产党), *gongdang* (共党), *gongfei* (共匪), *ganggong* (港共), *tugong* (土共), and *zhengzhiju* (政治局). Due to database access limitations, we only collected relevant articles published from 2002 to 2020.

[22] Gentzkow and Shapiro 2010.

The "Apple-Lization" of Hong Kong Media   137

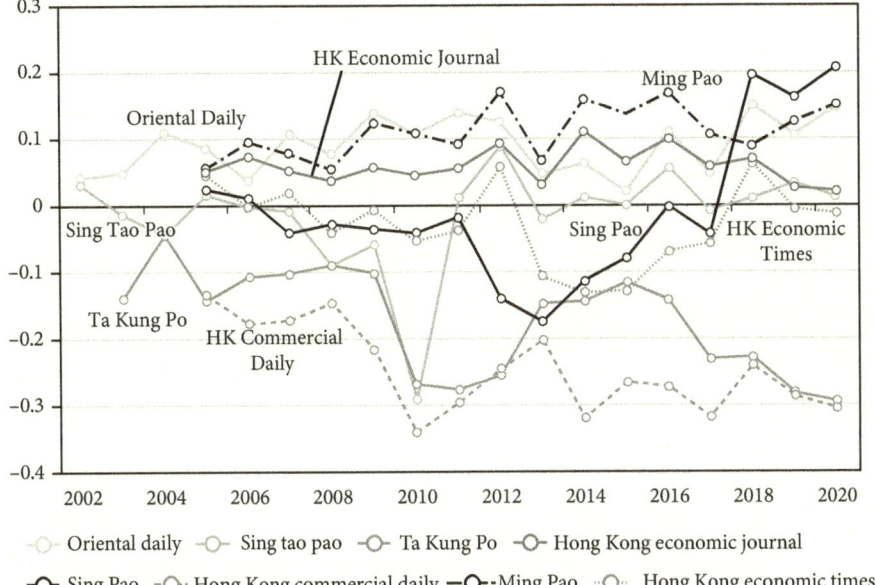

Figure 6.1 Media slant of Hong Kong newspapers, 2002–2020
Main findings: The figure shows the yearly changes of media slant of Hong Kong's eight major newspapers from 2002 to 2020, as compared to the two polars *Apple Daily* and *Wen Wei Po*. Positive values on the y-axis indicate that the newspaper's ideological stance is closer to *Apple Daily*, while negative values suggest a closer stance to *Wen Wei Po*. Several overall trends can be observed. First, the overall media slant has undergone a shift from turning to the left to turning to the right. The change took place around 2013. Second, the gap between the right and the left has been widening rapidly since 2013, showing the trend of ideological polarization in the Hong Kong press. Third, from 2002 to 2020, these newspapers can be roughly categorized into three groups. On the right with *Apple Daily* are *Oriental Daily*, *Hong Kong Economic Journal*, and *Ming Pao*; on the left with *Wen Wei Po* are *Hong Kong Commercial Daily* and *Ta Kung Pao*; and in the middle are *Sing Tao Daily*, *Hong Kong Economic Times*, and *Sing Pao*, while *Sing Pao* showed an alarming rightward turn since 2017.

Notes: The vertical axis represents the difference in linguistic similarity between a newspaper and two benchmark newspapers *Apple Daily* and *Wen Wei Po*, respectively. Linguistic similarity is a calculation of the cosine similarity between the texts of a newspaper and the two benchmark newspapers respectively in a given year. A positive number on the vertical axis indicates that the newspaper is more similar to *Apple Daily*, and the larger the value, the higher the similarity. A negative number indicates that the newspaper is more similar to *Wen Wei Po*, and the smaller the value, the higher the similarity.

Source: Based 539,381 unique articles on the CCP published by the 10 newspapers between 2002 and 2020.

First, the overall media slant has undergone a shift from turning to the left to turning to the right. The change took place approximately around 2013. Thereafter, most of the newspapers started to turn to the right, and only *Hong*

Kong Commercial Daily and *Ta Kung Pao*, the two newspapers with Mainland background, continued to move further to the left.

Second, the gap between the right and the left has been widening rapidly since 2013, showing the trend of ideological polarization in the Hong Kong press media in the last decade. In 2020, only *Hong Kong Commercial Daily* and *Ta Kung Pao* were with *Wen Wei Po* and on the leftist side. All the other major newspapers were far away from *Wen Wei Po*. Some newspapers, including *Sing Pao*, *Ming Pao*, and *Oriental Daily*, appeared to have media slant closest to that of *Apple Daily* in the past two decades.

Third, from 2002 to 2020, these newspapers can be roughly categorized into three groups. On the right with *Apple Daily* are *Oriental Daily, Hong Kong Economic Journal*, and *Ming Pao*; on the left with *Wen Wei Po* are *Hong Kong Commercial Daily* and *Ta Kung Pao*; and in the middle are *Sing Tao Daily, Hong Kong Economic Times*, and *Sing Pao*, while *Sing Pao* showed an alarming rightward turn since 2017.

Two "surprises" are worth mentioning. First, existing studies generally assume that some newspapers, such as *Ming Pao*, are centrist, but in fact they are much more critical of the CCP than one would expect. Another surprising finding is that *Oriental Daily*, which has always worn a moderate or even pro-China hat, has shown itself to be quite brave and critical on issues related to the CCP.

Table 6.2 sums up the findings in this section. As shown, the tendency to move leftward was exaggerated in the existing studies. Instead, the rightward move among the 10 newspapers was more obvious. Though this finding contradicts the existing studies about self-censorship, it nevertheless is based on more solid empirical evidence than previous studies. Furthermore, it seems to be consistent with the media's dumbing down effect in a market environment.[23]

Reader Preference: Evidence from Survey Data

The machine-aided text analysis in the previous section shows the media tendency of reporting negative news to attract more readers in the highly competitive Hong Kong market. This tendency only represents the supply of negative media content. It is yet to be confirmed if the demand side, the consumers of the media content, welcome such tactics. In other words, the

---

[23] Campbell 2004.

Table 6.2 Ideological Categories of Major Newspapers in Hong Kong

Ideological category	Representing newspapers (existing studies)	Representing newspapers (media slant 2020)	Representing newspapers (2021 survey)
Rightist	· *Apple Daily*	· *Apple Daily* · *Sing Pao* · *Ming Pao* · *Oriental Daily*	· *Apple Daily* · *Sing Pao* · *Ming Pao* · *Hong Kong Economic Times*
Moderate	· *Hong Kong Economic Times* · *Hong Kong Economic Journal* · *Ming Pao*	· *Sing Tao Daily* · *Hong Kong Economic Times* · *Hong Kong Economic Journal*	· *Sing Tao Daily* · *Oriental Daily* · *Ta Kung Pao*
Leftist	· *Oriental Daily* · *Ta Kung Pao* · *Hong Kong Commercial Daily* · *Wen Wei Po*	· *Ta Kung Pao* · *Hong Kong Commercial Daily* · *Wen Wei Po*	· *Wen Wei Po*

The table shows ideological groupings of major local newspapers by different criteria. The column on the left shows the categorization by mainstream studies. The column in the middle shows the results of the media slant measurement as presented in this chapter. The right column shows the respondents' self-grouping of major newspapers as found in the 2021 Hong Kong Political Culture Survey. Both the survey and the media slant measurements show that local newspapers' ideological positions are more rightist than the existing mainstream studies have concluded.

final step of this chapter is to show viewer preference of these newspapers based on the extent of the negative content.

In the 2021 Hong Kong Political Culture Survey, the respondents were asked about their preference among the 10 newspapers. As expected, the most popular print media outlet is *Apple Daily*, supposedly the only newspaper recognized in the existing studies as being critical of the CCP despite its political pressure. As shown in Figure 6.2, about half (49.9%) of the respondents reported that they read *Apple Daily* regularly, while the second most popular newspaper, *Oriental Daily*, attracted less than a quarter (23.3%) of the survey respondents. The popularity of the other newspapers, in descending order of readership share, were *Hong Kong Economic Times*, *Sing Tao Daily*, *Ming Pao*, *Tai Kung Po*, *Sing Pao*, and *Wen Wei Po*. The least popular newspaper, *Wen Wei Po*, had no more than 1% readership.

Coincidently, the popularity of these newspapers corresponds to how they have been categorized in previous studies. As early as in the 1990s, relevant studies have pointed out that the Hong Kong newspaper industry consisted

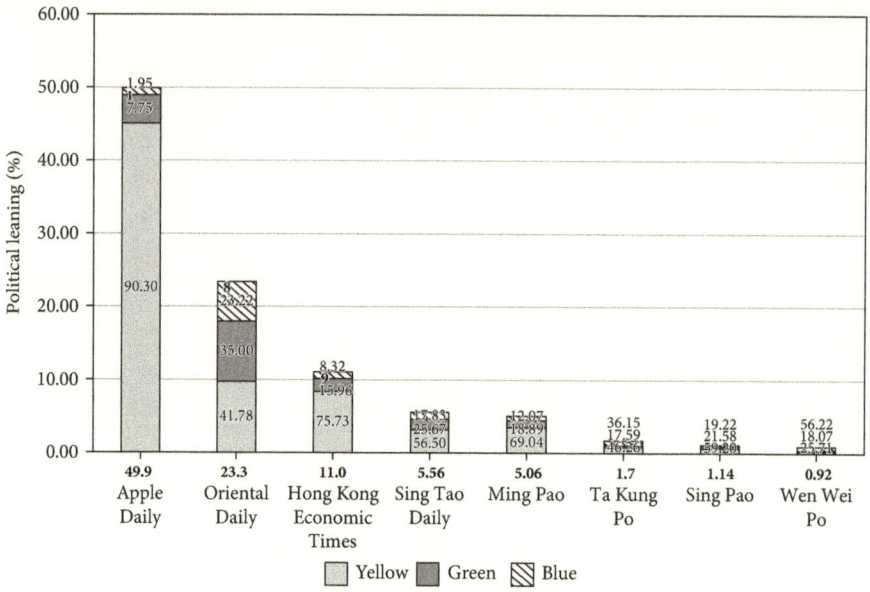

Figure 6.2 Reader preference of print media in Hong Kong, 2021

Main findings: The figure presents the preference of respondents with different political orientations to 10 major local newspapers. The most popular print media outlet is *Apple Daily*. About half (49.9%) of the respondents reported that they read *Apple Daily* regularly, while the second most popular newspaper, *Oriental Daily*, attracted less than a quarter (23.3%) of the survey respondents. The popularity of other newspapers, in descending order of readership share, were *Hong Kong Economic Times*, *Sing Tao Daily*, *Ming Pao*, *Tai Kung Po*, *Sing Pao*, and *Wen Wei Po*. The least popular newspaper, *Wen Wei Po*, had no more than 1% readership. When considering the respondents' political orientation, it shows that except for *Wen Wei Po*, all the news media had the largest proportion of readers with an anti-establishment orientation (yellow). Among all the media outlets, 90.30% of *Apple Daily*'s readers were disproportionately anti-establishment (yellow). Followers of *Hong Kong Economic Times*, *Sing Tao Daily, Ming Pao*, and *Sing Pao* were also majority yellow at 75.73%, 56.50%, 69.04%, and 59.20% respectively. Even for the moderate *Oriental Daily* and *Ta Kung Pao*, the largest groups of readers were still yellow at 42.78% and 46.26%; even their percentages did not pass majority. *Wen Wei Po* is the only paper whose readers were predominantly pro-establishment (65.22%).

Notes: Each bar represents the percentage of survey respondents who receive social and political news through that media channel. Political color: blue=pro-China, yellow=anti-China, green=neutral. All percentages are weighted by social desirability. Only paid Chinese-language newspapers are listed.

Source: Hong Kong Political Culture Survey 2021.

of elite newspapers, mass newspapers, and leftist newspapers,[24] which represented the three journalistic paradigms of professionalism, populism, and propaganda, respectively.[25] By examining the reports of local opinion polls, one study categorized *Apple Daily* as a populist paradigm, *Ming Pao* as a typical professional paradigm, and *Wen Wei Po* as a propaganda paradigm.[26] In this regard, we can say that populist newspapers dominated the local media after the Handover, while leftist or pro-China newspapers had very few supporters in the local community. In contrast, other centrist newspapers were much less popular than populist newspapers, but still more popular than the pro-China ones.

Another striking finding is unfolded when we relate individuals' political orientation with their media preferences. By inviting the respondents to self-identify with three major political orientations, pro-establishment (blue), politically neutral (green), and anti-establishment (yellow), we are able to outline the composition of political orientations among the readers of each media outlet.

As shown in Figure 6.2, except for *Wen Wei Po*, all the news media had the largest proportion of readers with an anti-establishment orientation (yellow). Among all the media outlets in Figure 6.2, 90.30% of *Apple Daily*'s readers were disproportionally anti-establishment (yellow). Followers of *Hong Kong Economic Times*, *Sing Tao Daily*, *Ming Pao*, and *Sing Pao* were also majority yellow at 75.73%, 56.50%, 69.04%, and 59.20% respectively. Even for the moderate *Oriental Daily* and *Ta Kung Pao*, the largest groups of readers were still yellow at 42.78% and 46.26%; even their percentages did not pass majority. *Wen Wei Po* is the only paper whose readers were predominantly pro-establishment (65.22%).

This finding is remarkably different from the existing studies that tend to focus on media control by the CCP (right column, Table 6.2).[27] It further confirms that except for *Wen Wei Po*, the supposedly leftist and neutral newspapers are actually more rightist than we usually think. For instance, the *Hong Kong Economic Times* and *Ming Pao*, which are usually regarded as centrists, have attracted readers from the rightist camp. Even *Ta Kung Pao* and *Oriental Daily*, which are usually regarded as leftist, have become moderates. Overall, unlike the consensus in the existing literature, our survey shows that the local media in Hong Kong attracted readers from the anti-establishment camp, possibly by following *Apple Daily* and tilting to the right.

---

[24] Lee 2000.
[25] Lee 2006.
[26] Lee 2006.
[27] Lee 2006; Lee and Lin 2006; Zhu, Krever, and Choi 2018; Yang et al. 2022.

142 Proud and Angry

Photo 6.1 Newsstand outside a convenience store in Hong Kong on a Sunday around noon in Wan Chai. Newspapers that were sold out included *Oriental Daily*, *Sing Tao Daily*, and *South China Morning Post*. At the bottom were Chinese government-sponsored papers, *Wen Wei Po*, *Ta Kung Pao*, and *China Daily*. Photo by Wenfang Tang, 12/10/2023.

Conclusions and Discussion

This chapter began by describing the market-oriented, highly competitive but only lightly regulated media environment in Hong Kong and the consensus in the existing literature about the CCPs supposed repression of media freedom.

In the first of the three empirical sections, this chapter compares the top topic keywords in the articles published by *Apple Daily* as one extreme on the right and *Wen Wei Po* as another extreme case on the left. The findings show a sharp contrast between the two. *Apple Daily* was able to blame Hong Kong's local problems on the CCP while *Wen Wei Po* was propagating Beijing's policies and rarely related its reporting to local issues.

There is also a big difference between the two papers in terms of language expression. While *Apple Daily* is good at using local Cantonese expressions and a more casual or even entertaining way of writing its reports, *Wen Wei Po* reproduces typical Mandarin expressions in a serious and official manner.

The second empirical section revealed a general tendency of becoming negative among Hong Kong's top-10 newspapers even for those that were considered neutral or leftist. These newspapers were probably compelled to do so because they needed to survive in a competitive media market by attracting more readers at the expense of political correctness.

The final empirical section confirms the supply-side story in the previous two sections by examining individual demand in media consumption by using survey data. It confirms the effectiveness of *Apple Daily*'s effort at cursing the PRC and how such effort explained other media outlets' tendency to turn right.

Overall, the analysis in this chapter shows the failure of the CCP in using media to integrate postcolonial Hong Kong,[28] where the local society is neither familiar with the Mainland narrative nor aware of Mainland politics. Communicating information of Chinese politics using a typical Mainland Chinese way is not well received by the local readers.

On the other hand, *Apple Daily* successfully cultivated the readers' need to "dumb down" while spreading its hatred of the CCP. Most of the other news outlets followed *Apple Daily*'s suit. This conclusion challenges the existing consensus that media were suppressed by the CCP. More importantly, it partially explains why public opinion in the first 23 years of Hong Kong's return to China was so anti-establishment, as was discussed in the previous chapters.

---

[28] Chan and Lee 2007b.

7
Conclusions and Discussion

The final chapter summarizes the main findings in the previous six chapters and offers some general discussion about the theoretical and methodological implications of Hong Kong's political culture in comparative political culture studies.

Summary of Main Findings

The previous six chapters in this book contribute to the understanding of the different dimensions of political culture in Hong Kong. Chapter 1 is a general discussion on political culture. It proposes directions and scopes of defining and measuring different dimensions of political culture and identifies the macro and micro conditions under which political cultures evolve. Of particular importance is the discussion about measurement errors. The chapter provides a general set of guidelines on how to study political cultures with quantitative and comparative data from public opinion surveys. By doing so, the chapter aims to benefit political culture research in general; it is not necessarily limited to Hong Kong. By reading this chapter, the reader should be able to position and compare Hong Kong or any other political culture in a broader framework of political cultural studies.

Chapter 2 describes how the Hong Kong Political Culture Survey was conducted, including sampling technique and questionnaire design. The focus is the survey's implementation of eight list experiments. These survey experiments were designed to detect the social desirability when the respondents were asked to answer politically sensitive questions such as their feelings toward Mainland China. Through a newly developed statistical weighting technique, a weight variable (activator) was created, and a significant amount of social desirability was found. Accordingly, the weighting technique was applied in the remaining chapters.

Chapter 3 is about Hongkongers' political identity. The survey data show that Hong Kong residents felt distant and cold toward Mainland China. Neither did they feel very warm toward the British and Americans. Instead, they showed a strong tendency to use Chinese cultural identity in place of their political identity, or indigenization of political identity. The chapter develops the concept of indigenization in place of localization because the latter reminds people of the colonial legacy.

Chapter 4 is about political trust and policy satisfaction. Hong Kong residents showed a significantly strong preference for the local political institutions over the central government agencies. In the meantime, they are relatively satisfied with government services in gender equality, Covid prevention, environment, welfare policy, healthcare, and education. Areas of dissatisfaction were in high housing prices, lack of job opportunities, and social inequality. Overall, Hong Kong residents were quite satisfied with the public services provided by the local government.

One interesting and seeming contradiction reflected in the above chapters is between a high level of recognition of Chinese sovereignty over Hong Kong and the acceptance of patriotism as one's responsibility (Chapter 2), and a low level of political identity and trust in the political institutions in China (Chapters 3 and 4). It seems that the majority of Hongkongers are saying: We agree to be part of you under the general framework, but please leave us alone and don't interfere in our daily life. The radical wing of the local population may not like this conclusion. Yet this is the best available evidence our survey data can provide.

Chapter 5 examines Hongkongers' political participation. The survey respondents were asked what actions they would take if they felt mistreated by the government, specifically:

1. Visit government bureaus/officials.
2. Express dissatisfaction through media or the internet.
3. Ask for help from members of the Legislative Council or district legislative council.
4. Express dissatisfaction through peaceful or violent protest.
5. Express dissatisfaction through voting in elections.
6. Ask for help from political parties.
7. Express dissatisfaction through legal channels.
8. I would do nothing.

One of the most interesting findings in this chapter is protest. Initially only less than 5% of the respondents would protest, but 30% of them would do so if their problems were not solved (see Figure 5.1). Another interesting finding in this chapter is that more than 90% of the respondents would take some form of political action and less than 10% said they would take no action. These findings suggest high levels of populism and political activism and willingness to engage in political confrontation. One may think that political activism can no longer be materialized given the tight political control in the post–National Security Law era. Yet the fact that many people still think protesting is the most effective problem-solving method suggests the potential of open political confrontation that can be triggered under the right conditions.

Chapter 6 discusses the role of press media in shaping Hong Kong people's identity in the postcolonial era. Applying text analysis methods, this chapter examines almost 540,000 unique articles on the Chinese Communist Party (CCP) published by 10 major local newspapers from 2002 to 2020. The results show that while *Apple Daily* was consistently the most critical of the CCP, all the other newspapers (except one) followed it closely and shifted away from the moderate ideological position of the local political spectrum. This is a surprising finding because most previous studies believed that the CCP was successful in controlling the local media. The chapter further discusses the reason underlying this pattern. By comparing *Apple Daily* on the far right and *Wen Wei Po* on the far left, it shows that the reporting style of *Apple Daily* managed to incorporate its criticism of the CCP with local news that is familiar to Hong Kong readers. In contrast, when *Wen Wei Po* tried to communicate positive news about the CCP to the local society, it failed to relate it to local circumstances, resulting in extremely low popularity among readers. It further implies that in a former colonial city like Hong Kong, the nationalization process requires a *localization* mechanism in which the message sent by the central government and its agents can be translated into the everyday language acceptable to the local society.

Together these chapters show an angry society, perhaps feeling abandoned by the British, but resentful of and willing to fight their newly rich monster neighbor Mainland China and its efforts to integrate them into the orbit of the CCP. In the meantime, they feel proud of their own accomplishments and are in a desperate search for self-identity.

Broader Implications for Political Culture Studies

The findings in this study have both theoretical and methodological implications for future studies of political culture in general and in Hong Kong in particular.

First, following the early literature, the discussion of quantitative studies of political culture with the latest public opinion survey data implies the feasibility and necessity of comparative studies of political cultures. Since Almond and Verba introduced quantitative and comparative methods to the study of political culture in the 1960s, researchers in this tradition have made great strides in the operationalization and measurement of political culture.[1] The contribution of this study to the literature is to propose a uniform and comprehensive set of outcome-based values and behaviors related to political and social life at the individual level and the macro conditions and demographic factors (independent variables) that can be used to explain the formation of cultural values and behaviors (dependent variables). This discussion can provide a convenient toolbox and facilitate researchers to compare and contrast different political cultures and trace any differences to their roots. A related contribution is the discussion of possible ways to avoid comparing apples to oranges. This is particularly important in cross-country comparisons of social scientific concepts such as democracy, civil society, and religiosity, among others.

The second contribution of this study is methodological. It embeds multiple list experiments in the Hong Kong Political Culture Survey to detect the hidden effect of social desirability. More importantly, it relies on an innovative and original technique of statistical weighting to detect further social desirability effects not revealed by the initial round of list experiments. This weighting technique improves the effectiveness of the traditional list experiment method. It can be used by other researchers in future survey experimental research.

Finally, and more importantly, this book contributes to the study of postcolonial political culture in general. As described in this book, Hong Kong's political culture in the first quarter century of the postcolonial era developed in a political vacuum under One Country, Two Systems, in which the British colonists no longer governed but the new ruler was blocked from entering. As defined in Chapter 1, political culture is conventionally viewed as a reflection of the official ideology and its related political institutional arrangements. Yet in the case of Hong Kong, a political culture grew in the absence of such official ideology and institutional arrangements. Consequently, in search of their political identity, the local residents turned to indigenous culture, which combined with their resentment of China that was nurtured by the British colonists before and after they left Hong Kong in 1997.[2]

In this sense, post-Handover Hong Kong represents a new type of postcolonial political culture. This political culture is unique because many other well-known postcolonial societies have a clearly defined sovereign national

---

[1] E.g., Inglehart 1990; Silver and Dowley 2000.
[2] Xia and Guan 2015.

government that either inherited the colonial political system or created their own system. New postcolonial cultures can develop under the new national government. While the national government in Beijing claims sovereignty over Hong Kong, the central government's ideology and institutional arrangements could not be implemented under the restrictions of the Basic Law. Without a trustworthy national government to fall back to, Hongkongers felt lost and confused.

In this environment, there were few ideological boundaries, institutional constraints, and legal restrictions. The indigenization of political identity is perhaps a way for the local residents to overcome feelings of political anxiety while voicing their anger and pride through social protests. While Hongkongers may have enjoyed unprecedented freedom that was not granted under the British rule, Hong Kong's political culture that grew out of the political vacuum was chaotic and destructive. This transitional political culture can be characterized as angry, distrustful, contentious, rebellious, and confused on the one hand, and proud and in desperate search of a political identity and a sense of belonging on the other hand. This unique transitional political culture can be added to the typology of existing postcolonial political cultures.

The passage of the National Security Law in 2020 and the related changes that followed in the electoral system,[3] the legal system,[4] education,[5] and media[6] have pulled the central government in Beijing closer to Hong Kong. They draw clearer boundaries, constraints, and restrictions. Accordingly, Hong Kong's political culture may reflect these changes. Yet cultural changes are slow; they take generations to manifest, and they may contain traditional elements such as political populism and local identity. They may be influenced by other factors, such as changes within China and in the international arena. It may be necessary to conduct a new study of Hong Kong's political culture in another 23 years.

---

[3] Young 2021.
[4] Deva 2020.
[5] Vickers 2023.
[6] Lee 2023.

Appendices

Appendix 2.1

Comparison of Socioeconomic Distributions Between the Survey and the Hong Kong 2016 Population By-Census (mean or percentage)

	Survey	Census
Age	46.68	47.45
Female (%)	0.54	0.55
Birthplace (%)		
Hong Kong	0.61	0.57
Mainland	0.32	0.33
Elsewhere	0.07	0.10
Education (%)		
Primary or below	0.20	0.20
Lower secondary	0.17	0.17
Upper secondary	0.30	0.30
Sub-degree	0.10	0.11
Degree or above	0.23	0.22
Ethnic Chinese (%)	0.94	0.92
N	3744	321,966

Notes: The sample of the Hong Kong 2016 Population By-census used here is restricted to age 16 and above. The numbers for a particular variable may not add up to 1 due to rounding error.

Sources: Hong Kong Political Culture Survey 2021 and Hong Kong 2016 Population By-Census (Hong Kong Census and Statistics Department 2017).

Appendix 2.2

Socioeconomic Statistics of List Experiment Groups (mean or percentage)

	Control Group	Group1	Group2	Group3	Group4	Group5	Group6	Group7	Group8
Age	47.55	46.28	46.56	45.38	46.52	46.21	46.84	47.24	47.13
Female	0.54	0.56	0.56	0.53	0.51	0.59	0.51	0.52	0.52
Birthplace									
Hong Kong	0.59	0.62	0.58	0.68	0.65	0.58	0.56	0.61	0.61
Mainland	0.33	0.32	0.35	0.26	0.30	0.34	0.35	0.33	0.31
Elsewhere	0.08	0.07	0.07	0.06	0.06	0.08	0.09	0.06	0.07
Education									
Primary or below	0.24	0.22	0.20	0.15	0.21	0.19	0.20	0.21	0.24
Lower secondary	0.17	0.14	0.18	0.18	0.17	0.19	0.17	0.17	0.17
Upper secondary	0.29	0.30	0.28	0.33	0.30	0.31	0.30	0.28	0.29
Sub-degree	0.10	0.10	0.10	0.10	0.10	0.12	0.11	0.10	0.09
Degree or above	0.21	0.25	0.24	0.25	0.23	0.20	0.22	0.24	0.20
Ethnic Chinese	0.93	0.94	0.93	0.94	0.94	0.93	0.92	0.94	0.92
N	419	424	411	433	404	424	410	415	402

Notes: In addition to the control group, each number represents different list experiment groups: group 1 is patriotism, 2 sovereignty, 3 imprison, 4 allegiance, 5 extradition, 6 election, 7 NSL, and 8 police. The numbers for a particular variable may not add up to 1 due to rounding error.

Source: Hong Kong Political Culture Survey 2021.

Appendix 2.3

Technical Notes on the Weight Variable's Construction and Applications

The goal of the weight is to adjust the proportions obtained from direct questions. With the results from both the list experiment questions and their direct questioning counterparts in the survey, we construct the weight variable W^{ij} by computing the ratio (R^{ij}) between the respondents' truthful supports and their overtly reported endorsement, i.e.,

$$W^{ij} = R^{ij} = \frac{PropY^{ij}_{list}}{PropY^{ij}_{direct}},$$

where i denotes one of the eight politically sensitive items (1 for patriotism, 2 sovereignty, 3 imprison, 4 allegiance, 5 extradition, 6 election, 7 NSL, and 8 police), while j one of the five political leanings (1 for blue, 2 light blue, 3 green, 4 light yellow, 5 yellow). As such, $PropY^{ij}_{list}$ is the proportion of respondents with the political leaning j who support item i according to the result of the list experiment, and $PropY^{ij}_{direct}$ is the proportion of respondents with the political leaning j who support item i according to the result of the direct questioning.

Below will demonstrate the process through which the constructed weight variable adjusts the proportions from direct questions.

To begin with, $NumY^{ij}_{true}$ denotes the number of respondents with the political leaning j who *truly* support item i in the direct question, and $NumY^{ij}_{reported}$ indicates the number of respondents with the political leaning j who *reported* to support item i in the direct question, then:

$$NumY^{ij}_{true} = NumY^{ij}_{reported} * W^{ij}$$

Then, Num^{ij}_{true} denotes the total number of respondents with the political leaning j in the list experiment group i who should have responded to the direct question, and $Num^{ij}_{reported}$ indicates the total number of respondents with the political leaning j in the list experiment group i who did respond to the direct question, then

$$Num^{ij}_{true} = Num^{ij}_{reported} * W^{ij}$$

Therefore, the proportion of respondents with the political leaning j who truly support item i in the direct question, $Prop^{ij}_{true}$, would be

$$Prop^{ij}_{true} = \frac{NumY^{ij}_{true}}{Num^{ij}_{true}} = \frac{NumY^{ij}_{reported} * W^{ij}}{Num^{ij}_{reported} * W^{ij}} = \frac{NumY^{ij}_{reported}}{Num^{ij}_{reported}} * W^{ij} = PropY^{ij}_{direct} * W^{ij}$$

Moreover, $Prop^{i}_{true}$, the proportion of respondents who truly support item i in the direct question, can also be obtained with the weight variable. To begin with, $NumY^{i}_{true}$ denotes the number of respondents who truly support item i in the direct question, then

$$NumY^{i}_{true} = \sum_{j=1}^{5} NumY^{ij}_{true} = \sum_{j=1}^{5} NumY^{ij}_{reported} * W^{ij}$$

And Num^i_{true} indicates the total number of respondents in the list experiment group i who should have responded to the direct question, then

$$Num^i_{true} = \sum_{j=1}^{5} Num^{ij}_{true} = \sum_{j=1}^{5} Num^{ij}_{reported} * W^{ij}$$

Therefore,

$$Prop^i_{true} = \frac{NumY^i_{true}}{Num^i_{true}} = \frac{\sum_{j=1}^{5} NumY^{ij}_{reported} * W^{ij}}{\sum_{j=1}^{5} Num^{ij}_{reported} * W^{ij}}$$

Finally, the constructed weight variable can be applied to other politically sensitive questions that are not in the list experiment groups, either to estimate $Prop^j_{others\_true}$, the proportion of respondents of the political leaning j who truly support each of these other questions, or $Prop_{others\_true}$ the proportion of all respondents who truly support each of these other questions. In such applications, since the sample containing all the eight list experiment groups are used and that these eight groups are randomly drawn from the full sample, the average of the weights of all eight list experiment items ($i=1$ to 8) for a particular partisan group j are effectively taken into consideration. Put in mathematic terms:

$$Prop^j_{others\_true} = \frac{NumY^j_{others\_true}}{Num^j_{others\_true}} = \frac{\sum_{i=1}^{8} NumY^{ij}_{others\_true}}{\sum_{i=1}^{8} Num^{ij}_{others\_true}} =$$

$$\frac{\sum_{i=1}^{8} W^{ij} * NumY^{ij}_{others\_reported}}{\sum_{i=1}^{8} W^{ij} * Num^{ij}_{others\_reported}} = \frac{\sum_{i=1}^{8} W^{ij} * (NumY^j_{others\_reported}/8)}{\sum_{i=1}^{8} W^{ij} * (Num^j_{others\_reported}/8)} =$$

$$\frac{(\sum_{i=1}^{8} W^{ij})/8 * NumY^j_{others\_reported}}{(\sum_{i=1}^{8} W^{ij})/8 * Num^j_{others\_reported}} = (\sum_{i=1}^{8} W^{ij})/8 * \frac{NumY^j_{others\_reported}}{Num^j_{others\_reported}}$$

$$Prop_{others\_true} = \frac{\sum_{j=1}^{5} NumY^j_{others\_true}}{\sum_{j=1}^{5} Num^j_{others\_true}} = \frac{\sum_{j=1}^{5} \sum_{i=1}^{8} NumY^{ij}_{others\_true}}{\sum_{j=1}^{5} \sum_{i=1}^{8} Num^{ij}_{others\_true}} =$$

$$\frac{\sum_{j=1}^{5} \sum_{i=1}^{8} W^{ij} * NumY^{ij}_{others\_reported}}{\sum_{j=1}^{5} \sum_{i=1}^{8} W^{ij} * Num^{ij}_{others\_reported}} = \frac{\sum_{j=1}^{5} \sum_{i=1}^{8} W^{ij} * (NumY^j_{others\_reported}/8)}{\sum_{j=1}^{5} \sum_{i=1}^{8} W^{ij} * (Num^j_{others\_reported}/8)} =$$

$$\frac{\sum_{j=1}^{5} (\sum_{i=1}^{8} W^{ij})/8 * NumY^j_{others\_reported}}{\sum_{j=1}^{5} (\sum_{i=1}^{8} W^{ij})/8 * Num^j_{others\_reported}} = \sum_{j=1}^{5} \left(\sum_{i=1}^{8} W^{ij} \right)/8 * \frac{NumY_{others\_reported}}{Num_{others\_reported}}$$

In sum, in all these applications, one can easily apply the weight variable to the variable concerned to get the adjusted proportion of the variable.[1]

---

[1] Note that one could argue that Numreportedij should not be multiplied by Wij since Numtrueij = Numreportedij and Numtruei = Numreportedi. Therefore, the alternative applications could be
Proptrueij = NumYtrueijNumtrueij = Wij * NumYreportedij Numreportedij
Proptruei = NumYtrueiNumtruei = j =15NumYreportedij * Wijj=15Numreportedij
Propothers_truej = (i=18 Wij)/8 * NumYothers_reportedjNumothers_reportedj
Propothers_true = j=15 (i=18 Wij)/8 * NumYothers_reported Numothers_reported

Appendix 3.1

Variables and Coding Scheme

Most of the below variables are coded as 0 (minimum) and 1 (maximum), except social class and birthplace.

> Cultural nationalism: Factor index of two variables related to support for Chinese civilization and Chinese culture.
>
> Political nationalism: Factor index of four variables about preferences for Chinese sports teams, Chinese movies and TV shows, Chinese political system, and Chinese Communist Party (CCP).
>
> Impression of Mainlanders: Ranging from the worst impression (0) to the best impression (1).
>
> Impression of British: Ranging from the worst impression (0) to the best impression (1).
>
> Immigrate intention: Intention to immigrate to North America, Europe, Japan, or Taiwan in the next two years (coded 1 and others coded 0).
>
> Pro-establishment: Political color ranging from deep yellow (0), yellow (0.167), light yellow (0.333), green (0.5), light blue (0.667), blue (0.833) and dark blue (1).
>
> Chinese identity: A categorical variable of three self-perceived identities coded as follows: Hong Konger (0), Chinese Hong Konger (0.5), or Chinese (1).
>
> Eastern values: Which set of values do you support?: (1) Freedom, democracy, human rights and rule of law (coded 0); (2) benevolence, integrity, filial piety, and restraint (coded 1); (3) both (coded 0.5).
>
> Putonghua ability: Factor index of four questions about Mandarin speaking, listening, reading, and writing.
>
> English ability: Factor index of four questions about English speaking, listening, reading, and writing.
>
> Education: Education level ranging from primary and below (0), lower secondary (0.25), upper secondary (0.5), sub-degree (0.75), and degree and above (1).
>
> Post97: pre97 cohort (age>40, coded 0) and post97 cohort (age≤40, coded 1)
>
> Post97#Education: interaction term between Post-97 cohort and education.
>
> Female: 0=male and 1=female
>
> Social class is a categorical variable of five levels of self-perceived social class, including upper, upper middle, middle, lower middle, and lower. Missing values are imputed using multiple imputations with an ordered logistic regression, which accounts for age, education level, occupation economic activity status, household income per capita, housing property ownership, and type of house.
>
> Birthplace is a categorical variable of three birthplace reported, including born in Hong Kong (1), born in Mainland (2), born elsewhere (3).
>
> *Apple Daily*: Frequency of reading (including hardcopy and online) at six levels: never, monthly, weekly, several times a week, daily, and several times daily.
>
> *Oriental Daily*: Frequency of reading (including hardcopy and online) at six levels: never, monthly, weekly, several times a week, daily, and several times daily.
>
> After *Apple Daily* closure: Respondent was interviewed after the closure of *Apple Daily* on June 24, 2021 (coded 1 and before coded 0)
>
> Source: Hong Kong Political Culture Survey 2021.

Appendix 3.2

Summary Statistics (HK Political Culture Survey 2021)

VARIABLES (unweighted)	Obs	Mean	Std. dev.	Min	Max
Cultural nationalism	3,714	0.669	0.226	0	1
Political nationalism	3,623	0.474	0.245	0	1
Impression of Mainlanders	3,743	0.609	0.221	0	1
Impression of British	3,743	0.608	0.243	0	1
Immigrate intention	3,744	0.087	0.282	0	1
Pro-establishment	3,722	0.490	0.181	0	1
Chinese identity	3,535	0.333	0.422	0	1
Eastern values	3,741	0.422	0.334	0	1
Putonghua ability	3,743	0.491	0.296	0	1
English ability	3,739	0.447	0.354	0	1
Education					
Primary or below	3,743	0.204	0.403	0	1
Lower secondary	3,743	0.170	0.376	0	1
Upper secondary	3,743	0.297	0.457	0	1
Sub-degree	3,743	0.103	0.305	0	1
Degree or above	3,743	0.225	0.418	0	1
Post97	3,744	0.341	0.474	0	1
Post97#Education	3,743	0.241	0.368	0	1
Female	3,744	0.539	0.499	0	1
Social Class					
1. Lower class	3,744	0.250	0.433	0	1
2. Lower middle class	3,744	0.373	0.484	0	1
3. Middle class	3,744	0.319	0.466	0	1
4. Upper middle class	3,744	0.055	0.228	0	1
5. Upper class	3,744	0.002	0.049	0	1
Birthplace					
1. Hong Kong	3,744	0.610	0.488	0	1
2. Mainland	3,744	0.320	0.467	0	1
3. Elsewhere	3,744	0.070	0.256	0	1
Apple Daily	3,738	0.191	0.317	0	1
Oriental Daily	3,738	0.225	0.325	0	1
After *Apple Daily* Closure	3,744	0.533	0.499	0	1

VARIABLES (weighted)	Obs	Mean	Std. dev.	Min	Max
Cultural nationalism	677,574	0.566	0.240	0	1
Political nationalism	663,282	0.331	0.238	0	1
Impression of Mainlanders	679,479	0.500	0.247	0	1
Impression of British	679,479	0.680	0.215	0	1
Immigrate intention	679,479	0.178	0.383	0	1
Pro-establishment	679,479	0.331	0.197	0	1
Chinese identity	658,708	0.166	0.339	0	1
Eastern values	679,400	0.258	0.318	0	1
Putonghua ability	679,479	0.501	0.274	0	1
English ability	679,113	0.533	0.334	0	1
Education					
Primary or below	679,389	0.112	0.315	0	1
Lower secondary	679,389	0.148	0.355	0	1
Upper secondary	679,389	0.302	0.459	0	1
Sub-degree	679,389	0.127	0.333	0	1
Degree or above	679,389	0.311	0.463	0	1
Post97	679,479	0.529	0.499	0	1
Post97#Education	679,389	0.384	0.409	0	1
Female	679,479	0.473	0.499	0	1
Social Class					
1. Lower class	679,479	0.209	0.407	0	1
2. Lower middle class	679,479	0.358	0.480	0	1
3. Middle class	679,479	0.368	0.482	0	1
4. Upper middle class	679,479	0.062	0.241	0	1
5. Upper class	679,479	0.002	0.049	0	1
Birthplace					
1. Hong Kong	679,479	0.756	0.429	0	1
2. Mainland	679,479	0.197	0.398	0	1
3. Elsewhere	679,479	0.047	0.211	0	1
Apple Daily	678,115	0.339	0.368	0	1
Oriental Daily	678,671	0.142	0.273	0	1
After *Apple Daily* Closure	679,479	0.502	0.500	0	1

Appendix 3.3

Robustness Check (full models, unweighted OLS & weighted OLS)

Unweighted VARIABLES	(1) Apple Daily	(2) Cultural nationalism	(3) Cultural nationalism	(4) Apple Daily	(5) Political nationalism	(6) Political nationalism
Putonghua ability	-0.075***	0.157***	0.151***	-0.078***	0.189***	0.184***
English ability	0.091***	-0.097***	-0.092***	0.097***	-0.103***	-0.098***
Education	0.116***	-0.055**	-0.046**	0.113***	-0.143***	-0.135***
Post97	0.154***	-0.131***	-0.120***	0.149***	-0.138***	-0.128***
Post97#Education	-0.062*	0.103***	0.099***	-0.056	0.083***	0.079***
female	-0.037***	0.003	-0.000	-0.038***	0.000	-0.003
Lower class (comparison)						
Lower-middle class	0.012	0.023**	0.023***	0.015	0.041***	0.042***
Middle class	-0.012	0.020*	0.019*	-0.010	0.050***	0.050***
Upper Middle class	-0.067***	0.020	0.015	-0.067***	0.046***	0.042**
Upper class	-0.227**	-0.167**	-0.187***	-0.227**	-0.088	-0.107
Born HK (comparison)						
Born Mainland	-0.069***	0.024**	0.019**	-0.067***	0.064***	0.059***
Born elsewhere	-0.216***	-0.037**	-0.054***	-0.213***	-0.071***	-0.087***

Oriental Daily	−0.048***	0.062***	0.058***	−0.050***	0.137***	0.133***
After Apple Daily Closure	−0.147***			−0.149***		
Apple Daily		−0.114**	−0.184***		−0.156***	−0.221***
Constant	0.242***	0.668***	0.680***	0.243***	0.472***	0.483***
Observations	3696	3696	3696	3605	3605	3605
R^2	0.200	0.211	0.219	0.201	0.425	0.431

*** $p<0.01$
** $p<0.05$
* $p<0.1$

Appendix 4.1a

Most of the below variables are coded as 0 (minimum) to 1 (maximum), except variables measuring the socioeconomic and political policies ranging from −1 (minimum) to 1 (maximum).

cntrust: Trust in national institutions is a factor index of the seven institutions, including Chinese media, Chinese Communist Party, Chinese government, Chinese People's Congress, Supreme People's Court, Chinese government offices in Hong Kong, and the People's Liberation Army stationed in Hong Kong.

hksystrust: Trust in local institutions is a factor index of five institutions, including Hong Kong police, Hong Kong's political system, the SAR government, the Legislative Council, and Hong Kong courts.

satsoc: Satisfaction with socioeconomic policies is another factor index of the nine policy items, including home prices, job opportunity, social equality, anti-Covid-19 policy, social welfare, healthcare, environmental protection, education opportunities, and gender equality.

satpol: Satisfaction with political policies is the fourth factor index of the eight items, including law enforcement, National Security Law, governance, freedom of speech, One Country, Two Systems, rule of law, social stability, and government cleanness.

homeprice2, job2, equality2, anticovid2, welfare2, healthcare2, env2, eduop2, and women2 are the measures of change in corresponding socioeconomic policy satisfaction, namely home price, job opportunity, social equality, anti-Covid-19 policy, social welfare, healthcare, environmental protection, education opportunities, and gender equality, scaled from −1 to 1.

police2 nsl2 freespeech2 governance2 onecountry2 ruleoflaw2 socialorder2 govclean2 are the measures of the change in corresponding political policies satisfaction namely law enforcement, National Security Law, governance, freedom of speech, One Country, Two Systems, rule of law, social stability, and government cleanness, scale from −1 to 1.

Appendix 4.1b

Summary Statistics of Four Factor Indices

Variable	Obs	Mean	Std. dev.	Min	Max
cntrust	3,630	0.478	0.259	0	1
hksystrust	3,719	0.531	0.209	0	1
satsoc	3,710	0.590	0.132	0	1
satpol	3,679	0.446	0.227	0	1

Appendix 4.1c

Summary Statistics of National and Local Institutions, Trust in Government Officials, Rating of Hong Kong Chief Executives and Political Activists, Socioeconomic and Political Policies Satisfactions, and Independent Variables

National institutions

Variable	Obs	Mean	Std. dev.	Min	Max
cnmedia	3,696	0.356	0.258	0	1
cngov	3,678	0.511	0.291	0	1
cnccp	3,659	0.398	0.298	0	1
cnhkoffice	3,677	0.496	0.273	0	1
cnnpc	3,667	0.511	0.293	0	1
cncourt	3,675	0.525	0.295	0	1
cnhkpla	3,657	0.504	0.290	0	1

Local institutions

Variable	Obs	Mean	Std. dev.	Min	Max
hkpolice	3,733	0.490	0.302	0	1
hkpolsystem	3,723	0.516	0.243	0	1
hksargov	3,735	0.523	0.247	0	1
hklegco	3,734	0.534	0.232	0	1
hkcourt	3,739	0.642	0.231	0	1
hkmedia	3,731	0.530	0.245	0	1
hksublegco	3,732	0.534	0.233	0	1

Trust in government officials

Variable	Obs	Mean	Std. dev.	Min	Max
bjreps	3,683	0.492	0.275	0	1
bjexecutive	3,679	0.504	0.285	0	1
hkexecutive	3,734	0.526	0.253	0	1
hklawmaker	3,728	0.518	0.234	0	1
hkdistrict	3,726	0.527	0.234	0	1

Rating of Hong Kong chief executives and political activists

Variable	Obs	Mean	Std. dev.	Min	Max
Tung Chee-hwa	3,611	0.541	0.263	0	1
Donald Tsang	3,633	0.446	0.257	0	1
Leung Chun-ying	3,661	0.366	0.279	0	1
Carrie Lam	3,717	0.348	0.301	0	1
Anson Chan	3,558	0.452	0.271	0	1
Martin Lee	3,535	0.449	0.294	0	1
Albert Ho	3,584	0.381	0.284	0	1
Benny Tai	3,548	0.369	0.320	0	1
Jimmy Lai	3,639	0.337	0.325	0	1
Joshua Wong	3,621	0.312	0.314	0	1

continued

continued

Socioeconomic and political policies satisfactions

Variable	Obs	Mean	Std. dev.	Min	Max
satsoc	3,710	0.590	0.132	0	1
changesoc	3,710	0.491	0.156	0	1
homeprice	3,723	0.236	0.212	0	1
job	3,738	0.295	0.222	0	1
equality	3,736	0.341	0.231	0	1
anticovid	3,743	0.516	0.239	0	1
welfare	3,738	0.548	0.210	0	1
healthcare	3,739	0.600	0.199	0	1
env	3,736	0.620	0.194	0	1
eduop	3,736	0.656	0.186	0	1
women	3,739	0.671	0.168	0	1
homeprice2	3,724	−0.661	0.519	−1	1
job2	3,737	−0.799	0.429	−1	1
equality2	3,735	−0.538	0.546	−1	1
anticovid2	3,742	0.177	0.695	−1	1
welfare2	3,738	−0.095	0.624	−1	1
healthcare2	3,739	−0.051	0.631	−1	1
env2	3,736	−0.015	0.554	−1	1
eduop2	3,736	0.018	0.459	−1	1
women2	3,739	0.046	0.415	−1	1
satpol	3,679	0.446	0.227	0	1
changepol	3,679	0.324	0.278	0	1
police	3,734	0.426	0.280	0	1
nsl	3,690	0.431	0.289	0	1
freespeech	3,730	0.429	0.270	0	1
governance	3,728	0.399	0.257	0	1
onecountry	3,696	0.450	0.267	0	1
ruleoflaw	3,726	0.458	0.259	0	1
socialorder	3,737	0.489	0.250	0	1
govclean	3,732	0.504	0.234	0	1
police2	3,734	−0.261	0.757	−1	1
nsl2	3,691	−0.242	0.793	−1	1
freespeech2	3,730	−0.546	0.550	−1	1
governance2	3,728	−0.466	0.674	−1	1
onecountry2	3,699	−0.356	0.711	−1	1
ruleoflaw2	3,727	−0.398	0.692	−1	1
socialorder2	3,735	−0.206	0.811	−1	1
govclean2	3,730	−0.305	0.581	−1	1

Independent variables

Variable	Obs	Mean	Std. dev.	Min	Max
age4					
1. 16–24	3,744	0.118	0.323	0	1
2. 25–44	3,744	0.349	0.477	0	1
3. 45–64	3,744	0.355	0.479	0	1
4. >65	3,744	0.177	0.382	0	1
edu					
1. Primary or below	3,743	0.204	0.403	0	1
2. Lower Secondary	3,743	0.170	0.376	0	1
3. Upper secondary	3,743	0.297	0.457	0	1
4. Sub-degree	3,743	0.103	0.305	0	1
5. Degree or above	3,743	0.225	0.418	0	1
female	3,744	0.539	0.499	0	1
religiosity	3,744	0.432	0.250	0	1
married	3,701	0.699	0.459	0	1
class5					
1. lower class	3,744	0.250	0.433	0	1
2. lower middle class	3,744	0.373	0.484	0	1
3. middle class	3,744	0.319	0.466	0	1
4. upper middle class	3,744	0.055	0.228	0	1
5. upper class	3,744	0.002	0.049	0	1
Ethnic identity					1
1. Hong Konger	3,743	0.546	0.498	0	1
2. Chinese	3,743	0.231	0.422	0	1
3. Chinese Hong Kong	37,43	0.167	0.373	0	1
4. Others	3,743	0.056	0.229	0	1
Political color	3,722	0.510	0.181	0	1
Mandarin ability	3,743	0.491	0.296	0	1
appledaily	3,738	0.191	0.317	0	1
orientdaily	3,738	0.225	0.325	0	1
district18					
1. Central and Western	3,744	0.039	0.194	0	1
2. Wan Chai	3,744	0.027	0.161	0	1
3. Eastern	3,744	0.067	0.250	0	1
4. Southern	3,744	0.040	0.196	0	1
5. Yau Tsim Mong	3,744	0.041	0.197	0	1
6. Sham Shui Po	3,744	0.054	0.225	0	1
7. Kowloon City	3,744	0.062	0.241	0	1
8. Wong Tai Sin	3,744	0.053	0.225	0	1
9. Kwun Tong	3,744	0.080	0.272	0	1
10. Kwai Tsing	3,744	0.067	0.250	0	1
11. Tsuen Wan	3,744	0.040	0.196	0	1
12. Tuen Mun	3,744	0.067	0.251	0	1
13. Yuen Long	3,744	0.081	0.272	0	1
14. North	3,744	0.053	0.224	0	1
15. Tai Po	3,744	0.041	0.197	0	1
16. Sha Tin	3,744	0.094	0.292	0	1
17. Sai Kung	3,744	0.067	0.251	0	1
18. Islands	3,744	0.027	0.163	0	1

Appendix 4.2

Detailed Multilevel Regression Analysis for Chinese Institutions

VARIABLES	(1) cntrust	(2) NATMEDIA	(3) NATGOV	(4) CCP	(5) PRECREP	(6) NPC	(7) NATCOURT	(8) PLA
age4								
4. >65 (comparison)								
1. 16–24	−0.012	0.003	−0.015	−0.007	−0.007	−0.012	−0.023	−0.038**
2. 25–44	−0.013	−0.002	−0.018	−0.014	−0.007	−0.010	−0.023*	−0.024
3. 45–64	0.002	0.001	0.001	−0.011	0.009	0.008	−0.001	0.007
edu								
1. Primary or below (comparison)								
2. Lower secondary	−0.011	−0.006	−0.012	−0.020	−0.016	−0.010	−0.011	−0.007
3. Upper secondary	−0.021**	−0.030**	−0.015	−0.038***	−0.022*	−0.020	−0.023*	0.005
4. Sub-degree	−0.037***	−0.030*	−0.032*	−0.057***	−0.038**	−0.035**	−0.028	−0.029*
5. Degree or above	−0.040***	−0.039**	−0.033**	−0.053***	−0.040***	−0.038**	−0.041**	−0.025
female	0.012**	0.023***	0.005	0.002	0.016**	0.012*	0.013*	0.018**
religiosity	0.018	−0.035**	0.046***	0.001	0.035**	0.034**	0.052***	−0.062***
married	0.002	0.012	−0.000	−0.001	0.000	−0.001	0.012	−0.002

class						
1. Lower (comparison)						
2. Lower middle	0.027***	0.025***	0.031***	0.054***	0.029***	0.020**	0.016*	-0.001
3. Middle	0.026***	0.031***	0.008	0.078***	0.018*	0.008	0.014	0.031***
4. Upper middle	0.028*	0.039**	-0.003	0.083***	0.015	0.021	0.007	0.037*
5. Upper	-0.034	-0.084	-0.036	-0.080	-0.016	-0.028	-0.028	0.026
Ethnic Identity								
1. Hong Konger (comparison)								
2. Chinese	0.107***	0.097***	0.096***	0.143***	0.089***	0.114***	0.092***	0.116***
3. Chinese Hong Konger	0.085***	0.066***	0.080***	0.135***	0.063***	0.080***	0.065***	0.101***
4. Others	0.080***	0.070***	0.084***	0.080***	0.086***	0.086***	0.074***	0.039**
yellow01	-0.741***	-0.653***	-0.740***	-0.791***	-0.727***	-0.736***	-0.760***	-0.752***
putonghua	0.082***	0.069***	0.107***	0.054***	0.091***	0.097***	0.115***	0.021
appledaily	-0.153***	-0.086***	-0.192***	-0.117***	-0.167***	-0.189***	-0.153***	-0.118***
orientdaily	0.002	-0.021*	0.006	0.027**	0.002	-0.001	0.002	-0.009

continued

continued

VARIABLES	(1) cntrust	(2) NATMEDIA	(3) NATGOV	(4) CCP	(5) PRECREP	(6) NPC	(7) NATCOURT	(8) PLA
District level								
dcbornml_2016	0.722***	0.437**	1.069***	0.298	0.708***	0.759***	0.825***	0.971***
dchighhin_2016	0.199***	0.136	0.311***	0.234**	0.234***	0.093	0.182*	0.243**
dcmedianage	0.010**	0.005	0.018***	-0.003	0.010*	0.016***	0.013***	0.011*
dcpop	-0.003	-0.007	0.039	-0.004	-0.005	-0.012	0.002	-0.011
vote2019y	-0.374*	-0.190	-0.811***	0.442**	-0.381	-0.705***	-0.540**	-0.388
dcpopdensity2	-0.002***	-0.001**	-0.003***	-0.000	-0.002***	-0.002***	-0.002***	-0.002***
elderlyresidence2	-0.023**	-0.010	-0.040***	0.009	-0.026**	-0.035***	-0.020**	-0.030**
erdensity2	0.147**	0.074	0.281***	-0.009	0.109	0.234***	0.153**	0.188**
Constant	0.370**	0.400**	0.188	0.464**	0.422**	0.365*	0.349*	0.392*
Observations	3,567	3,624	3,610	3,594	3,610	3,599	3,607	3,591
Number of groups	18	18	18	18	18	18	18	18

*** $p<0.01$
** $p<0.05$
* $p<0.1$

Appendix 4.3

Detailed Multilevel Regression Analysis for Hong Kong Institutions

VARIABLES	(1) HKPOLICE	(2) HKPOLSYSTEM	(3) SARGOV	(4) HKLEGCO	(5) HKCOURTS	(6) HKMEDIA	(7) HKSUBLEGCO
age4							
4. >65 (comparison)							
1. 16–24	−0.069***	−0.010	−0.047***	−0.045**	−0.046**	−0.046**	−0.044**
2. 25–44	−0.044***	−0.008	−0.018	−0.025*	−0.030**	−0.019	−0.022
3. 45–64	−0.020*	−0.001	−0.014	−0.010	0.000	−0.012	−0.017
edu							
1. Primary or below (comparison)							
2. Lower secondary	0.043***	−0.015	0.017	0.026**	0.032**	−0.010	0.010
3. Upper secondary	0.054***	−0.026**	−0.005	0.033***	0.028**	−0.017	0.012
4. Sub-degree	0.055***	−0.045***	−0.025	0.028*	0.035*	−0.020	0.016
5. Degree or above	0.054***	−0.029**	−0.008	0.005	0.039**	−0.049***	−0.018
female	0.033***	0.020**	0.020***	0.026***	0.018**	0.008	0.018**
religiosity	−0.040***	0.071***	−0.023**	−0.054***	−0.009	−0.107***	−0.085***
married	0.008	0.002	0.005	−0.014	−0.025**	−0.025**	−0.020*
Class							
1. Lower (comparison)							
2. Lower middle	−0.007	0.025***	0.020**	−0.021**	−0.018*	−0.024**	−0.018*
3. Middle	0.007	0.016	0.016*	0.002	0.007	0.009	0.009
4. Upper middle	0.045**	0.005	0.025	0.062***	0.066***	0.052**	0.063***
5. Upper	0.134*	0.141**	0.131**	0.092	0.017	0.080	0.000

continued

continued

VARIABLES	(1) HKPOLICE	(2) HKPOLSYSTEM	(3) SARGOV	(4) HKLEGCO	(5) HKCOURTS	(6) HKMEDIA	(7) HKSUBLEGCO
Ethnic identity							
1. Hong Konger (comparison)							
2. Chinese	0.166***	0.056***	0.067***	0.057***	0.049***	-0.117***	-0.057***
3. Chinese Hong Konger	0.120***	0.058***	0.077***	0.046***	0.057***	0.011	0.050***
4. Others	0.088***	0.129***	0.100***	0.052***	-0.004	-0.020	0.012
yellow01	-0.836***	-0.534***	-0.632***	-0.509***	-0.306***	0.089***	-0.113***
putonghua	-0.067***	0.058***	-0.002	-0.028**	-0.100***	-0.033**	-0.086***
appledaily	-0.087***	-0.126***	-0.117***	-0.055***	-0.060***	-0.040***	-0.051***
orientdaily	0.052***	0.026**	0.004	-0.023**	-0.027**	-0.112***	-0.074***
District level							
dcbornml_2016	0.433*	0.599***	0.617***	0.552***	0.765***	0.747*	0.429
dchighin_2016	0.136	0.159*	0.164*	0.242***	0.218**	0.016	0.100
dcmedianage	0.003	0.002	0.008*	0.008	0.008	0.015*	0.003
dcpop	-0.079***	-0.001	0.022	-0.037	-0.006	-0.003	0.074*
vote2019y	-0.323	-0.476*	-0.523**	-0.332	-0.520*	-0.653	-0.316
dcpopdensity2	-0.001	-0.001**	-0.002***	-0.001	-0.001**	-0.002	-0.001
elderlyresidence2	-0.011	-0.024**	-0.028***	-0.013	-0.024**	-0.023	-0.005
erdensity2	-0.004	0.159***	0.227***	0.033	0.105	0.038	0.086
Constant	0.833***	0.737***	0.617***	0.515***	0.587***	0.219	0.611**
Observations	3,658	3,651	3,661	3,660	3,664	3,657	3,659
Number of groups	18	18	18	18	18	18	18

***p<0.01
**p<0.05
*p<0.1

Appendix 4.4

Detailed Multilevel Regression Analysis for Hong Kong Policies Satisfaction and Change in Two Years

VARIABLES	(1) satsoc	(2) changesoc	(3) satpol	(4) changepol	(5) homeprice	(6) homeprice2	(7) job
age4							
4. >65 (comparison)							
1. 16–24	0.001	-0.007	0.020	0.024	0.015	-0.021	0.017
2. 25–44	-0.008	-0.003	0.005	0.001	-0.023*	-0.052	-0.003
3. 45–64	-0.007	0.003	0.000	0.000	0.001	-0.001	-0.008
edu							
1. Primary or below (Comparison)							
2. Lower secondary	-0.001	0.020**	-0.011	0.002	-0.016	-0.046	-0.001
3. Upper secondary	-0.002	0.031***	-0.018*	0.001	-0.031**	-0.053	-0.011
4. Sub-degree	-0.005	0.030***	-0.034***	-0.013	-0.068***	-0.092**	-0.007
5. Degree or above	0.017*	0.044***	-0.026**	-0.022	-0.039**	-0.015	0.016
female	0.004	0.000	0.001	-0.006	-0.015**	-0.020	-0.001
religiosity	0.003	0.017	0.065***	0.073***	0.025*	-0.100***	0.040***
married	0.006	0.006	0.034***	0.025***	-0.002	-0.006	0.008
class							
1. Lower (comparison)							
2. Lower middle	0.028***	-0.037***	0.038***	0.020**	0.068***	0.056**	0.070***
3. Middle	0.022***	-0.050***	0.023***	0.021**	0.084***	0.036	0.071***
4. Upper middle	0.012	-0.066***	-0.004	0.006	0.123***	0.061	0.087***
5. Upper	-0.002	-0.014	-0.145***	-0.082	-0.080	-0.349*	0.015

continued

continued

VARIABLES	(1) satsoc	(2) changesoc	(3) satpol	(4) changepol	(5) homeprice	(6) homeprice2	(7) job
Ethnic identity							
1. Hong Konger (comparison)							
2. Chinese	0.034***	0.041***	0.089***	0.135***	−0.044***	−0.107***	−0.009
3. Chinese Hong Konger	0.037***	0.033***	0.062***	0.054***	0.020*	−0.000	0.046***
4. Others	0.059***	0.027**	0.138***	0.102***	0.029*	0.028	0.072***
yellow01	−0.255***	−0.244***	−0.584***	−0.706***	−0.195***	−0.273***	−0.249***
putonghua	0.004	0.003	0.087***	0.106***	0.077***	0.183***	−0.032**
appledaily	−0.037***	−0.065***	−0.107***	−0.129***	−0.076***	−0.136***	−0.020
orientdaily	0.012*	−0.013*	0.062***	0.044***	−0.050***	−0.133***	0.010
District level							
dcbornml_2016	0.494***	0.599***	0.482***	0.361	0.691***	1.028*	−0.778*
dchighhin_2016	0.091*	0.112**	0.190***	0.159	0.043	0.243	−0.199
dcmedianage	0.008***	0.013***	0.015***	0.004	0.018***	0.021	−0.009
dcpop	−0.044***	−0.042**	−0.056***	−0.080**	−0.036	−0.196***	−0.007
vote2019y	−0.327***	−0.376***	−0.239	0.143	−0.310	0.598	0.189
dcpopdensity2	−0.001***	−0.001***	−0.001	−0.001	−0.002***	−0.001	0.001
elderlyresidence2	−0.028***	−0.015**	−0.025***	0.002	−0.033***	−0.001	0.014
erdensity2	0.072*	0.121**	0.111**	0.134	0.157**	0.104	−0.182
Constant	0.415***	0.114	−0.014	0.176	−0.437**	−1.961***	0.883**
Observations	3,639	3,639	3,607	3,607	3,651	3,651	3,663
Number of groups	18	18	18	18	18	18	18

VARIABLES	(8) job2	(9) equality	(10) equality2	(11) anticovid	(12) anticovid2	(13) welfare	(14) welfare2
age4							
4. >65 (comparison)							
1. 15-24	0.049	0.027	0.062	-0.039**	-0.030	0.022	0.030
2. 25-44	0.042	0.005	0.012	-0.015	0.031	-0.001	-0.017
3. 45-64	0.028	-0.003	0.021	-0.010	0.050	-0.011	-0.044
edu							
1. Primary or below (comparison)							
2. Lower secondary	-0.012	-0.006	-0.023	0.011	0.060	-0.021*	0.014
3. Upper secondary	-0.045*	-0.018	-0.033	0.020	0.067*	-0.011	0.065*
4. Sub-degree	-0.016	-0.042**	-0.038	0.013	0.114**	-0.014	0.070
5. Degree or above	-0.018	0.008	0.050	0.035**	0.197***	-0.011	0.096**
female	-0.025*	0.002	0.004	0.017**	0.010	0.019***	0.019
religiosity	0.008	0.029*	-0.039	-0.065***	0.108**	0.020	-0.008
married	-0.028	0.017	0.037	0.003	0.013	0.028***	0.078***
class							
1. Lower (comparison)							
2. Lower middle	0.060***	0.082***	0.123***	-0.001	-0.060**	0.020**	-0.059**
3. Middle	0.083***	0.074***	0.073***	0.010	-0.120***	0.014	-0.128***

continued

continued

VARIABLES	(8) job2	(9) equality	(10) equality2	(11) anticovid	(12) anticovid2	(13) welfare	(14) welfare2
4. Upper middle	0.138***	0.048**	0.070	−0.005	−0.242***	−0.033*	−0.257***
5. Upper	0.246	−0.148*	−0.052	0.041	−0.194	−0.316***	−0.467**
Ethnic identity							
1. Hong Konger (comparison)							
2. Chinese	−0.008	0.021*	0.060**	0.091***	0.280***	0.052***	0.223***
3. Chinese Hong Konger	0.037*	0.060***	0.096***	0.083***	0.128***	0.020**	0.039
4. Others	0.086***	0.094***	0.159***	0.091***	0.150***	0.091***	0.231***
yellow01	−0.384***	−0.265***	−0.602***	−0.488***	−0.993***	−0.261***	−0.702***
putonghua	−0.030	−0.016	0.016	−0.047***	0.005	0.055***	0.173***
appledaily	−0.096***	0.054***	0.115***	−0.083***	−0.339***	−0.019	−0.064*
orientdaily	−0.067***	0.062***	0.064**	−0.016	−0.088***	0.054***	0.128***
District level							
dcbornml_2016	−0.801*	0.135	0.615	0.544**	1.696**	0.695***	2.377***

	(1)	(2)	(3)	(4)	(5)
dchighhin_2016	0.027	0.043	0.040	0.157*	0.428	0.172**	0.343
dcmedianage	-0.019*	0.001	0.010	0.011**	0.031	0.014***	0.050***
dcpop	0.030	-0.023	-0.106	-0.034	-0.157	-0.085***	-0.253***
vote2019y	1.180**	0.047	0.319	-0.636**	-1.686*	-0.594**	-1.491*
dcpopdensity2	0.001	0.001	-0.001	-0.001**	-0.004*	-0.001***	-0.006***
elderlyresidence2	0.058**	-0.017	-0.013	-0.018	-0.039	-0.040***	-0.100***
erdensity2	-0.124	-0.187**	-0.056	0.167**	0.326	0.151**	0.666***
Constant	-0.309	0.310	-1.133**	0.515***	-0.205	0.189	-1.709***
Observations	3,662	3,661	3,660	3,665	3,665	3,663	3,663
Number of groups	18	18	18	18	18	18	18

VARIABLES	(15) healthcare	(16) healthcare2	(17) env	(18) env2	(19) eduop	(20) eduop2	(21) women
age4							
4. >65 (comparison)							
1. 16–24	0.055***	0.139***	−0.043***	−0.131***	−0.036**	−0.018	−0.029**
2. 25–44	0.010	0.048	−0.014	−0.048	−0.027**	−0.023	−0.007
3. 45–64	0.003	0.010	−0.003	0.016	−0.014	0.002	0.001
edu							
1. Primary or below (comparison)							
2. Lower secondary	0.002	0.025	0.007	0.077**	0.018	0.046	−0.001
3. Upper secondary	−0.011	0.011	0.012	0.110***	0.029**	0.065**	0.019*
4. Sub-degree	−0.014	−0.012	0.033**	0.107**	0.052***	0.063*	0.011
5. Degree or above	−0.011	−0.026	0.038***	0.117***	0.068***	0.095***	0.045***
female	0.001	−0.014	−0.001	−0.010	0.009	−0.004	−0.001
religiosity	−0.003	0.004	−0.006	0.015	−0.006	0.050	−0.016
married	0.024***	0.124***	−0.011	−0.037	−0.014	−0.030	−0.017**
class							
1. Lower (comparison)							
2. Lower middle	0.031***	−0.072**	−0.021**	−0.123***	−0.013	−0.091***	−0.010
3. Middle	0.032***	−0.091***	−0.040***	−0.140***	−0.036***	−0.100***	−0.024***
4. Upper middle	0.008	−0.121**	−0.037**	−0.144***	−0.038***	−0.092**	−0.028*
5. Upper	−0.040	−0.089	0.188***	0.302	0.237***	0.190	0.130**

	(1)	(2)	(3)	(4)	(5)	(6)
Ethnic identity						
1. Hong Konger (comparison)						
2. Chinese	0.055***	0.042	0.036***	0.052*	0.027***	0.030***
3. Chinese Hong Konger	0.037***	0.073**	0.002	0.053*	0.023**	0.008
4. Others	0.077***	0.177***	0.036**	0.052	0.001	0.014
yellow01	−0.155***	−0.415***	−0.154***	−0.415***	−0.149***	−0.098***
putonghua	0.054***	0.256***	−0.024**	−0.074***	−0.035***	−0.018*
appledaily	−0.045***	−0.195***	−0.059***	−0.203***	−0.036***	−0.029***
orientdaily	0.032***	−0.045	0.008	−0.067***	−0.011	−0.026***
District level						
dcbornml_2016	0.497***	0.595	0.788***	2.027***	0.668***	0.622***
dchighhin_2016	0.093	0.064	0.064	0.149	0.151*	0.068
dcmedianage	0.008*	0.026	0.018***	0.042***	0.002	0.007*
dcpop	−0.056**	−0.097	−0.049*	−0.077	−0.026	−0.025
vote2019y	−0.156	−0.331	−0.642**	−0.826	−0.168	−0.522**
dcpopdensity2	−0.000	−0.003*	−0.002***	−0.005***	−0.001**	−0.001***
elderlyresidence2	−0.031***	−0.010	−0.042***	−0.073***	−0.022**	−0.033***
erdensity2	0.077	0.176	0.137*	0.385***	0.101	0.163***
Constant	0.237	−1.054*	0.184	−1.445***	0.613***	0.625***
Observations	3,662	3,662	3,660	3,660	3,661	3,663
Number of groups	18	18	18	18	18	18

VARIABLES	(22) women2	(23) police	(24) police2	(25) nsl	(26) nsl2	(27) freespeech	(28) freespeech2
age4							
4. >65 (comparison)							
1. 16–24	−0.065*	−0.010	−0.050	0.009	0.065	0.005	−0.044
2. 25–44	−0.019	−0.000	−0.056	0.006	0.024	−0.005	−0.049*
3. 45–64	−0.001	0.003	−0.054	0.007	0.024	−0.013	−0.020
edu							
1. Primary or below (comparison)							
2. Lower secondary	0.034	−0.006	0.061*	−0.002	0.037	−0.009	0.027
3. Upper secondary	0.071***	0.007	0.061*	−0.008	0.025	−0.009	0.031
4. Sub-degree	0.051	−0.002	0.076	−0.016	0.021	−0.040**	−0.032
5. Degree or above	0.074**	0.008	0.069	−0.008	0.017	−0.022	−0.020
female	0.009	0.013*	0.042**	−0.000	−0.014	0.006	−0.011
religiosity	0.039	−0.013	0.081***	0.088***	0.222***	0.060***	0.067**
married	−0.018	0.030***	0.064**	0.024***	0.042	0.024**	0.029
class							
1. Lower (comparison)							
2. Lower middle	−0.071***	0.006	−0.025	0.026***	0.024	0.041***	0.026
3. Middle	−0.094***	0.003	−0.009	−0.001	0.008	0.032***	0.063***
4. Upper middle	−0.067*	0.003	−0.074	−0.049***	−0.095*	−0.012	0.050
5. Upper	−0.104	−0.038	−0.025	−0.200***	−0.317	−0.154**	−0.134

	(1)	(2)	(3)	(4)	(5)	(6)
Ethnic identity						
1. Hong Konger (comparison)						
2. Chinese	0.004	0.134***	0.389***	0.118***	0.440***	0.309***
3. Chinese Hong Konger	0.054***	0.115***	0.087***	0.066***	0.169***	0.131***
4. Others						
yellow01	−0.077**	0.119***	0.232***	0.143***	0.223***	0.211***
putonghua	−0.206***	−0.715***	−1.639***	−0.708***	−1.675***	−1.005***
appledaily	−0.057**	−0.015	0.130***	0.105***	0.287***	0.133***
orientdaily	−0.056**	−0.119***	−0.314***	−0.131***	−0.296***	−0.188***
	−0.068***	0.095***	0.172***	0.067***	0.130***	0.040*
District level						
dcbornml_2016	0.558	0.241	0.842	0.242	1.348*	−0.349
dchighhin_2016	0.101	0.024	0.056	0.192**	0.505	−0.077
dcmedianage	0.011	0.015***	0.028	0.010*	0.017	−0.013
dcpop	0.003	−0.046**	−0.220**	−0.071***	−0.270**	−0.185**
vote2019y	−0.202	−0.568**	−0.855	0.182	0.684	1.363***
dcpopdensity2	−0.001	−0.001	−0.002	0.000	−0.001	0.001
elderlyresidence2	−0.000	−0.019*	−0.010	−0.011	−0.010	0.035
erdensity2	0.094	0.092	0.359	0.048	0.443	0.214
Constant	−0.334	0.376**	−0.535	0.040	−1.308*	−0.322
Observations	3,663	3,658	3,658	3,616	3,617	3,654
Number of groups	18	18	18	18	18	18

VARIABLES	(29) governance	(30) governance2	(31) onecountry	(32) onecountry2	(33) ruleoflaw	(34) ruleoflaw2	(35) socialorder
age4							
4. >65 (comparison)							
1. 16–24	0.048***	0.157***	0.020	0.026	0.026	0.047	0.023
2. 25–44	0.011	0.064*	−0.004	−0.013	0.003	−0.031	0.016
3. 45–64	0.007	0.041	−0.009	−0.030	−0.001	−0.006	0.010
edu							
1. Primary or below (comparison)							
2. Lower secondary	−0.036***	−0.075**	0.000	0.015	−0.011	−0.003	−0.029**
3. Upper secondary	−0.065***	−0.070*	−0.007	0.044	−0.019	−0.012	−0.038***
4. Sub-degree	−0.095***	−0.113**	−0.008	0.035	−0.035**	−0.059	−0.063***
5. Degree or above	−0.086***	−0.114***	−0.014	0.013	−0.024	−0.076*	−0.047***
female	−0.006	−0.058***	−0.005	−0.012	0.002	−0.026	−0.007
religiosity	0.087***	0.208***	0.083***	0.140***	0.065***	0.168***	0.052***
married	0.044***	0.059**	0.040***	0.010	0.039***	0.091***	0.041***
Class							
1. Lower (comparison)							
2. Lower middle	0.069***	0.114***	0.037***	0.095***	0.060***	0.075***	0.049***
3. Middle	0.076***	0.174***	0.013	0.042	0.036***	0.031	0.042***
4. Upper middle	0.070***	0.164***	−0.017	0.044	0.012	0.015	0.022
5. Upper	−0.067	−0.021	−0.145**	−0.208	−0.153**	−0.162	−0.148**

	(1)	(2)	(3)	(4)	(5)	(6)
Ethnic identity						
1. Hong Konger (comparison)						
2. Chinese	0.024**	0.101***	0.104***	0.358***	0.064***	0.066***
3. Chinese Hong Konger	0.036***	0.146***	0.069***	0.138***	0.054***	0.032***
4. Others	0.152***	0.230***	0.139***	0.170***	0.157***	0.140***
yellow01	−0.590***	−1.494***	−0.561***	−1.551***	−0.541***	−0.449***
putonghua	0.072***	0.153***	0.113***	0.238***	0.098***	0.118***
appledaily	−0.087***	−0.242***	−0.119***	−0.228***	−0.100***	−0.062***
orientdaily	0.025**	0.002	0.061***	0.073**	0.058***	0.071***
District level						
dcbornml_2016	0.543**	−1.310**	0.740***	0.698	0.518**	0.045
dchighhin_2016	0.123	−0.028	0.236**	0.310	0.203**	0.088
dcmedianage	0.019***	−0.046***	0.016***	0.011	0.013**	0.007
dcpop	−0.005	0.030	−0.076**	−0.155	−0.023	−0.055*
vote2019y	−0.630**	1.012	−0.220	0.642	−0.001	−0.281
dcpopdensity2	−0.001**	0.003	−0.001*	−0.001	−0.000	0.000
elderlyresidence2	−0.027**	0.092***	−0.038***	−0.015	−0.027**	−0.012
erdensity2	0.095	−0.332	0.164**	0.299	0.121	0.059
Constant	−0.032	1.660***	−0.172	−0.910	−0.143	0.428*
Observations	3,653	3,653	3,622	3,624	3,650	3,661
Number of groups	18	18	18	18	18	18

VARIABLES	(36) socialorder2	(37) govclean	(38) govclean2
age4			
4. >65 (comparison)			
1. 16–24	0.117*	0.016	0.055
2. 25–44	0.110**	0.005	0.009
3. 45–64	0.082**	0.003	0.018
edu			
1. Primary or below (comparison)			
2. Lower secondary	−0.107**	0.000	−0.004
3. Upper secondary	−0.119***	−0.001	0.006
4. Sub-degree	−0.187***	−0.024	−0.002
5. Degree or above	−0.298***	−0.005	−0.025
female	−0.015	0.009	0.008
religiosity	0.045	0.043***	0.131***
married	0.132***	0.035***	0.019
Class			
1. Lower (comparison)			
2. Lower middle	0.015	0.002	−0.021
3. Middle	0.130***	−0.008	−0.053**
4. Upper middle	0.148**	−0.019	−0.075*
5. Upper	−0.270	−0.218***	−0.268

Ethnic identity			
1. Hong Konger (comparison)			
2. Chinese	0.106***	0.068***	0.139***
3. Chinese Hong Konger	0.024	0.046***	0.079***
4. Others	0.216***	0.116***	0.149***
yellcw01	−1.240***	−0.453***	−1.094***
putonghua	0.448***	0.047***	0.043
appledaily	−0.366***	−0.077***	−0.187***
orientdaily	0.061	0.051***	0.097***
District level			
dcbornml_2016	2.201*	1.058***	2.202***
dchighhin_2016	0.522	0.337***	0.651***
dcmedianage	0.062**	0.024***	0.042***
dcpop	−0.162	−0.049	−0.039
vote2019y	−1.724	−0.614**	−2.021***
dcpopdensity2	−0.006**	−0.002***	−0.005***
elde-1yresidence2	−0.059	−0.040***	−0.074***
erdensity2	0.848**	0.169**	0.411**
Constant	−2.124**	−0.303	−1.120**
Observations	3,659	3,658	3,657
Number of groups	18	18	18

*p<0.1
**p<0.05
***p<0.01

Appendix 4.5

Detailed Multilevel Regression Analysis for the Rating of National and Local Officials and Local Political Activists

VARIABLES	(1) bjofficial	(2) hkofficial	(3) Tung Chee-hwa	(4) Donald Tsang	(5) Leung Chun-ying	(6) Carrie Lam	(7) bjreps
age4							
4. >65 (comparison)							
1. 16–24	-0.008	-0.037***	-0.076***	-0.097***	-0.002	0.022	-0.009
2. 25–44	0.004	-0.005	-0.055***	-0.050***	-0.020	-0.007	0.001
3. 45–64	0.011	0.001	-0.018	-0.015	-0.022*	-0.003	0.009
edu	-0.008	-0.037***	-0.076***	-0.097***	-0.002	0.022	-0.009
1. Primary or below (comparison)							
2. Lower secondary	-0.017	0.014	0.008	0.044***	0.012	0.002	-0.012
3. Upper secondary	-0.014	0.012	-0.002	0.056***	0.004	-0.015	-0.010
4. Sub-degree	-0.031**	0.001	-0.008	0.056***	0.002	-0.015	-0.030**
5. Degree or above	-0.021	-0.003	-0.008	0.077***	-0.026	-0.023	-0.015
female	0.007	0.021***	0.019**	0.000	0.001	0.014*	0.005
religiosity	0.045***	-0.034***	0.058***	0.026	0.067***	0.078***	0.030**
married	0.011	-0.011	0.007	-0.028**	0.040***	0.016*	0.016*
class5							
1. Lower (comparison)							
2. Lower middle	0.019**	-0.013*	-0.023**	-0.065***	0.010	0.050***	0.015*
3. Middle	0.005	0.010	-0.007	-0.074***	-0.002	0.057***	0.003
4. Upper middle	-0.013	0.060***	0.001	-0.069***	0.000	0.059***	-0.012

	(1)	(2)	(3)	(4)	(5)	(6)	(7)
5. Upper	−0.046	0.082		0.200***	0.347***	−0.049	−0.079	−0.044
Ethnic identity							
1. Hong Konger (comparison)							
2. Chinese	0.096***	0.042***	0.075***	0.039***	0.097***	0.152***	0.101***
3. Chinese Hong Konger	0.063***	0.058***	0.034***	0.014	0.044***	0.096***	0.064***
4. Others	0.078***	0.046***	0.028	−0.005	0.111***	0.169***	0.080***
yellow01	−0.728***	−0.462***	−0.465***	−0.144***	−0.574***	−0.768***	−0.726***
putonghua	0.080***	−0.054***	−0.001	−0.037**	0.114***	0.022	0.069***
appledaily	−0.202***	−0.082***	−0.109***	−0.094***	−0.123***	−0.049***	−0.192***
orientdaily	−0.002	−0.015*	0.036***	−0.090***	0.073***	0.105***	−0.002
District level							
dcbornml_2016	0.710***	0.581***	0.205	−0.400	0.321	0.046	0.591***
dchighin_2016	0.103	0.122*	0.187*	−0.027	0.202	0.092	0.072
dcmedianage	0.016***	0.008*	0.014**	−0.004	0.014*	0.009	0.013***
dcpop	−0.031	−0.008	0.035	0.038	−0.027	0.054*	−0.029
vote2019y	−0.729***	−0.530**	−0.654**	−0.342	−0.070	−0.309	−0.711***
dcpopdensity2	−0.002***	−0.001**	−0.002***	0.000	−0.001	−0.000	−0.002***
elderlyresidence2	−0.033***	−0.021**	0.001	0.019	−0.003	−0.015	−0.027**
erdensity2	0.183***	0.112*	0.028	−0.043	0.002	0.116	0.147**
Constant	0.374**	0.620***	0.453**	1.070***	−0.129	0.321	0.535***
Observations	3,607	3,645	3,545	3,567	3,595	3,649	3,615
Number of groups	18	18	18	18	18	18	18

*** $p<0.01$
** $p<0.05$
* $p<0.1$

VARIABLES	(8) hkexecutive	(9) hklawmaker	(10) hkjudge	(11) hkdistrict	(12) Anson Chan	(13) Martin Lee	(14) Albert Ho
age4							
4. >65 (comparison)							
1. 16–24	−0.037**	−0.032*	−0.040**	−0.053***	−0.047**	−0.042*	−0.029
2. 25–44	−0.010	0.002	−0.002	−0.021	−0.032*	−0.025	−0.018
3. 45–64	−0.001	0.004	0.006	−0.012	−0.019	−0.017	−0.020
edu							
1. Primary or below (comparison)							
2. Lower secondary	0.006	0.022*	0.017	0.003	−0.012	−0.008	−0.008
3. Upper secondary	0.003	0.020	0.016	0.002	−0.037**	−0.010	−0.036**
4. Sub-degree	−0.013	0.016	0.002	−0.008	−0.049**	0.001	−0.027
5. Degree or above	−0.003	−0.001	0.012	−0.030**	−0.063***	−0.014	−0.033*
female	0.019***	0.028***	0.019**	0.017**	−0.007	−0.005	−0.005
religiosity	−0.028**	−0.060***	0.018	−0.066***	0.002	−0.092***	−0.007
married	0.009	−0.016*	−0.016	−0.023**	0.009	−0.033**	−0.033***
class5							
1. Lower (comparison)							
2. Lower middle	0.005	−0.023**	−0.019*	−0.010	−0.012	−0.029**	−0.006
3. Middle	0.001	0.008	0.017	0.015	0.026*	0.012	0.031**
4. Upper middle	0.025	0.049***	0.092***	0.084***	0.034	0.065***	0.046**
5. Upper	0.124*	0.105	0.032	0.025	−0.046	0.171**	−0.021

	(1)	(2)	(3)	(4)	(5)
Ethnic identity					
1. Hong Konger (comparison)					
2. Chinese	0.075***	0.061***	0.039***	-0.057***	-0.126***	-0.088***	-0.116***
3. Chinese Hong Konger	0.080***	0.055***	0.053***	0.033***	0.002	-0.023*	-0.023*
4. Others	0.083***	0.059***	0.009	0.014	-0.011	-0.068***	-0.005
yellow01	-0.669***	-0.501***	-0.382***	-0.119***	0.367***	0.580***	0.567***
putonghua	0.002	-0.054***	-0.095***	-0.080***	-0.001	-0.076***	0.004
appledaily	-0.131***	-0.055***	-0.086***	-0.054***	0.039**	0.090***	0.064***
orientdaily	0.007	-0.009	-0.016	-0.066***	-0.055***	-0.086***	-0.074***
District level							
dcbornml_2016	0.749***	0.306	0.946***	0.371	1.095***	0.633*	0.092
dchighhin_2016	0.086	0.177*	0.204*	-0.063	-0.102	0.006	-0.122
dcmedianage	0.011**	0.008	0.009	0.005	0.023***	0.016**	-0.001
dcpop	-0.004	-0.034	-0.021	0.067**	0.026	0.080**	0.091**
vote2019y	-0.766***	-0.438***	-0.433	-0.519	-1.405***	-0.814***	-0.425
dcpopdensity2	-0.002***	-0.000	-0.002**	-0.001*	-0.003***	-0.002***	-0.001
elderlyresidence2	-0.036***	-0.006	-0.033**	-0.013	-0.058***	-0.029**	-0.016
erdensity2	0.229***	-0.011	0.151	0.120	0.212**	0.199*	0.013
Constant	0.676***	0.611***	0.468*	0.687***	-0.016	-0.067	0.465*
Observations	3,661	3,655	3,658	3,655	3,493	3469	3520
Number of groups	18	18	18	18	18	18	18

***p<0.01
**p<0.05
*p<0.1

VARIABLES	(15) Benny Tai	(16) Jimmy Lai	(17) Joshua Wong
age4			
4. >65 (comparison)			
1. 16–24	−0.035	0.018	0.043**
2. 25–44	−0.006	0.016	0.018
3. 45–64	−0.026*	−0.012	−0.003
edu			
1. Primary or below (comparison)			
2. Lower secondary	0.027*	0.005	0.003
3. Upper secondary	0.035**	−0.002	0.010
4. Sub-degree	0.064***	0.015	0.030
5. Degree or above	0.090***	0.031*	0.062***
female	−0.010	−0.011	−0.015*
religiosity	−0.088***	−0.124***	−0.097***
married	−0.037***	−0.006	−0.015

class5			
1. Lower (comparison)			
2. Lower middle	−0.053***	−0.029***	−0.015
3. Middle	−0.075***	−0.032**	−0.042***
4. Upper middle	−0.060***	−0.032	−0.028
5. Upper	0.127	−0.133	0.108
Ethnic identity			
1. Hong Konger (comparison)			
2. Chinese	−0.095***	−0.118***	−0.099***
3. Chinese Hong Konger	−0.031**	−0.070***	−0.052***
4. Others	−0.058***	−0.073***	−0.039*
yellow01	0.665***	0.751***	0.683***
putonghua	−0.110***	−0.035**	−0.077***
appledaily	0.102***	0.138***	0.166***
orientdaily	−0.104***	−0.104***	−0.089***

continued

continued

VARIABLES	(15) Benny Tai	(16) Jimmy Lai	(17) Joshua Wong
age4			
District level			
dcbornml_2016	−0.214	0.069	−0.340
dchighhin_2016	−0.113	−0.028	−0.204*
dcmedianage	−0.002	−0.004	−0.006
dcpop	0.059	0.024	0.059*
vote2019y	−0.293	0.106	−0.034
dcpopdensity2	−0.000	0.000	0.001
elderlyresidence2	0.008	−0.010	−0.001
erdensity2	−0.092	−0.030	−0.173*
Constant	0.508	0.176	0.468**
Observations	3,484	3,572	3,557
Number of groups	18	18	18

*** $p<0.01$
** $p<0.05$
* $p<0.1$

Appendix 4.6

Summary Statistics and Sources of District-Level Variables

Variable	Obs	Mean	Std. dev.	Min	Max
dcbornml_2016	18	0.288	0.056	0.190	0.386
dchighhin_2016	18	0.188	0.077	0.098	0.344
dcmedianage	18	44.111	1.231	41.000	46.000
dcpop	18	0.416	0.162	0.175	0.692
vote2019y	18	0.568	0.025	0.531	0.611
dcpopdensity2	18	20.675	19.672	1.040	61.410
elderlyresidence2	18	1.614	0.671	0.497	3.257
erdensity2	18	0.077	0.084	0.011	0.287

Data Sources and Variable Construction for Multilevel Analysis

Variables used at the 18 district level are from two Census and Statistics Department sources and Legco commission document, namely the 2016 Population By-Census, mid-2020 population estimates report, Finance Committee (Agenda).

The 18-DC level variable used	
dcbornml_2016	The proportion of the Mainland-born population by 18 districts is from the 2016 Population By-Census.
dchighhin_2016	The proportion of high household income, over 60k, by 18 districts is from the 2016 Population By-Census.
dcmedianage	The median age by 18 districts is from mid-2020 population estimates.
dcpop	Mid-year population (in 1 million) by 18 districts is from mid-2020 population estimates.
vote2019y	The proportion of votes garnered by the anti-establishment camp in 2019 district council elections. It is the result of the aggregated vote to the anti-establishment camp divided by the total number of the valid ballots of each district, excluding the voids and abstains. Each candidate's camp/political affiliation follows the news report by the StandNews web page. Link: https://dce2019.thestandnews.com/
dcpopdensity2	Population density (1,000 people per km square) by 18 districts is from mid-2020 population estimates.
elderlyresidence2	The number of subsidized places offered by various types of residential care homes for the elderly (RCHEs) by 18 districts from the Legislative Council (in thousands).
erdensity2	The density of subsidized places offered by various types of residential care homes for the elderly (RCHEs) (1,000 per km square) by 18 districts from the Legislative Council and further calculated by the authors.

Appendix 5.1

Sources of Political Action (OLS)

VARIABLES	(1) actgov	(2) actprotest	(3) boycott01	(4) actleg	(5) actmedia
disatsoc	−0.064*	0.038**	−0.081*	0.019	0.082**
disatpol	−0.134***	0.039***	0.148***	0.189***	−0.030
yellow5 0-1	−0.038*	0.065***	0.123***	−0.143***	0.141***
appledaily0-1	−0.044***	0.050***	0.194***	−0.036***	−0.041***
16**24	0.000	0.000	0.000	0.000	0.000
25–44	0.037***	−0.022***	−0.055***	0.051***	−0.065***
45–64	0.042**	−0.031***	−0.092***	0.097***	−0.107***
>65	0.042**	−0.035***	−0.112***	0.115***	−0.152***
Primary or below	−0.026	0.017**	0.005	0.001	0.012
Lower secondary	−0.017	0.004	−0.011	0.004	0.002
Upper secondary	−0.025**	0.012**	−0.017	−0.006	−0.004
Sub-degree	−0.029**	0.024***	0.017	−0.012	0.016
Degree or above	0.000	0.000	0.000	0.000	0.000
Female (see: m6)	−0.000	−0.006	−0.037***	0.021***	−0.015**
Atheism	0.000	0.000	0.000	0.000	0.000
Eastern	−0.033***	0.003	−0.039***	0.040***	−0.028***
Western	−0.022*	0.001	−0.012	0.031***	0.007
Religiosity	0.093***	−0.038***	0.051***	−0.057***	0.019
Marital status (~31)	−0.014	−0.014***	−0.015	−0.005	0.009
class5=1	0.000	0.000	0.000	0.000	0.000
class5=2	−0.170**	0.015	0.189**	0.123*	0.014
class5=3	−0.161**	0.006	0.148*	0.140*	−0.024
class5=4	−0.153**	0.001	0.136	0.158**	−0.027
class5=5	−0.147*	−0.010	0.071	0.182**	−0.056
1. 中西區	0.000	0.000	0.000	0.000	0.000
2. 灣仔	0.023	0.005	−0.032	0.012	−0.000
3. 東區	−0.058**	0.028**	0.039	−0.017	0.055***
4. 南區	−0.000	0.000	0.038	−0.051**	0.050**
5. 深水埗	−0.042*	0.033***	0.072***	−0.043*	0.041*
6. 油尖旺	−0.005	−0.005	−0.009	−0.030	0.051**
7. 九龍城	−0.016	0.033***	0.060**	−0.007	0.017
8. 黃大仙	−0.006	0.026**	0.034	−0.031	0.048**
9. 觀塘	−0.017	0.013	0.064**	−0.011	0.005
10. 葵青	−0.027	0.001	0.025	−0.007	0.047**
11. 荃灣	−0.048*	−0.005	0.046	−0.013	0.060***
12. 屯門	−0.028	0.010	0.068**	−0.011	0.044**
13. 元朗	−0.008	−0.014	0.064**	0.000	0.040**
14. 北區	−0.020	0.003	0.019	−0.029	0.023
15. 大埔	−0.053*	0.005	0.083**	−0.045*	0.030
16. 沙田	−0.000	0.002	0.039	−0.011	0.025
17. 西貢	0.001	0.000	0.076***	−0.002	0.024
18. 離島	0.041	0.002	0.124***	−0.013	0.002
constant	0.589***	0.007	0.223**	−0.043	0.192***

VARIABLES	(1) actgov	(2) actprotest	(3) boycott01	(4) actleg	(5) actmedia
Adj R^2	0.093	0.191	0.249	0.088	0.126
N	3,365	3,365	3,371	3,365	3,365
bic	−593.7	−5356.7	197.3	−922.8	−1473.6

*$p<0.10$
**$p<0.05$
***$p<0.01$

VARIABLES	(6) actvote	(7) actparty	(8) actcourt
disatsoc	0.000	0.064**	−0.049***
disatpol	0.077***	−0.122***	−0.002
yellow5 0–1	−0.025*	0.018	−0.021***
appledaily0–1	0.009	0.017*	0.055***
16–24	0.000	0.000	0.000
25–44	0.008	0.005	−0.003
45–64	0.004	0.002	0.005
>65	0.014	0.013	0.011
Primary or below	−0.040***	0.020*	−0.011*
Lower secondary	−0.020**	0.029***	−0.006
Upper secondary	−0.001	0.018**	0.001
Sub-degree	−0.008	0.014	−0.008
Degree or above	0.000	0.000	0.000
Female (see: m6)	0.004	−0.009	−0.000
Atheism	0.000	0.000	0.000
Eastern	−0.005	0.025***	−0.018***
Western	−0.015*	−0.006	−0.004
Religiosity	0.009	−0.035***	0.032***
Marital status (~31)	−0.002	0.029***	−0.007*
class5=1	0.000	0.000	0.000
class5=2	−0.045	0.058	−0.002
class5=3	−0.026	0.048	0.007
class5=4	−0.037	0.040	0.004
class5=5	−0.036	0.043	−0.000
1. 中西區	0.000	0.000	0.000
2. 灣仔	0.037*	−0.063***	0.007
3. 東區	0.009	−0.002	0.007
4. 南區	0.027	−0.017	−0.009
5. 深水埗	0.024	−0.031*	0.006
6. 油尖旺	0.006	−0.023	0.003
7. 九龍城	0.010	−0.050***	0.013

continued

continued

VARIABLES	(6) actvote	(7) actparty	(8) actcourt
8. 黃大仙	−0.001	−0.031*	0.001
9. 觀塘	0.012	−0.023	0.015*
10. 葵青	0.001	−0.005	−0.005
11. 荃灣	0.011	−0.020	0.008
12. 屯門	0.003	−0.014	−0.005
13. 元朗	0.011	−0.015	−0.007
14. 北區	0.012	0.011	−0.001
15. 大埔	0.048**	−0.051**	0.045***
16. 沙田	0.012	−0.020	−0.002
17. 西貢	−0.001	−0.020	0.004
18. 離島	0.023	−0.061***	0.021*
constant	0.079	0.070	0.039
Adj R^2	0.032	0.053	0.077
N	3365	3365	3365
bic	−3246.4	−2866.0	−7205.1

*$p<0.10$
**$p<0.05$
***$p<0.01$

Notes: Logit results the same (check). OLS is used to compare results with boycot01 which is a continuous variable.

Appendix 5.2

Summary Statistics of Variables

VARIABLES	Obs	Mean	Std. dev.	Min	Max
actgov	3,720	0.325224	0.2240738	0	1
actprotest	3,720	0.0550627	0.1227397	0	1
boycot01	3,726	0.4501029	0.2742794	0	1
actnone	3,720	0.0359319	0.1184074	0	1
actmedia	3,720	0.1872312	0.1979543	0	1
actleg	3,720	0.191129	0.210809	0	1
actvote	3,720	0.0858871	0.1483159	0	1
actparty	3,720	0.0906362	0.1582026	0	0.8333333
actcourt	3,720	0.0288979	0.083665	0	0.5
disatsoc	3,710	0.4100749	0.1316955	0	1
disatpol	3,679	0.554017	0.2273734	0	1
yellow5	3,722	0.5147098	0.2645305	0	1
appledaily	3,738	0.1906367	0.317078	0	1

VARIABLES	Obs	Mean	Std. dev.	Min	Max
age					1
16–24	3,744	0.1180556	0.322717	0	1
25–44	3,744	0.349359	0.4768312	0	1
45–64	3,744	0.355235	0.4786484	0	1
>65	3,744	0.1773504	0.382016	0	1
edu					1
Primary or below	3,743	0.2043815	0.4033028	0	1
Lower secondary	3,743	0.1701843	0.3758449	0	1
Upper secondary	3,743	0.2965536	0.456799	0	1
Sub-degree	3,743	0.103393	0.3045122	0	1
female	3744	0.5392628	0.4985226	0	1
rel3					1
Atheism	3,741	0.6583801	0.4743162	0	1
Eastern	3,741	0.2076985	0.405714	0	1
Western	3,741	0.1339214	0.3406134	0	1
Religiosity	3,744	0.4323023	0.2502801	0	1
Married	3,701	0.6987301	0.4588717	0	1
class5					1
2	3,546	0.0566836	0.2312696	0	1
3	3,546	0.322899	0.4676504	0	1
4	3,546	0.3708404	0.4830979	0	1
5	3,546	0.2470389	0.4313504	0	1
district18					1
1. 中西區	3,744	0.0392628	0.1942455	0	1
2. 灣仔	3,744	0.0267094	0.1612543	0	1
3. 東區	3,744	0.0667735	0.2496627	0	1
4. 南區	3,744	0.0400641	0.1961358	0	1
5. 深水埗	3,744	0.0536859	0.2254269	0	1
6. 油尖旺	3,744	0.0405983	0.1973841	0	1
7. 九龍城	3,744	0.0619658	0.2411257	0	1
8. 黃大仙	3,744	0.0534188	0.2248972	0	1
9. 觀塘	3,744	0.0803953	0.2719405	0	1
10. 葵青	3,744	0.0667735	0.2496627	0	1
11. 荃灣	3,744	0.0400641	0.1961358	0	1
12. 屯門	3,744	0.0673077	0.2505876	0	1
13. 元朗	3,744	0.0806624	0.2723523	0	1
14. 北區	3,744	0.0531517	0.2243659	0	1
15. 大埔	3,744	0.0405983	0.1973841	0	1
16. 沙田	3,744	0.0940171	0.2918915	0	1
17. 西貢	3,744	0.0673077	0.2505876	0	1
18. 離島	3,744	0.0272436	0.1628142	0	1

Appendix 6.1

The Big Ten Newspapers in Hong Kong.

Among the ten best-known newspapers, *Ta Kung Pao*, *Wen Wei Po*, and *Hong Kong Commercial Daily* are regarded as China's propaganda mouthpieces.[2] They are sponsored by Chinese capital and have a distinctly pro-China political stance. They are also among the few Hong Kong newspapers that can be distributed in Mainland China. The other seven newspapers are essentially market oriented and privately run by Hong Kong businessmen. Depending on their reporting focus, they can be furthered categorized into five newspapers that cover general issues including *Sing Tao Daily*, *Sing Pao*, *Oriental Daily*, *Ming Pao*, and *Apple Daily*; and two that focus on financial news including *Hong Kong Economic Journal* and *Hong Kong Economic Times*.

1. Propaganda Newspapers

1.1 Ta Kung Pao

In 1938, *Ta Kung Pao*, already a very influential newspaper in Mainland China, started its Hong Kong edition. During the Second World War, the publication was suspended for a while, then resumed in 1948 and has been in operation since then. Along with *Hong Kong Commercial Daily* and *Wen Wei Po*, *Ta Kung Pao* is considered a leftist (Chinese-funded) newspaper in Hong Kong. In 2016, *Ta Kung Pao* and *Wen Wei Po* merged to form Hong Kong Ta Kung Wen Wei Media Group. On the official website of this media group, it is stated: "Hong Kong Ta Kung Wen Wei Media Group is a comprehensive media conglomerate with three major newspapers, including *Ta Kung Pao*, *Wen Wei Po*, *Lion Rock Daily*, and various new-media platforms. The Group pledges its loyalty to the homeland, to loving China, and to loving Hong Kong."

1.2 Wen Wei Po

Another newspaper with a strong Chinese background is *Wen Wei Po*. It was founded in 1948 by the Shanghai-based *Wen Wei Po*, with the support of Hong Kong patriots. Since its inception, *Wen Wei Po* has always adhered to a distinctly pro-China political stance. Now it is part of the Hong Kong Ta Kung Wen Wei Media Group.

1.3 Hong Kong Commercial Daily

Founded in 1952, *Hong Kong Commercial Daily* is a major financial newspaper that focuses on economic reports about China and Hong Kong. It was developed from the *Hong Kong Standard Department Store Fiancial Quotation* (in Chinese: 香港标准百货金融行情), a tabloid of the pro-China newspaper, *Hong Kong Economic Herald*. In 1989, Sino United Publishing injected HK$150 million into the newspaper and became its major shareholder. In 1999, *Shenzhen Special Zone Daily* (in Chinese: 深圳特区报) took a stake in the paper and became its owner. Subsequently, *Hong Kong Commercial Daily* was authorized by the central government of China to publish in the Mainland. Since then, it has fully entered the Mainland market. Its readers are mainly businesspeople in Hong Kong and the Pearl River region adjacent to Hong Kong.

[2] Lee 2006.

2. Market-Oriented General Newspapers

2.1 Sing Tao Daily

Sing Tao Daily is one of the longest surviving newspapers in Hong Kong. It was founded in 1938 by Mr. Aw-Boon Haw, a Chinese entrepreneur and philanthropist, famously known as the founder of Tiger Balm. During the colonial period, *Sing Tao* had a close relationship with the British colonial government and often published government notices in addition to the weekly Friday *Government Gazette*. Later, with the return of Hong Kong to China, *Sing Tao* turned into a pro-China newspaper, with editorials and news articles often in support of the Chinese regime. In 2001, a prominent Hong Kong tobacconist, Tsu-kwok Ho, bought *Sing Tao Daily* and its parent company and became the owner until it was sold to another Hong Kong businessman in 2021. *Sing Tao* is now operated by Sing Tao News Corporation Limited, which is a Hong Kong–listed company. The newspaper is headquartered in Hong Kong, with branches in the United States, Canada, the United Kingdom, and Australia, and its readership is mainly Chinese people who have settled overseas.

2.2 Sing Pao

Sing Pao was founded in 1939 by Hong Kong newspaper tycoon Man-fat Ho. It was one of the most successful market-oriented newspapers in colonial Hong Kong. Within half a year of its launch, *Sing Pao* jumped to the top of the Hong Kong media market in terms of sales and remained there for decades until it was overtaken by *Oriental Daily* in the 1980s. Sales of *Sing Pao* began to decline into the late 1990s, a decline that was exacerbated by the emergence of *Apple Daily*. In 2000, the ownership of *Sing Pao* changed for the first time and several times thereafter. In 2016, *Sing Pao* publicly published articles criticizing the then-Chief Executive Chun-ying Leung. Since then, the reporting stance has gradually shifted in favor of the pro-democracy camp.

2.3 Ming Pao

Ming Pao was founded in 1959 by the famous Hong Kong novelist Leung-yung Cha (金庸) and Pao-sing Shen. It focused on local news in Hong Kong. In 1991, Ming Pao Enterprise Corporation was listed on the Stock Exchange of Hong Kong. In 1995, Mr. Cha sold *Ming Pao* to Malaysian businessman Hiew-King Tiong. Ming Pao Enterprise Corporation was later merged with other companies and renamed to Media Chinese International.

2.4 Oriental Daily

Oriental Daily was founded in 1969 by Hong Kong gangster and businessman Sik-chun Ma and his brother Sik-yu Ma. The newspaper claims to be "Hong Kong's top-selling newspaper for 30 consecutive years." On December 16, 1995, the newspaper set a daily record of 838,487 copies sold in Hong Kong.[3] *Oriental Daily* is a popular newspaper among grassroots readers as it focuses on local community news. The paper is now owned by the Oriental Press Group, a Hong Kong–listed company chaired by Ching-fat Ma, the son of one of the founders, Sik-chun Ma. *Oriental Daily*'s main competitor is *Apple Daily*.

2.5 Apple Daily

Apple Daily was founded by Jimmy Lai in 1995 and is part of the publicly listed Next Media Group. The newspaper is completely market oriented. In 1995, when *Apple Daily* was first published, it started a price war by selling at half the market price at that time. Many newspapers closed down in this price war. *Apple Daily* won readers with sensationalism, pornography, and

---

[3] Oriental Enterprise Holdings Limited 2006.

gory reports. As the market became more competitive, otherwise serious newspapers began to compete for readers with similar stories.[4] This led to the total "Apple-ization" of the local newspaper industry.

3. Market-Oriented Financial Newspapers

3.1 Hong Kong Economic Journal

Hong Kong Economic Journal, the first financial newspaper in Hong Kong, was founded in 1973 by Mr. and Mrs. Shan-muk Lam, local journalism professionals, with readers mainly from the financial sector and intellectuals. It focuses on economic reporting and analysis, covering four major categories: China, industry, stock market, and finance. *Hong Kong Economic Journal* is the only one of the seven private newspapers under study that has not developed into a large media conglomerate. In 2006, Tzar-kai Li, son of Hong Kong billionaire business magnate Ka-shing Li, bought the paper and became its owner.

3.2 Hong Kong Economic Times

Hong Kong Economic Times was founded in 1988 by Siu-por Fung and Perry Mak, and Perry Mak raised HK$20 million to launch the newspaper in 1988 in response to the demand for financial and business information in Hong Kong. It mainly covers news on the stock market, real estate, and information technology, and its readers are mainly middle-class Hong Kong businessmen, executives, and investors. In 2005, *Hong Kong Economic Times* was listed on the Hong Kong Stock Exchange.

Table A6.1 summarizes the basic information of these newspapers. From Table A6.1, it can be seen that the development of private newspapers in Hong Kong is characterized by one obvious feature, that is, with the exception of the *Hong Kong Economic Journal*, most of the private newspapers have developed into large-scale media conglomerates and have been listed on the stock market. These media conglomerates at the same time operate a wide range of media products other than newspapers. However, they have not merged with each other to form a larger media group but have developed separately and maintained competition with each other. This mode of media development is very different from that of Mainland China. In Mainland China, the party started to vigorously promote newspaper conglomeration around 2003 by merging the major newspapers within a certain region into a newspaper group, through which the party could better control the local newspapers.[5] From this perspective, the development of the media in Hong Kong is clearly market oriented, which is very different from the situation in Mainland China.

---

[4] Chen, Chen, and Yang 2014.
[5] Zhao 2006. Lee, He, and Huang 2006.

Table A6.1 Ten Legacy Newspapers in Hong Kong

Newspaper	Founding year	Founder	Current owner	Parent news group
Propaganda newspapers				
Ta Kung Pao	1938	Ta Kung Pao (Mainland China)	Unpublicized	Hong Kong Ta Kung Wen Wei Media Group
Wen Wei Po	1948	Wen Wei Po (Mainland China)	Unpublicized	
Hong Kong Commercial Daily	1952	*Hong Kong Economic Herald*	Shenzhen Special Zone Daily	Shenzhen Press Group
Market-oriented general newspapers				
Sing Tao Daily	1938	Aw-Boon Haw	Tsu-kwok Ho (2001–2021); Ying-shing Kwok and Karson Choi (2022–present)	Sing Tao News Corporation (listed company, 1986–present)
Sing Pao	1939	Man-fat Ho	Zhuo-heng Gu	Sing Pao Media Enterprises (listed company; 2001–2015)
Ming Pao	1959	Leung-yung Cha (金庸) and Pao-sing Shen	Hiew-King Tiong	Media Chinese International (listed company, 1991–present)
Oriental Daily	1969	Sik-chun Ma and Sik-yu Ma	Ching-fat Ma	Oriental Press Group (listed company, 1987–present)
Apple Daily	1995–2021	Jimmy Chee-ying Lai	Jimmy Chee-ying Lai	Next Digital (listed company, 2000–2023)
Market-oriented financial newspapers				
Hong Kong Economic Journal	1973	Shan-muk Lam couple	Tzar-kai Li	Clermont Media
Hong Kong Economic Times	1988	*Siu-por Fung and Perry Mak*	*Siu-por Fung*	Hong Kong Economic Times Holdings (listed company, 2005–present)

Appendix 6.2

Top-10 Topic Keywords on CCP by *Apple Daily* and *Wen Wei Po* (2002–2020)

Year	Apple Daily	Wen Wei Po
2002	Bush, June 4th, Article 23, democracy movements, repression, Uncle Tung, confidants, Zhao Ziyang, monopoly party, demonstration;	construction, promote, Western China, formulate, Bush, system, accelerate, improve, modernization, innovation;
2003	June 4th, Uncle Tung, Article 23, Bush, hide, Aha-Tung, local CCP (*tu gong*), Zhao Ziyang, July 1st, protest on the street (*shangjie*);	CPPCC (Chinese People's Political Concultative Conference, *renmin zhengxie*), spacecraft, the Ninth Conference, Bush, opportunity, Li Zongren, Tibetan, Yu Youren, Hui minority, Li Kenong;
2004	June 4th, Bush, Longhair (Leung Kwok-hung, *changmao*), repression (*zhen ya*), Jiang Yanyong, Aha-Tung, Zhao Ziyang, 1989 (Tiananmen Square protests and massacre), suppress (*da ya*), democracy movements;	institution, industry, Pan Pearl River Delta, economic zone, Pearl River Delta, Sheng Shicai, Western Taiwan Straits Economic Zone, CPPCC, Lu Zhangong, prevention and control;
2005	Zhao Ziyang, Zhao Family, repression, dissent, Ziyang, democracy movements, condolences, year 1989, Bush, 1989;	formulate, improve, Ye Ting, Western Taiwan Straits Economic Zone, Wei Lihuang, economy-and society, CPPCC, Gu Zhun, Bush;
2006	June 4th, North Korea, frostiness, Ching Cheong, Bush, Culture Revolution, defend human rights, Zhao Ziyang, democrats, Youth League Faction;	industry, comprehensive, construction, Western Taiwan Straits Economic Zone, Yiwu, promote, formulate, economy-and-society, Taiwan-funded, complete;
2007	June 4th, left-wing politics, anti-rightist, right-wing politics, Youth League Faction, princelings, netizen, democracy movements, Mrs. Chan (Anson Maria Elizabeth Chan Fang On Sang), Yahoo;	construction, promote, industry, Western Taiwan Straits Economic Zone, Tsui Sze Man, economy-and-society, Buddhism, formulate, economic zone, Putian;
2008	June 4th, police, Bush, Hu Jia, the Hu–Wen regime, repression, pan-democrats, Ching Cheong, democrats, Zhao Ziyang;	industry, construction, Guangdong–Hong Kong, promote, Guangdong–Hong Kong-Macau, service industry, Shishi, cartoons and comics, Taiwan and the Mainland (*haixialiang'an*), Haining;<?TeX

2009	June 4th, authorities, Liu Xiaobo, Zhao Ziyang, police, repression, democracy movements, rehabilitate, human rights, Hong Kong Letters Patent;	construction, industry, financial crisis, accelerate, promotion, Pearl River Delta, Xiamen, opportunity, service industry, economy-and-society;
2010	June 4th, Liu Xiaobo, authorities, North Korea, Liu Xia, Confucius, dissent, Nobel Peace Prize, Zhao Ziyang, defend human rights;	construction, economy-and-society, get to know, CPC Central Committee Political Bureau Standing Committee, research, enforcement, Workers' Party of Korea (WPK), Municipal Party Committee, implement, 12th Five-Year Plan;
2011	Ai Weiwei, June 4th, authorities, Uncle Wah, chief executive, pan-democrats, Liu Xiaobo, dissent, Tang Ying-yen, defend human rights;	construction, promote, cross-Straits relations, accelerate, 12th Five-Year Plan, our country, party group, innovation, get to know, implement;
2012	June 4th, Li Wangyang, brain-washing, Leung Chun-ying, National Education Reform, Tang Ying-yen, march, chief executive, the government, protest on the street;	construction, promote, socialism, innovation, economy-and-society, *xiaokang* society, implement, improve, our country, anti-corruption;
2013	June 4th, march, local, assembly, pan-democrats, Charles K. Djou, China-Hong Kong, North Korea, democrats, 1st July;	construction, inspection, North Korea, inspection group, promote, Central Commission for Discipline Inspection, Municipal Party Committee, research, implement, formulate;
2014	June 4th, pan-democrats, hongkongers, the government, resistance, the establishment, suppress, march, vote, repression;	construction, cadres, inspection, promote, North Korea, Party integrity, Central Commission for Discipline Inspection, our country, party committee, get to know;
2015	June 4th, Leung Chun-ying, pan-democrats, Umbrella Movement, authorities, North Korea, the establishment, democrats, facebook, HKFS (Hong Kong Federation of Students);	promote, cadres, Central Commission for Discipline Inspection, Municipal Party Committee, party group, innovation, Party integrity, get to know, Provincial Party Committee, party committee;
2016	Leung Chun-ying, June 4th, Paul Lee, Books, Culture Revolution, Causeway Bay, democrats, 689, reelection, missing;	promote, innovation, construction, cadres, party group, Secretary of the Party Group, deepen, Provincial Party Committee, Municipal Party Committee, strict governance over the Party;

continued

continued

Year	Apple Daily	Wen Wei Po
2017	Liu Xiaobo, June 4th, North Korea, democrats, Liu Xia, elites, Guo Wengui, Political Bureau of the CPC Central Committee, Carrie Lam Cheng Yuet-ngor, South Korea;	construction, promote, poverty alleviation, comrade, deepen, innovation, improve, ecology, attack, construct;
2018	June 4th, Liu Xia, democrats, North Korea, bishop, Liu Xiaobo, church, the Curia, Culture Revolution, defend human rights;	construction, innovation, our country, promote, poverty alleviation, Guangdong-Hong Kong-Macau, modernization, carry out, ecology, CPPCC;
2019	Call for action, go to vote, 11.24, kick off, free Kong Kong (*guangfu hongkong*), June 4th, resistance, anti-extradition-law, one-hundred days, summer of freedom;	development, construction, socialism, promote, Guangdong-Hong Kong-Macau, innovation, Greater Bay Area, improve, with Chinese characteristics, governance;
2020	Hong Kong, China, CCP, America, Apple, Taiwan, Nation, the Hong Kong national security law, government, Covid-19.	development, China, Hong Kong, Covid-19, country, task, Xi Jinping, prevent and control, economy, construction.

Appendix 6.3

Data Analysis Strategy for Media Stance

First, we used *jieba*, one of the best Chinese word segmentation methods, to segment news report containing content related to the Chinese Communist Party (CCP). *Jieba*'s training corpus includes news articles from the *People's Daily*, which ensures strong performance in processing news data. To further evaluate and enhance word segmentation accuracy, we randomly sampled 20 to 40 news reports every year in two decades from 2000 to 2019. Two research assistants reviewed and annotated the segmentation results of *jieba* on news reports, adding any unrecognized words to a custom dictionary. After this refinement, we re-processed the news text again. The improved *jieba* segmentation yielded more accurate results for news data.

After the completion of the word segmentation, each document can be treated as a bag of words containing a number of vocabularies. The analysis of different media reports was transformed into bag-of-words analysis. After that, we set *Wen Wei Po* and *Apple Daily* as benchmarks for comparison. For each year from 2000 to 2019, we took seven days (one week) as the time window and calculated the cosine similarity between the reports of different media and the benchmark media in different time windows of the year on a day-by-day basis. Specifically, for each benchmark media, we computed the cosine similarity between the compared media's reports and the benchmark media's reports across 359 different time windows per year.

In order to make the cosine similarity between different media reports better reflect the degree of similarity or difference between the news reports in their time windows and those of the benchmark media, we further cleaned the results of the cosine similarity of each report after word splitting. First, we removed the stop words in the segmentation results to improve the quality of the text features. Next, we excluded the single-character words to further improve the quality of textual features, so as to ensure that only words with actual meanings are retained in the bag of words.

After cleaning, we aggregated the bag of words for all reports from the same media within each time window, extracted the high-frequency words, and vectorized them. We then aligned the dimensions of these high-frequency word vectors with those of the benchmark media in the same time window, and calculated the cosine similarity between them. The result of this cosine similarity calculation represents our measure of the similarity of the topics, contents, and stances of different media reports.

Calculating Text Similarity
We calculated the similarity between the reports of different media and those of the benchmark media in the same way as described in the previous section, and in practice, we set the time window to seven days in order to exclude the influence of random fluctuations. More specifically, we calculated the day-by-day cosine similarity of all Hong Kong media reports except the benchmark media (i.e., *Apple Daily* and *Wen Wei Po*) with the benchmark media over the past two decades. In order to better characterize the overall consistency of reporting across different media, for each Hong Kong media, we computed the difference in text similarity between this media and the two different benchmark media for each time window and then sorted the differences.

We then extracted the upper and lower quartiles of the difference sequence to determine the relative position of each media relative to the benchmarks. Simply put, as shown in Figure A6.1, the closer to the upper right corner of the chart, the closer to the pan-Democratic camp (*Apple Daily*) the position of the media outlet is; the closer to the lower left corner of the chart, the closer to the pro-establishment camp (*Wen Wei Po*) the position of the media outlet is.

200 Appendices

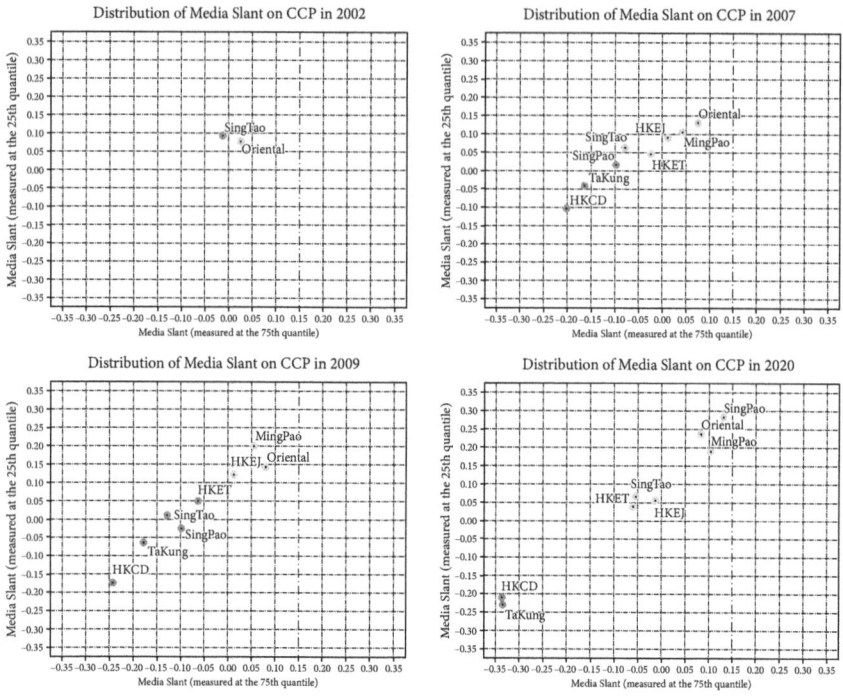

Figure A6.1 Media Slant in Selective Years on CCP

Bibliography

Adler, Paul S., Adly, Amr, Armanios, Daniel E., et al. 2023. Authoritarianism, populism, and the global retreat of democracy: a curated discussion. *Journal of Management Inquiry* 32(1), 3–20.

AFP. 2019. China step up war of words over Hong Kong. *Hong Kong Free Press*, August 11, 2019. http://hongkongfp.com/2019/08/11/us-china-step-war-words-hong-kong/

Almond, Gabriel A. 1956. Comparative political systems. *Journal of Politics* 18(3), 391–409.

Almond, Gabriel A., and Verba, Sidney. 1963. *The civic culture: political attitudes and democracy in five nations*. Princeton, NJ: Princeton University Press.

Amies, Nick. 2009. EU's uneasy relationship with China endures 20 years on. *Deutsche Welle*, June 4, 2009. https://www.dw.com/en/eus-uneasy-relationship-with-china-endures-20-years-on/a-4290281

Anderson, Benedict, R. 2016. *Imagined communities: reflections on the origin and spread of nationalism*. Rev. ed. London: Verso.

Ang, Ien. 2001. *On not speaking Chinese: living between Asia and the West*. London: Routledge.

Arranz, Adolfo, and Lam, Jeffie. 2019. From Occupy 2014 to protests 2019. *South China Morning Post*, September 28, 2019. https://multimedia.scmp.com/infographics/news/hong-kong/article/3030696/from-occupy-to-hong-kong-protests/index.html

Arts, Will, Hagenaars, Jacques, and Halman, Loek, eds. 2003. *The cultural diversity of European unity*. Berlin, Germany: Brill.

Ashcroft, Bill, Griffiths, Gareth, and Tiffin, Helen. 1995. *The post-colonial studies reader*. London: Routledge.

Bahri, Deepika. 2003. *Native intelligence: aesthetics, politics, and postcolonial literature*. Minneapolis: University of Minnesota Press.

Baker, Hug D. R. 1983. Life in the cities: the emergence of Hong Kong man. *The China Quarterly* 95, 469–479.

Bammer, Angelika. 1994. *Displacements: cultural identities in question*. Bloomington: Indiana University Press.

BBC. 2019. 香港逃犯条例游行:民阵称近200万人参与,再次破纪录 [Hong Kong fugitive offenders ordinance march: the democratic front said nearly 2 million people participated, breaking another record]. *BBC News*, June 15, 2019. https://www.bbc.com/zhongwen/simp/live/chinese-news-48634220

Benford, Robert D., and Snow, David A. 2000. Framing processes and social movements: an overview and assessment. *Annual Review of Sociology* 26, 611–639.

Berman, Sheri. 1997. Civil society and the collapse of the Weimar Republic. *World Politics* 49(3), 401–429.

Bhabha, Homi K. 1990. *Nation and narration*. London: Routledge.

Bhabha, Homi. K. 1994. *The location of culture*. London: Routledge.

Bishop, George F., Oldendick, Robert W., and Tuchfarber, Alfred J. 1984. Interest in political campaigns: the influence of question order and electoral context. *Political Behavior* 6(2),159–169.

Blair, Graeme, and Imai, Kosuke. 2012. Statistical analysis of list experiments. *Political Analysis* 20 (1), 47–77.

Blair, Graeme, Coppock, Alexander, and Moor, Margaret. 2020. When to worry about sensitivity bias: a social reference theory and evidence from 30 years of list experiments. *American Political Science Review* 114(4), 1297–1315.

Blanchard, Ben. 2019. Chinese paper says "foreign forces" using Hong Kong havoc to hurt China. *Reuters*, June 10, 2019. https://www.reuters.com/article/us-hongkong-extradition-march-china-idUSKCN1TA0U4

Bloomberg. 2019. High-flying Chinese professionals in Hong Kong living like fugitives. *Street Times*, October 22, 2019. https://www.nst.com.my/world/world/2019/10/532228/high-flying-chinese-professionals-hong-kong-living-fugitives

Bressler, Charles E. 2007. *Literary criticism: an introduction to theory and practice*. Upper Saddle River, NJ: Pearson Prentice Hall.

Brinton, Crane. 1965. *The anatomy of revolution*. Rev. and expanded ed. New York: Vintage books.

Brunnstorm, David. 2019. Chinese reports on U.S. diplomat in Hong Kong "have gone from irresponsible to dangerous": State Department. *Reuters*, August 9, 2019. https://www.reuters.com/article/us-hongkong-protests-usa-idUSKCN1UZ2HK

Brynen, Rex, Korany, Bahgat, and Noble, Paul. 1995. *Political liberalization and democratization in the Arab world*. Boulder, CO: Lynne Rienner.

Brysk, Alison, Parsons, Craig, and Sandholtz, Wayne. 2002. After empire: national identity and post-colonial families of nations. *European Journal of International Relations* 8, 267–305.

Bush, Richard C. 2014. Hong Kong: examining the impact of the "umbrella movement." *Brookings*, December 3, 2014. https://www.brookings.edu/testimonies/hong-kong-examining-the-impact-of-the-umbrella-movement/

Cai, Yongshun. 2017. *The Occupy movement in Hong Kong: sustaining decentralized protest*. London and New York: Routledge

Campbell, Angus, Converse, Philip E., Miller, Warren E., et al. 1980. *The American voter*. Chicago: University of Chicago Press.

Campbell, Vincent. 2004. *Information age journalism: journalism in an international context*. London and New York: Arnold; distributed in the US by Oxford University Press.

Carroll, John. M. 2005. *Edge of empires: Chinese elites and British colonials in Hong Kong*. Cambridge, MA: Harvard University Press.

Carvalho, Raquel. 2019. Amid protests for democracy, Hong Kong's ethnic minorities strive to be heard. *South China Morning Post*, October 26, 2019. https://www.scmp.com/week-asia/politics/article/3034525/amid-protests-democracy-hong-kongs-ethnic-minorities-strive-be

CDC (Curriculum Development Council). 2017. 中國語文教育學習領域:普通話科課程指引(小一至中三)(2017) [Chinese language education key learning area: Putonghua curriculum guide (primary one to secondary three) (2017)]. Education Bureau, HKSAR. https://www.edb.gov.hk/attachment/tc/curriculum-development/kla/chi-edu/curriculum-documents/PTH_Curriculum_guide_for_upload_final.pdf/

Chan, H. M. 1994. Culture and identity. In D. H. McMillen and S. W. Man, eds. *The other Hong Kong Report 1994*. Hong Kong: Chinese University Press.

Chan, Joseph M., and Lee, Francis L. F. 2007a. Media and large-scale demonstrations: the pro-democracy movement in post-handover Hong Kong. *Asian Journal of Communication* 17(2), 215–228.

Chan, Joseph M., and Lee, Francis L. F. 2007b. Re-nationalization, internationalization and localization: media and politics in Hong Kong [再国族化、国际化与本土化的角力:香港的传媒和政治]. *21st Century* [二十一世纪评论] 101(1), 43–55.

Chan, Michael, Lee, Francis and Lee, Hsuan-Ting. 2021. Hong Kong. In Nic Newman, et al. eds. *Reuters Institute Digital News Report 2021*, 10th ed., The Reuters Institute for the Study of Journalism.

Chan, P. Y. 2022. Legco election: 3 reasons the low voter turnout is no failure. *South China Morning Post*, Jan 1, 2022. https://www.scmp.com/comment/letters/article/3161568/legco-election-3-reasons-low-voter-turnout-no-failure?utm_source=rss_feed

Chan, Selina C. 1998. Politicizing tradition: the identity of Indigenous inhabitants in Hong Kong. *Ethnology* 37, 39–54.

Chan, Yun-Nam, and Lau, Siu-Fung. 2021. Hong Kong to fire 129 civil servants who refused to pledge allegiance. *Radio Free Asia*, June 4., 2021. https://www.rfa.org/english/news/china/pledge-04192021115920.html

Chatterjee, Partha. 2004. *The politics of the governed: reflections on popular politics in most of the world*. New York: Columbia University Press.

Chau, Candice. 2020. Hong Kong liberal studies to be renamed and reformed—more China content, less focus on current affairs. *Hong Kong Free Press*, November 27, 2020. https://hongkongfp.com/2020/11/27/hong-kong-liberal-studies-to-be-renamed-and-reformed-more-china-content-less-focus-on-current-affairs/

Chau, Candice. 2021. Explainer: Hong Kong's first legislative election since Beijing's "patriots-only" overhaul. *Hong Kong Free Press*, November 27, 2021. https://hongkongfp.com/2021/11/27/explainer-hong-kongs-first-legislative-election-since-beijings-patriots-only-overhaul/

Chen, Jie, Huhe, Narisong, and Yan, Ting. 2022. Is a "silent revolution" in the making in China? *Asian Survey* 62(2), 302–329.

Chen, Jie. 2004. *Popular political support in urban China*. Washington, DC: Woodrow Wilson Center Press.

Chen, Qingqing, Cui, Fandio, and Leng, Shumei. 2021. Largest HK opposition group likely to disband; city no longer secessionism hotbed. *Global Times*, August 12, 2021. https://www.globaltimes.cn/page/202108/1231368.shtml

Chen, Zhizhong, Chen, Juan, and Yang, Guang. 2014. *Press industry in Hong Kong, Macao and Taiwan [港澳台报业]*. Guangzhou: Jinan University Press.

Cheng, Kris. 2019. Beijing deems Hong Kong protests "colour revolution," will not rule out intervention. *Hong Kong Free Press*, August 8, 2019. https://hongkongfp.com/2019/08/08/beijing-deems-hong-kong-protests-colour-revolution-will-not-rule-intervention/

Cheng, Sara, and Alun, John. 2021. Hong Kong's first "patriots-only" election kicks off. *Reuters*, September 19, 2021. https://www.reuters.com/world/asia-pacific/hong-kongs-first-patriots-only-election-kicks-off-2021-09-18/

Cheng, Joseph Y. S., ed. 2014. *New trends of political participation in Hong Kong*. Hong Kong: City University of Hong Kong Press.

Cheung, Gary K. W. 2012. 六七暴動: 香港戰後歷史的分水嶺 [Hong Kong's watershed: the 1967 riots]. Hong Kong: Hong Kong University Press.

Cheung, Gary. 2019. International Chamber of Commerce—Hong Kong calls on government to halt extradition bill, saying global companies might reconsider locating offices in the city. *South China Morning Post*, May 8, 2019. https://www.scmp.com/news/hong-kong/politics/article/3009421/international-chamber-commerce-hong-kong-calls-government

Cheung, Gary, Lam, Jeffie, and Lau, Jack. 2020. Veteran Australian judge James Spigelman resigns from Hong Kong's top court, citing national security law. *South China Morning Post*, September 18, 2020. https://www.scmp.com/news/hong-kong/law-and-crime/article/3102051/veteran-australian-judge-james-spigelman-resigns-hong

Cheung, Kwai-Yeung. 2007. *Jinyong and the press* [金庸与报业]. Hong Kong: Commercial Press.

Chinoy, Mike. 2003. Doubts over HK security law. *CNN*, July 14, 2003. https://edition.cnn.com/2003/WORLD/asiapcf/east/07/13/hk.protest/index.html

Choi, Po K. 1990. *"Popular culture" in the other Hong Kong report: 1990*, edited by Richard Y. C. Wong and Joseph Y. S. Cheng. Hong Kong: Chinese University Press.

Citrin, Jack, and Luks, Samantha. 2001. Political trust revisited: déjà vu all over again? In John R. Hibbing and Elizabeth Theiss-Morse, eds. *What is it about government that Americans dislike?* Cambridge: Cambridge University Press.

Coleman, James. 2000. *Foundations of social theory*. Cambridge, MA: Belknap Press of Harvard University Press.

Congressional Research Service. 2014. Protests in Hong Kong: the "umbrella movement" (update). *EveryCRSReport.com*, November 28, 2014. https://www.everycrsreport.com/reports/IF10005.html

Converse, Philip E. 1964. The nature of belief systems in mass publics. In D. E. Apter, ed. *Ideology and discontent*. New York: Free Press.

Cou, M. 2007.回顧保衛天星碼頭清拆運動 — 一場自發的運動 [Review the campaign to defend the demolition of the Star Ferry Pier—a spontaneous movement]. *Cultural Studies*, March 2007. https://www.ln.edu.hk/mcsln/archive/4th_issue/criticism_04.html

Crozier, Michel, Huntington, Samuel P., and Watanuki, Joji. 1975. *The crisis of democracy: report on the governability of democracies to the Trilateral Commission*. New York: New York University Press.

Davidson, Helen. 2020. Hong Kong primaries: China declares pro-democracy polls "illegal." *The Guardian*, July 14. 2020. https://www.theguardian.com/world/2020/jul/14/hong-kong-primaries-china-declares-pro-democracy-polls-illegal

Davis, Michael C., and Kellogg, Thomas E. 2019. *The promise of democratization in Hong Kong*. National Democratic Institute, Washington DC. https://www.ndi.org/sites/default/files/Final_04.11.20_The%20Promise%20of%20Democratization%20in%20Hong%20Kong.pdf

Dekker, Paul, and Uslaner, Eric M., eds. 2001. *Social capital and participation in everyday life*. London and New York: Routledge.

Deva, Surya. 2020. Threats to Hong Kong's autonomy from the NPC's Standing Committee: the role of courts and the basic structure doctrine. *Hong Kong Law Journal* 50(1), 901–934.

Diamond, Larry. 2008. The democratic rollback: the resurgence of the predatory state. *Foreign Affairs* 87(2), 36–48.

Dickson, Bruce. 2016. *The dictator's dilemma: the Chinese Communist Party's strategy for survival*. New York: Oxford University Press.

Dickson, Bruce J. 2021. *The party and the people: Chinese politics in the 21st century*. Princeton, NJ: Princeton University Press.

Dickson, Bruce J., Landry, P. F., Shen, Mingming, et al. 2016. Public goods and regime support in urban China. *The China Quarterly* 228, 859–880.

District Council Election. 2020. *Voter turnout rate*. Registration and Electoral Office, HKSAR. https://www.elections.gov.hk/dc2019/eng/contact.html

District Council Election. 2021. *Voter turnout rate*. Registration and Electoral Office, HKSAR. https://www.elections.gov.hk/legco2021/eng/turnout.html

Dizayi, Saman, A. H. 2019. Locating identity crisis in postcolonial theory: Fanon and Said. *Journal of Advanced Research in Social Sciences* 2.

Druckman, James N., Green, Donald P., Kuklinski, James H., et al. 2011. Experiments: an introduction to core concepts. In James N. Druckman et al., eds. *Cambridge handbook of experimental political science*. New York: Cambridge University Press.

Easton, David. 1965. *A systems analysis of political life*. New York: John Wiley & Sons.

Eckstein, Harry. 1998. Congruence theory explained. In Eckstein et al., eds. *Can democracy take root in post-Soviet Russia?* Lanham, Md.: Rowman & Littlefield.
Edelman. 2020. *Edelman 2020 Trust Barometer Report.* https://www.edelman.com/sites/g/files/aatuss191/files/2022-01/2022%20Edelman%20Trust%20Barometer%20FINAL_Jan25.pdf
Edelman. 2022. *Edelman 2022 Trust Barometer Report.* https://www.edelman.com/sites/g/files/aatuss191/files/2022-01/2022%20Edelman%20Trust%20Barometer%20Global%20Report_Final.pdf.
Elam, J. Daniel. 2019. Postcolonial theory. *Oxford Bibliographies in Literary and Critical Theory.* https://www.oxfordbibliographies.com/view/document/obo-9780190221911/obo-9780190221911-0069.xml
Elkins, David J., and Richard, E. B. Simeon. 1979. A cause in search of its effects, or what does political culture explain? *Comparative Politics* 1(11), 127–146.
Evers, Adalbert. 1995. Part of the welfare mix: the third sector as an intermediate area. *International Journal of Voluntary and Nonprofit Organizations* 6(2), 159–182.
Fang, Kecheng. 2022. The social movement was live streamed: a relational analysis of mobile live streaming during the 2019 Hong Kong protests. *Journal of Computer-Mediated Communication.* 28(1), zmac033.
Fanon, Frantz. 1967. *Black skin, white masks.* New York: Grove Press.
Fanon, Frantz. 2004. *The wretched of the earth.* Translated from the French by Richard Philcox; introductions by Jean-Paul Sartre and Homi K. Bhabha. New York: Grove Press.
FCCHK. 2017. *Fifty years on: the riots that shook Hong Kong in 1967.* Foreign Correspondents' Club Hong Kong, May 18, 2017. https://www.fcchk.org/correspondent/fifty-years-on-the-riots-that-shook-hong-kong-in-1967/
Fewston, C. G. 2019. What Hongkongers think but cannot say. *Washington Examiner*, October 30, 2019. https://www.washingtonexaminer.com/opinion/op-eds/what-hongkongers-think-but-cannot-say
Finchelstein, Federico. 2022. *A brief history of fascist lies.* Berkeley: University of California Press.
Finifter, Ada W. 1970. Dimensions of political alienation. *American Political Science Review* 64(2), 389–410.
Fitzgerald, Jennifer. 2018. *Close to home: local ties and voting radical right in Europe.* Cambridge: Cambridge University Press
Foley, Michael W., and Edwards, Bob. 1996. The paradox of civil society. *Journal of Democracy* 7(3), 38–52.
Foran, John. 1994. *A century of revolution: social movements in Iran.* Minneapolis: University of Minnesota Press.
Fox, James Alan, and Tracy, Paul E. 1986. *Randomized response: a method for sensitive surveys.* Los Angeles: SAGE.
Freeden, Michael. 1996. *Ideologies and political theory: a conceptual approach.* Oxford: Clarendon Press.
Freedom House. 2021. *Freedom in the world 2021: Democracy under siege.* https://freedomhouse.org/sites/default/files/2021-02/FIW2021_World_02252021_FINAL-web-upload.pdf
Freedom House. 2023. *Reports.* (Relevant data can be requested via https://freedomhouse.org/reports)
Frisch, Nicholas, Belair-Gagnon, Valerie, and Agur, Colin. 2017. Media capture with Chinese characteristics: changing patterns in Hong Kong's news media system. *Journalism* 19(8), 1165–1181.

Frosina, Silvia. 2021. Digital revolution: how social media shaped the 2019 Hong Kong protests. *ISPI*, June 8, 2021. https://www.ispionline.it/en/publication/digital-revolution-how-social-media-shaped-2019-hong-kong-protests-30756

Fuchs, Dieter. 2007. The political culture paradigm. In Russell J. Dalton and Hans-Dieter Klingemann, eds. *The Oxford handbook of political behavior*. Oxford Handbooks Online, https://academic.oup.com/edited-volume/28179.

Fukuyama, Francis. 1992. *The end of history and the last man*. London: Hamilton.

Fukuyama, Francis. 1995. *Trust: the social virtues and the creation of prosperity*. New York: Free Press.

Fung, Anthony. 2001. What makes the local? A brief consideration of the rejuvenation of Hong Kong identity. *Culture Studies* 15, 501–560.

Fung, Anthony Y. H. 2007. Political economy of Hong Kong media: producing a hegemonic voice. *Asian Journal of Communication* 17(2), 159–171.

Gainous, Jason, Abbott, Jason P., and Wagner, Kevin M. 2019. Traditional versus Internet media in a restricted information environment: how trust in the medium matters. *Political Behavior* 41(2), 401–422.

Gandhi, Leela. 1998. *Postcolonial theory: a critical introduction*. St. Leonards, N.S.W.: Allen & Unwin.

Gellner Ernest. 1983. *Nations and nationalism*. Ithaca, NY: Cornell University Press.

Gentzkow, Matthew, and Shapiro, Jesse M. 2010. What drives media slant? Evidence from U.S. daily newspapers. *Econometrica* 78(1), 35–71.

Government of the Hong Kong Special Administrative Region (GHKSAR). 2020. The law of the People's Republic of China on safeguarding national security in the Hong Kong Special Administrative Region gazetted and takes immediate effect. Press release. https://www.info.gov.hk/gia/general/202108/18/P2021081800330.htm

GHKSAR. 2021a. *Annex I—Method for the selection of the chief executive of the Hong Kong Special Administrative Region*. https://www.basiclaw.gov.hk/en/basiclaw/annex1.html (accessed October 17, 2023)

GHKSAR. 2021b. *Public's Putonghua standard*. Press release. https://www.info.gov.hk/gia/general/202108/18/P2021081800330.htm

GHKSAR. 2021c. *Some facts about the Basic Law*. https://www.basiclaw.gov.hk/en/basiclaw/facts.html

GHKSAR. 2024. *Hong Kong: the Facts: the Media*. https://www.gov.hk/en/about/abouthk/factsheets/docs/media.pdf.

Gibson, James L. 2009. Political intolerance in the context of democratic theory. In R. J. Dalton and H. Klingemann H., eds. *The Oxford handbook of political behavior*. New York: Oxford University Press.

Gilens, Martin, Sniderman, Paul M., and Kuklinski, James H. 1998. Affirmative action and the politics of realignment. *British Journal of Political Science* 28 (1), 159–183.

Global Times. 2020. HK has never adopted Western "separation of powers" concept: State Council. *Global Times*, September 7, 2020. https://www.globaltimes.cn/content/1200196.shtml

Glynn, Adam N. 2013. What can we learn with statistical truth serum? Design and analysis of the list experiment. *Public Opinion Quarterly* 77(S1), 159–172.

Goldstone, Jack A. 2023. *Revolutions: a very short introduction*. 2nd ed. New York: Oxford University Press.

Gopalakrishnan, Raju, and Doyle, Gerry. 2021. The impact of the national security law on Hong Kong. *Reuters*, June 4, 2021. https://www.reuters.com/world/asia-pacific/impact-national-security-law-hong-kong-2021-05-31/

Graham-Harrison, Emma. 2019. Hong Kong voters deliver landslide victory for pro-democracy campaigners. *The Guardian*, November 25, 2019. https://www.theguardian.com/world/2019/nov/24/hong-kong-residents-turn-up-for-local-elections-in-record-numbers

Greeley, Andrew M. 1977. *The American Catholic: A social portrait*. New York: Basic Books.

Greenberg, Alissa. 2015. Hong Kong lawmakers reject electoral-reform proposal backed by Beijing. *Time*, June 18, 2015. https://time.com/3923968/hong-kong-election-reform-bill/

Groseclose, Tim, and Milyo, Jeffrey. 2005. A measure of media bias. *The Quarterly Journal of Economics* CXX(4), 1192–1237.

Guha, Ranajit. 1982. On some aspects of the historiography of colonial India. In R. Guha, ed. *Subaltern studies: writings on South Asian history and society*. New York: Oxford University Press.

Gunia, Amy. 2021. Hong Kong sees lowest ever voter turnout after Beijing's new election rules. *Time*, December 20, 2021. https://time.com/6130028/hong-kong-patriots-only-election/

Gurr, Ted R. 2016. *Why men rebel*. 40th anniversary paperback ed. London and New York: Routledge, Taylor & Francis Group.

Hall, Stuart. 1990. Cultural identity and diaspora. In J. Rutherford, ed. *Identity: community, culture, difference*. London: Lawrence & Wishart.

Han, Enze. 2016. *Contestation and adaptation: the politics of national identity in China*. New York: Oxford University Press.

Han, Enze. 2019. *Asymmetrical neighbors: borderland state building between China and Southeast Asia*. New York: Oxford University Press.

Hao, Shou. 2019. 黄之锋罗冠聪承认与美领事会面 见面翌日扬言策动罢课 [Joshua Wong and Law admitted to meet with the US consul to meet and discuss the strike]. *Ta Kung Pao*, August 8, 2019. http://www.takungpao.com/news/232109/2019/0808/333028.html

Higgins, Andrew. 2019. China's theory for Hong Kong protests: secret American meddling. *The New York Times*, August 8, 2019. https://www.nytimes.com/2019/08/08/world/asia/hong-kong-black-hand.html

Hoadley, J. Stephen. 1970. Hong Kong is the lifeboat: notes on political culture and socialization. *Journal of Oriental Studies* 8, 206–218.

Hofstede, Geert. 1980. *Culture's consequences: international differences in work-related values*. London: SAGE.

Hofstede, Geert. 2001. *Culture's consequences: comparing values, behaviors, institutions and organizations across nations*. London: SAGE.

Hofstede, Geert. 2011. Dimensionalizing cultures: The Hofstede model in context. *Online Readings in Psychology and Culture* 2(1), 2307–2919.

Hofstede, Geert, Hofstede, Gert Jan, and Minkov, Michael. 2010. *Cultures and organizations software of the mind: intercultural cooperation and its importance for survival*. New York: McGraw-Hill.

Hong Kong Census and Statistics Department. 2017. *Hong Kong 2016 population by-census*. HKSAR. (Relevant data can be requested via https://www.bycensus2016.gov.hk/en/)

Hong Kong Police Force. 2019. Statement from the Hong Kong police in response to questions from *The Washington Post*. *The Washington Post*, December 24, 2019. https://www.washingtonpost.com/world/asia_pacific/statement-from-the-hong-kong-police-in-response-to-questions-from-the-washington-post/2019/12/24/e91d3e96-25a9-11ea-b2ca-2e72667c1741_story.html

Hong Kong Court of Final Appeal. 2021. *The judges: non-permanent judges*. HKSAR. https://www.hkcfa.hk/en/about/who/judges/npjs/index.html

Hong Kong Journalists Association. 2016. *One country, two nightmares, Hong Kong media caught in ideological battleground.* https://www.hkja.org.hk/site/Host/hkja/UserFiles/file/annualreport/Annual_report_2016_Final%20V.pdf.

HKEAA (Hong Kong Examinations and Assessment Authority). 2021a. *Hong Kong diploma of secondary education examination 2022: registration for Category A and Category B subjects instructions to applicants (school candidates).* HKSAR. https://www.hkeaa.edu.hk/DocLibrary/HKDSE/Exam_Registration/Instructions_to_Applicants_SepReg_2022_SchoolCand_Eng.pdf

HKEAA. 2021b. *Subject information.* HKSAR. https://www.hkeaa.edu.hk/en/hkdse/assessment/subject_information/

HKPORI (Hong Kong Public Opinion Research Institute). 2021a. *Categorical ethnic identity.* HKSAR. https://www.pori.hk/pop-poll/ethnic-identity-en/q001.html?lang=en

HKPORI. 2021b. *POP releases popularities of trust and confidence indicators as well as rankings of people's most familiar political figures.* March 9, 2021. https://www.pori.hk/press-release-en/2021-03-09-pm.html?lang=en

Hong, Ying-yi et al. 2004. Predicting intergroup bias: the interactive effects of implicit theory and social identity. *Personality and Social Psychology Bulletin* 30(8), 1035–1047.

Hu, Caitlin. 2019. What Hong Kong's masked protesters fear. *CNN*, September 12, 2019. https://edition.cnn.com/2019/09/09/asia/smart-lamp-hong-kong-hnk-intl/index.html

Hu, Yue. 2020. Culture marker versus authority marker: how do language attitudes affect political trust? *Political Psychology* 41(4), 699–716.

Hu Fu Center for East Asia Democratic Studies. 2023. *Asian Barometer.* National Taiwan University. (Relevant data can be requested via https://www.asianbarometer.org)

Huang, Haifeng, Intawan, Chanita, and Nicholson, Stephen P. 2023. In government we trust: implicit political trust and regime support in China. *Perspectives on Politics* 21(4), 1357–1375.

Huang, Kristin. 2019. Meet the Mainland Chinese who are living in fear in Hong Kong. *South China Morning Post*, October 8, 2019. https://www.scmp.com/news/china/society/article/3031883/meet-mainland-chinese-who-are-living-fear-hong-kong

Huang, Minxuan. 2024. Confucian culture and democratic values: an empirical comparative study in East Asia. *Journal of East Asian Studies* 24(1), 71–101.

Hui, Mary. 2020. Beijing is breaching Hong Kong's final line of defense: its judiciary. *Quartz*, December 29, 2020. https://qz.com/1944464/hong-kongs-judges-are-its-final-line-of-defense-from-beijing/

Human Rights Watch. 2021. *Dismantling a free society: Hong Kong one year after the National Security Law.* June 25, 2021. https://www.hrw.org/feature/2021/06/25/dismantling-free-society/hong-kong-one-year-after-national-security-law

Huntington, Samuel P. 1993a. The clash of civilizations? *Foreign Affairs* 72(3), 22.

Huntington, Samuel P. 1993b. *The third wave: democratization in the late twentieth century.* Norman: University of Oklahoma.

Huntington, Samuel P. 1996. *The clash of civilizations and the remaking of world order.* New York: Simon & Schuster.

Imai, Kosuke. 2011. Multivariate regression analysis for the item count technique. *Journal of the American Statistical Association* 106(494), 407–416.

Inglehart, Ronald. 1990. *Culture shift in advanced industrial society.* Princeton, NJ: Princeton University Press.

Inglehart, Ronald, and Baker, Wayne E. 2000. Modernization, cultural change, and the persistence of traditional values. *American Sociological Review* 65(1),19.

Inglehart, Ronald, and Welzel, Christian. 2001. *Modernization, cultural change, and democracy: the human development sequence.* Cambridge: Cambridge University Press.

Inkeles, Alex, and Smith, David H. 1974. *Becoming modern: individual change in six developing countries*. Cambridge, MA: Harvard University Press.
Ip, Regina. 2020. Hong Kong still paying the price for Britain's failure to bring democracy when it had the chance. *South China Morning Post*, December 21, 2020. https://www.scmp.com/comment/letters/article/3114457/hong-kong-still-paying-price-britains-failure-bring-democracy-when?module=perpetual_scroll_0&pgtype=article&campaign=3114457
ISSP Research Group. 2012. *International social survey programme: citizenship—ISSP 2004*. GESIS Data Archive, Cologne. A3950 Data file Version 1.3.0. (Relevant data can be requested via https://search.gesis.org/research_data/ZA3950?)
ISSP Research Group. 2015. *International social survey programme: national identity III*. GESIS Data Archive, Cologne. ZA5950 Data file Version 2.0.0. (Relevant data can be requested via https://search.gesis.org/research_data/ZA5950)
Ives, Mike. 2019. Hong Kong police, once called "Asia's finest," are now a focus of anger. *The New York Times*, June 24, 2019. https://www.nytimes.com/2019/06/24/world/asia/hong-kong-police-protest.html
Jackman, Robert W., and Ross, A. Miller. 2005. *Before norms: institutions and civic culture*. Ann Arbor: University of Michigan Press.
Jaffer, Sue, Knaudt, Susanna, and Morris, Nicholas. 2014. Failures of regulation and governance. In Nicholas Morris and David Vines, eds. *Capital failure: rebuilding trust in financial services*. New York: Oxford University Press.
Judiciary of HKSAR. 2021. *Judiciary fact sheet*. https://www.judiciary.hk/en/publications/judfactsheet.html
Kaase, Max, and Newton, Kenneth. 1995. *Beliefs in government*. New York: Oxford University Press.
Kane, James G., Craig, Stephen C., and Wald, Kenneth D. 2004. Religion and presidential politics in Florida: a list experiment. *Social Science Quarterly* 85(2), 281–293.
Kaphle, Anup. 2013. Chinese tourists' bad manners harming country's reputation, says senior official. *The Washington Post*, May 17, 2013. https://www.washingtonpost.com/news/worldviews/wp/2013/05/17/chinese-vice-premier-says-chinese-tourists-bad-manners-is-harming-china/
Kennedy, John J., and Shi, Yaojiang. 2019. *Lost and found: the "missing girls" in rural China*. New York: Oxford University Press.
Khan, Zia. 2017. *The ugly truth about fake news: fragility of liberal democracies in the internet age*. Australian Institute of International Affairs. December 26, 2017. https://www.internationalaffairs.org.au/ugly-truth-fake-news-fragility-liberal-democracies-internet-age/
King, Ambrose Y. 1975. Administrative absorption of politics in Hong Kong: emphasis on the grass roots level. *Asian Survey* 15, 422–439.
Kornhauser, William. 1960. *The politics of mass society*. London: Routledge and Kegan Paul.
Ku, Agnes S. 2004. Immigration policies, discourses, and the politics of local belonging in Hong Kong (1950–1980). *Modern China* 30, 326–360.
Ku, Agnes S. 2009. Review of *Hong Kong, China: learning to belong to a nation*, by Gordon Mathews, Eric Kit-wai Ma, and Tai-lok Lui. *The China Journal* 61, 258–259.
Ku, Agnes S-M. 2012. Remaking places and fashioning an opposition discourse: struggle over the Star Ferry Pier and the Queen's Pier in Hong Kong. *Environment and Planning D: Society and Space* 30(1), 5–22.
Ku, Agnes S-M., and Pun, Ngai, eds. 2006. *Remaking citizenship in Hong Kong: community, nation, and the global city*. Routledge Studies in Asia's Transformations. London: Routledge.

Kuan, Hsin-chi, and Lau, S. K. 1989. The civic self in a changing polity: The case of Hong Kong. In M. Mushkat and K. Cheek-Milby, eds. *Hong Kong: the challenge of transformation*. Hong Kong: Centre of Asian Studies, University of Hong Kong.

Kuan, Hsin-chi, and Lau, Siu-kai. 1995. The partial vision of democracy in Hong Kong: a survey of popular opinion. *The China Journal* 34(July), 239–264.

Kuan, Hsin-chi, and Lau, Siu-kai. 2002. Cognitive mobilization and electoral support for the Democratic Party in Hong Kong. *Electoral Studies* 21(4), 561–582.

Kuklinski, James H., Cobb, Michael D., and Gilens, Martin. 1997. Racial attitudes and the "New South." *The Journal of Politics* 59(2), 323–349.

Kuklinski, James H., Sniderman, Paul M., Knight, Katheleen, et al. 1997. Racial prejudice and attitudes toward affirmative action. *American Journal of Political Science* 41(2), 402.

Kuo, Lily. 2019. Hong Kong police and demonstrators clash as tensions escalate. *The Guardian*, September 22, 2019. https://www.theguardian.com/world/2019/sep/22/hong-kong-pro-democracy-protests-turn-violent-again

Kuo, Lily. 2020. China fires two senior Hubei officials over coronavirus outbreak. *The Guardian*, February 11, 2020. https://www.theguardian.com/world/2020/feb/11/china-fires-two-senior-hubei-officials-over-coronavirus-outbreak

Kwok, Tony. 2019. Lenient sentencing for rioters could only prolong the protests and lead to a loss of faith in Hong Kong's courts. *South China Morning Post*, September 22, 2019. https://www.scmp.com/comment/opinion/article/3029636/lenient-sentencing-rioters-could-only-prolong-protests-and-lead

Kwong, Ying-ho. 2015. The dynamics of mainstream and internet alternative media in Hong Kong: a case study of the Umbrella movement. *International Journal of China Studies* 6(3), 273–298.

Kwong, Ying-ho. 2016. The growth of "localism" in Hong Kong: A new path for the democracy movement? *China Perspectives* 3, 63–68.

Lai, Yan-ho, and Chan, Yuen. 2022. Hong Kong: How colonial-era laws are being used to shut down independent journalism. *The Conversation*, January 10, 2022. https://theconversation.com/hong-kong-how-colonial-era-laws-are-being-used-to-shut-down-independent-journalism-174375

Lam, Jeffie, and Zhao, Shirley. 2017. Who's afraid of Chinese history lessons? *South China Morning Post*, November 1, 2017. https://www.scmp.com/news/hong-kong/education/article/2117899/explain-why-do-chinese-history-lessons-get-bad-reputation

Lam, Wai-man. 2004. *Understanding the political culture of Hong Kong: the paradox of activism and depoliticization*. New York: M.E. Sharpe.

Lam, Wai-man. 2018. Hong Kong's fragmented soul: exploring brands of localism. In W. M. Lam and L. Cooper, eds. *Citizenship, identity and social movements in the new Hong Kong localism after the Umbrella movement*. London: Routledge.

Lane, Ruth. 1992. Political culture: residual category or general theory? *Comparative Political Studies* 25, 362–387.

Landry, Pierre. 2019. *Interviewer effect in public opinion surveys*. Paper presented at the American Political Science Association annual meeting, Washington DC, August 2019.

Lau, S. K. 1992. *Indicators of social development: Hong Kong, 1990*. Hong Kong: Hong Kong Institute of Asia-Pacific Studies, Chinese University of Hong Kong.

Lau, S. K. 1997. "Hong Konger" or "Chinese": the identity of Hong Kong Chinese 1985–1995. *Twenty First Century* 41, 43–58.

Lau, S. K. 2017. 香港人的政治心態 [The political mentality of Hong Kong people]. Hong Kong: Commercial Press.

Lau, S. K., and Kuan, Hsin-chi. 1988. *The ethos of the Hong Kong Chinese*. Hong Kong: Chinese University Press.

Lau, Shirley. 2021. Will Beijing's education reforms succeed in "brainwashing" Hong Kong's rebellious youth? *Equal Times*, January 22, 2021. https://www.equaltimes.org/will-beijing-s-education-reforms

Lau, Siu-Kai. 1984. *Society and politics in Hong Kong*. 2nd ed. Hong Kong: Chinese University Press.

Lau, Siu-kai, and Kuan, Hsin-chi. 1995. The attentive spectators: political participation of the Hong Kong Chinese. *Journal of Northeast Asian Studies* 14, 3–24.

Lau, Stuart, and Delaney, Robert. 2019. If Beijing puts troops in Hong Kong, Washington should suspend the city's trade status, US commission says. *South China Morning Post*, November 14, 2019. https://www.scmp.com/news/china/diplomacy/article/3037805/if-china-puts-troops-hong-kong-us-should-end-citys-trade

Lee, Alice Y. L., and Ting, Ka Wan. 2015. Media and information praxis of young activists in the Umbrella movement. *Chinese Journal of Communication* 8(4), 376–392.

Lee, C. C. 2000. The paradox of political economy: media structure, press freedom, and regime change in Hong Kong. In C. C. Lee, ed. *Power, money, and media*. Evanston, IL: Northwestern University Press.

Lee, Francis L. F. 2005. Collective efficacy, support for democratization, and political participation in Hong Kong. *International Journal of Public Opinion Research* 18(3), 297–317.

Lee, Francis, L. F. 2006. Poll reporting and journalistic paradigm: a study of popularity poll coverage in Hong Kong newspapers. *Asian Journal of Communication* 16(2), 132–151.

Lee, Francis L. F. 2010. The perceptual bases of collective efficacy and protest participation: the case of pro-democracy protests in Hong Kong. *International Journal of Public Opinion Research* 22(3), 392–411.

Lee, Francis, L. F. 2018. Changing political economy of the Hong Kong media. *China Perspective* 3(1), 9–18.

Lee, Francis, L. F. 2023. Beyond self-censorship: Hong Kong's journalistic risk culture under the National Security Law. *The China Journal*, 90(July), 129–153.

Lee, Francis L. F., and Chan, Joseph M. 2008. Making sense of participation: the political culture of pro-democracy demonstrators in Hong Kong. *The China Quarterly* 193(March), 84–101.

Lee, Francis L. F., and Chan, Joseph M. 2009. Organizational production of self-censorship in the Hong Kong media. *International Journal of Press/Politics* 14(1), 112–133.

Lee, Francis L. F., and Chan, Joseph M. 2011. *Media, social mobilization, and mass protests in post-colonial Hong Kong: the power of a critical event*. London: Routledge.

Lee, Francis L. F., and Lin, Angel M. Y. 2006. Newspaper editorial discourse and the politics of self-censorship in Hong Kong. *Discourse & Society* 17(3), 331–358.

Lee, Chin-chuan, He, Zhou, and Huang, Yu. 2006. Chinese party publicity inc. conglomerated: the case of the Shenzhen Press Group. *Media, Culture & Society* 28(4), 581–602.

Lee, Francis L. F., Tang, Gary K. Y., Yuen Samson, W. H., et al. 2019. 《[反逃犯條例修訂示威]現場調查報告》 [An on-site survey report on the anti-extradition law amendment bill movement]. Centre for Communication and Public Opinion Survey, HKSAR. https://www.academia.edu/10714053/_%E5%8F%8D%E9%80%83%E7%8A%AF%E6%A2%9D%E4%BE%8B%E4%BF%AE%E8%A8%82%E7%A4%BA%E5%A8%81_%E7%8F%BE%E5%A0%B4%E8%AA%BF%E6%9F%A5%E5%A0%B1%E5%91%8A

Lee, Francis L. F., Yuen, Samson, Tang, Gary, et al. 2019. Hong Kong's summer of uprising: from anti-extradition to anti-authoritarian protests. *China Review* 19(4),1–32.

Lee, Jo. 2021. Official unmasking of the HK Professional Teachers' Union. *Chinadailyhk*, August 3, 2021. https://www.chinadailyhk.com/article/231559#Official-unmasking-of-the-HK-Professional-Teachers

Lee, L. F., and Chen, Hsuan-Ting, and Chan, Michael. 2017. Social media use and university students' participation in a large-scale protest campaign: the case of Hong Kong's Umbrella movement. *Telematics and Informatics* 34(2), 457–469.

Leicester, John. 2019a. For Hong Kong protesters, masks shield against big brother. *Associated Press News*, October 5, 2019. https://apnews.com/b411b9c205da4b34a5aafded7ae50122

Leicester, John. 2019b. Pro-China protesters in Hong Kong denounce anti-government "rioters." *Associated Press News*, December 7, 2019. https://apnews.com/article/618adcc5cf34a1412c3fe5d0f65b54e6

Leonardi, Robert, Raffaella, Nanetti Y., and Putnam, Robert D. 1993. *Making democracy work: civic traditions in modern Italy*. Princeton, NJ: Princeton University Press.

Leung, Christy, and Lee, Danny. 2019. Hundreds of doctors side with police over Hong Kong protests, exposing deep divisions in medical profession. *South China Morning Post*, September 16, 2019. https://www.scmp.com/news/hong-kong/politics/article/3027405/hundreds-doctors-side-police-over-hong-kong-protests

Leung, Hillary. 2019. Then and now: 79 days of protest in Hong Kong. *Time*, August 27, 2019. https://time.com/5661211/hong-kong-protests-79-days/

Leung, Kanis. 2019. Thousands rally in support of Hong Kong's embattled police force, as extradition bill unrest rumbles on. *South China Morning Post*, August 3, 2019. https://www.scmp.com/news/hong-kong/politics/article/3021321/thousands-rally-support-hong-kongs-embattled-police-force

Leung, Kwok-leung. 2014. It is time for "Occupy" protesters to move on. *China Daily*, November 19, 2014. https://snapshot.factiva.com/Search/SSResults

Leung, S. W. 1997. Social construction of Hong Kong identity: a partial account. In S. K. Lau, M. K. Lee, P. S. Wan, and S. L. Wong, eds. *Indicators of social development: Hong Kong 1997*. Hong Kong: Hong Kong Institute of Asia-Pacific Studies, Chinese University of Hong Kong.

Lewis-Beck, Michael, Tang, Wenfang, and Martini, Nicholas. 2014. A Chinese popularity function: sources of government support. *Political Research Quarterly* 67(1),16–25.

Li, Amy. 2013. Why are Chinese tourists so rude? A few insights. *South China Morning Post*, June 1, 2013. https://www.scmp.com/news/china/article/1251239/why-are-chinese-tourists-so-rude

Li, Amy. 2014. Rude awakening: Chinese tourists have the money, but not the manners. *South China Morning Post*, December 31, 2014. https://www.scmp.com/news/china/article/1671504/rude-awakening-chinese-tourists-have-means-not-manners#

Li, Lianjiang. 2013. *Hierarchical trust in China*. Paper presented at the Iowa Conference on the Rise of Public Opinion in China, October 18–19, 2013.

Lia, Brynjar, and Kjøk, Åshild. 2001. Islamist insurgencies, diasporic support networks, and their host states—the case of the Algerian GIA in Europe 1993–2000. *FFI, Kjeller*. https://www.ffi.no/publikasjoner/arkiv/islamist-insurgencies-diasporic-support-networks-and-their-host-states-the-case-of-the-algerian-gia-in-europe-1993-2000

Lichbach, Mark I. 1995. *The rebel's dilemma*. Ann Arbor: University of Michigan Press.

Liddiard, Patrick. 2019. *Is populism really a problem for democracy?* Wilson Center. September 3, 2019. https://www.wilsoncenter.org/article/populism-really-problem-for-democracy

Lin, Zuwei. 2019a.[不是中國人]:港獨]青年揭示的中港撕裂 ["Not Chinese": The tear between China and Hong Kong revealed by the youth of "Hong Kong independence camp"]. *BBC News Chinese*, April 1, 2019. https://www.bbc.com/zhongwen/trad/chinese-news-47353234

Lin, Zuwei. 2019b. 香港佔中五週年:從雨傘運動的[和理非]到[反送中]的[勇武] [Hong Kong's fifth anniversary of Occupy Central: from the "peaceful, rational and non-violent" of the Umbrella movement to the "courage" of the "Anti-E CLAB movement"]. *BBC*

News Chinese, September 27, 2019. https://www.bbc.com/zhongwen/trad/chinese-news-49753070

Liu, Caiyu. 2022. At least 26 officials dismissed for poor performance in dealing with COVID-19. *Global Times*, March 13, 2022. https://www.globaltimes.cn/page/202203/1254740.shtml

Liu, Melinda. 2019. 30 Years after Tiananmen: how the West still gets China wrong. *Foreign Policy*, June 4, 2019. https://foreignpolicy.com/2019/06/04/30-years-after-tiananmen-how-the-west-still-gets-china-wrong/

Liu, Xiaoyan, and Tang, Wenfang. 2020. Sexism in Mainland China and Taiwan: a social experimental study. *China: An International Journal* 18(3), 1–21.

Lo, Sonny Shiu Hing. 2001. Citizenship and participation in Hong Kong. *Citizenship Studies* 5(2), 127–142.

Lo, Sonny Shiu Hing. 2021. The 2021 Legislative Council elections in Hong Kong: mobilization, divided society and implications for Taiwan. *Macau Business*, December 25, 2021. https://www.macaubusiness.com/opinion-the-2021-legislative-council-elections-in-hong-kong-mobilization-divided-society-and-implications-for-taiwan/

Lo, Wing-sang. 2015. 告別七一嘉年華:從虛擬自由主義到公民共和論的後殖主體性 [Farewell to the July 1st carnival: from the virtual liberalism to the postcolonial subjectivity of the citizen republic]. In Editorial Committee of the Journal of Local Discourse and SynergyNet, eds. *Journal of local discourse 2013–2014: The China factor*. Taipei: Azoth Books.

Lo, Wing-sang. 2018. Decolonisation deferred: Hong Kong identity in historical perspective. In W. Lam and L. Cooper, eds. *Citizenship, identity and social movements in the new Hong Kong: localism after the Umbrella movement*. London: Routledge.

LOCPG (Liaison Office of the Central People's Government in HKSAR). 2021. Full text: Luo's speech on CPC and "One Country, Two Systems." *China Daily*, June 12, 2021. https://www.chinadailyhk.com/article/223434#Full-text:-Luo's-speech-on-CPC-and-'one-country-two-systems

Loomba, Ania. 1998. *Colonialism/postcolonialism*. London: Routledge.

Lum, Alvin, and Lam, Jeffie. 2019. Hong Kong Bar Association calls government's extradition proposal a "step backward," while extradition lawyer says it does not offer sufficient protections. *South China Morning Post*, April 2, 2019. https://www.scmp.com/news/hong-kong/politics/article/3004370/hong-kong-bar-association-calls-governments-extradition

Luo, Huining. 2020. *Let patriotism flourish in Hong Kong*. Liaison Office of the Central People's Government in the HKSAR. September 30, 2020. http://www.locpg.gov.cn/jsdt/2020-10/01/c_1210825856.htm

Ma, K. 2008. 不是經濟奇蹟的香港故事:保衛天星、皇后碼頭的歷史意義 [The story of Hong Kong that is not an economic miracle: the historical significance of defending the Star Ferry Pier and Queen's Ferry Pier]. *Cultural Studies*, January 2008. https://cms1.ln.edu.hk/mcsln/archive/9th_issue/criticism_01.shtml

Ma, Kit W., and Fung, Anthony Y. 2007. Negotiating local and national identifications: Hong Kong identity surveys 1996–2006. *Asian Journal of Communication* 17, 172–185.

Ma, Ngok. 2015. The rise of "anti-China" sentiments in Hong Kong and the 2012 Legislative Council elections. *China Review* 15(1), 39–66.

Ma, Ngok. 2018. Changing identity politics: the democracy movement in Hong Kong. In W. M. Lam, ed. *Citizenship, identity and social movements in the new Hong Kong: localism after the Umbrella movement*. London: Routledge.

Mahtani, Shibani, McLaughlin, Timothy, Liang, Tiffany, et al. 2019. Hong Kong: leaked police manuals show officers often ignored guidelines in protest crackdown. *The Washington Post*,

December 24, 2019. https://www.washingtonpost.com/graphics/2019/world/hong-kong-protests-excessive-force/

Maizland, Lindsay, and Albert, Eleanor. 2021. *Hong Kong's freedoms: what China promised and how it's cracking down.* Council on Foreign Relations. May 19, 2022. https://www.cfr.org/backgrounder/hong-kong-freedoms-democracy-protests-china-crackdown

Mao, Tse-Tung. 1965. Report on an investigation of the peasant movement in Hunan. In *Selected works of Mao Tse-Tung*, vol. 1. Online: https://www.marxists.org/reference/archive/mao/selected-works/volume-1/index.htm.

March, James G., and Olsen, Johan P. 1983. The new institutionalism: organizational factors in political life. *American Political Science Review* 78(3), 734–749.

Marcolini, Barbara. 2019. Police dressed as protesters: how undercover police in Hong Kong severely injured people. *New York Times*, September 22, 2019. https://www.nytimes.com/2019/09/22/world/hong-kong-police-protests.html

Mathews, Gordon. 2019. South Asians and Africans are no longer Hong Kong's "ethnic other"—now it's the Mainland Chinese. *Hong Kong Free Press*, October 30, 2019. https://hongkongfp.com/2019/10/30/south-asians-africans-no-longer-hong-kongs-ethnic-now-mainland-chinese/

Mathews, Gordon, Ma, Eric K. W., and Lui, Tai-Lok. 2008. *Hong Kong, China: learning to belong to a nation.* London: Routledge.

McAdam, Doug. 1999. *Political process and the development of Black insurgency, 1930–1970.* 2nd ed. Chicago: University of Chicago Press.

McCarthy, John D., and Zald, Mayer N. 1977. Resource mobilization and social movements: a partial theory. *American Journal of Sociology* 82(6), 1212–1241.

McFarland, Sam G. 1981. Effects of question order on survey responses. *The Public Opinion Quarterly* 45(2), 208–215.

McLellan, David. 1986. *Ideology.* Minneapolis, MN: University of Minnesota Press.

Meng, Shuqiang. 2018.回归二十年香港新闻传媒的发展 [Press development in post-Handover Hong Kong]. 澳门理工学报 [*Macau Polytech University Journal*]. Vol. 69, issue 1, 46–56.

Mo, Xiaoning, and Zhou, Christina. 2018. "Everyone is feeling more despair": a look back at Hong Kong's handover to China 21 years later. *ABC News*, July 1, 2018. https://www.abc.net.au/news/2018-07-01/21-years-on-after-hong-kong-handover-to-china/9918508?nw=0&r=HtmlFragment

Molloy, Antonia. 2014. Hong Kong protests in pictures: The "Umbrella Revolution." *The Independent*, September 30, 2014. https://www.independent.co.uk/news/world/asia/hong-kong-protests-in-pictures-the-umbrella-revolution-9761617.html

Morelock, Jeremiah. 2018. *Critical theory and authoritarian populism.* West Sussex, UK: University of Westminster Press.

Morris, Nicholas, and Vines, David. 2016. *Capital failure.* Oxford: Oxford University Press.

Muller, Edward N., and Seligson, Mitchell A. 1994. Civic culture and democracy: the question of causal relationships. *American Political Science Review* 88(3), 635–652.

National Survey Research Center. 2023. *Chinese general social survey.* Renmin University, China. (Relevant data can be requested via http://cgss.ruc.edu.cn/English/Home.htm)

Needler, Chardonnay. 2020. Scared silent: Hong Kong National Security Law forces Penn students to rethink future plans. *The Daily Pennsylvanian*, July 27, 2020. https://www.thedp.com/article/2020/07/hong-kong-students-penn-protest-national-security-law

Ng, Angela, Yi, Yeung, and Lee, Gloria. 2017. Cantonese, Putonghua or English? The language politics of Hong Kong's school system. *Hong Kong Free Press*, April 9, 2017. https://hongkongfp.com/2017/04/09/cantonese-putonghua-english-language-politics-hong-kongs-school-system/

Nicholson, Stephen P., and Huang, Haifeng. 2023. Making the list: reevaluating political trust and social desirability in China. *American Political Science Review* 117(3), 1158–1165.

NORC. 2023. *The General Social Survey*. University of Chicago, Chicago. (Relevant data can be requested via https://gss.norc.org)

Norman, Laurence, and Marson, James. 2020. EU levels sanctions over Hong Kong Security Law, inching toward tough U.S. stance on China. *The Wall Street Journal*, July 28, 2020. https://www.wsj.com/articles/eu-countries-sanction-china-over-hong-kong-security-law-11595957097

Norris, Pippa. 2011. *Democratic deficit critical citizens revisited*. Cambridge: Cambridge University Press.

NPC. 2020. The Law of the People's Republic of China on Safeguarding National Security in the Hong Kong Special Administrative Region. The National People's Congress of the People's Republic of China. http://www.npc.gov.cn/englishnpc/c23934/202009/eb3d12a9d34045f9a94de9a32d0d5433.shtml

O'Leary, John, Welle, Angela, and Agarwal, Sushumna. 2021. Improving trust in state and local government. *Deloitte Insights*, September 22, 2021. https://www2.deloitte.com/xe/en/insights/industry/public-sector/trust-in-state-local-government.html

OECD. 2021. Internal and external political efficacy. In *Government at a glance 2021*. Organisation for Economic Co-operation and Development.

Olson, Mancur. 2003. *The logic of collective action: public goods and the theory of groups*. Harvard Economic Studies. Cambridge, MA: Harvard University Press.

On.cc. 2018. 七一遊行民陣稱5萬人參加 警指最高峰僅9800人 [The Democratic Front said 50,000 people participated in the July 1st rally, but the police said the peak number was only 9,800]. 東網, July 1, 2018. https://hk.on.cc/hk/bkn/cnt/news/20180701/bkn-20180701144605246-0701_00822_001.html

Oriental Enterprise Holding Limited. 2006. Operation Statement. https://oeh.on.cc/en/pdf/corpsite_report/2006/2006_02_en.pdf.

Otto, Lukas, Glogger, Isabella, and Boukes, Mark. 2016. Comprehensive framework model of sensationalism, soft news, infotainment, and tabloidization. Communication Theory 27(2), 136–155.

Paolini, Albert J., Elliott, Anthony, and Moran, Anthony, eds. 1999. *Navigating modernity: postcolonialism, identity, and international relations*. Boulder, CO: Lynne Rienner.

Pateman, Carole. 1971. Political culture, political structure and political change. *British Journal of Political Science* 1(3), 291–305.

Pepper, Suzanne. 2022. Beijing's White Paper on Hong Kong democracy—a pledge renewed or a promise betrayed? *Hong Kong Free Press*, January 9, 2022. https://hongkongfp.com/2022/01/09/beijings-white-paper-on-hong-kong-democracy-a-pledge-renewed-or-a-promise-betrayed/

Perry, Elizabeth J., Ekiert, Grzegorz, and Yan, Xiaojun. 2020. *Ruling by Other means: state-mobilized movements*. Cambridge: Cambridge University Press.

Pew Research Center. 2008. *The 2008 Pew Global Attitudes Survey in China: The Chinese celebrate their roaring economy, as they struggle with its costs near universal optimism about Beijing Olympics*. The Pew Global Project Attitudes. July 22, 2008. https://www.pewresearch.org/wp-content/uploads/sites/2/2008/07/2008-Pew-Global-Attitudes-Report-2-July-22-2pm.pdf

Pew Research Center. 2020. *Americans' views of government: Low trust, but some positive performance ratings*. https://www.pewresearch.org/politics/2020/09/14/americans-views-of-government-low-trust-but-somepositive-performance-rating

Pew Research Center. 2023. *Politics & policy*. Relevant data can be requested via: https://www.pewresearch.org/topic/politics-policy/

Pharr, Susan. 1990. *Losing face: status politics in Japan*. Berkeley: University of California Press.
Pokropek, Artur. 2016. Introduction to instrumental variables and their application to large-scale assessment data. *Large-Scale Assessments in Education* 4, 1–20.
Polletta, Francesca, and Jasper, James M. 2001. Collective Identity and social movements. *Annual Review of Sociology* 27, 283–305.
Putnam, Robert D. 2000. *Bowling alone: the collapse and revival of American community*. New York: Simon & Schuster.
Putnam, Robert D., Leonardi, Robert, and Nonetti, Raffaella Y. 1994. *Making democracy work: civic traditions in modern Italy*. Princeton, NJ: Princeton University Press.
Pye, Lucian W. 1991. Political culture revisited. *Political Psychology* 12(3), 487–508.
Lee, Rainie, Keeter, Scott, and Perrin, Andrew. 2019. Trust and distrust in America. Pew Research Center. https://www.pewresearch.org/politics/wp-content/uploads/sites/4/2019/07/PEW-RESEARCH-CENTER_TRUST-DISTRUST-IN-AMERICA-REPORT_2019-07-22-1.pdf
Ramanathan, Vaidehi. 2005. *The English-vernacular divide: postcolonial language politics and practice*. Clevedon: Multilingual Matters.
Redlawsk, David P., Tolbert, Caroline J., and Franko, William. 2010. Voters, emotions, and race in 2008: Obama as the first black president. *Political Research Quarterly* 63(4), 875–889.
Reuters Graphics. 2015. Hong Kong public opinion. *Reuters*, June 15, 2015. (Relevant data can be requested via http://graphics.thomsonreuters.com/14/hk/index.html)
Richards, David. 2010. Framing identities. In S. Chew and D. Richards, eds. *A concise companion to postcolonial literature*. Malden, MA: Wiley-Blackwell.
Roan, Anne M. 2019. "I miss colonial times": Hong Kong protest regular Grandma Wong on the city's uncertain future. *Reuters*, July 12, 2019. https://hongkongfp.com/2019/07/12/i-miss-colonial-times-hong-kong-protest-regular-grandma-wong-citys-uncertain-future/
Rose, Richard. 2007. Perspectives on political behavior in time and space. In Russell J. Dalton and Hans-Dieter Klingemann, eds. *The Oxford handbook of political behavior*. Oxford Handbooks Online, https://academic.oup.com/edited-volume/28179.
Rose, Richard, Mishler, William, and Munro, Neil. 2006. *Russia transformed: developing popular support for a new regime*. New York: Cambridge University Press.
Ross, Marc H. 1997. Culture and identity in comparative political analysis. In Mark I. Lichbach and Alan S. Zuckerman, eds. *Comparative politics: rationality, culture, and structure*. Cambridge, MA: Harvard University Press.
Rothstein, Bo. 1998. Political institutions: an overview. In Robert E. Goodin and H.-D. Klingemann, eds. *A new handbook of political science*. Oxford: Oxford University Press.
Rukundwa, Lazar S., and Aarde, Andries V. 2007. The formation of postcolonial theory. *HTS Teologiese Studies/Theological Studies* 63, 1171–1194. http://www.ajol.info/index.php/hts/article/view/41235
Said, Edward. W. 1994. *Orientalism*. New York: Vintage Books.
Schaefer, David Lewis. 2007. Procedural versus substantive justice: Rawls and Nozick. *Social Philosophy and Policy* 24(1), 164–186.
Schreiber, E. M. 1976. Anti-war demonstrations and American public opinion on the war in Vietnam. *The British Journal of Sociology* 27(2), 225.
Schuman, Howard, Presser, Stanley, and Ludwig, Jacob. 1981. Context effects on survey responses to questions about abortion. *The Public Opinion Quarterly* 45(2), 216–223.
Schumpeter, Joseph A. 1942. *Capitalism, socialism, and democracy*. New York: Harper & Brothers.
SCOLAR (Standing Committee on Language Education and Research). 2018. *Scheme to support schools in using Putonghua to teach Chinese language subject*. HKSAR. https://

scolarhk.edb.hkedcity.net/en/project/2008/scheme-support-schools-using-putonghua-teach-chinese-language-subject?menu=main-menu&mlid=752

Scoones, Ian, Edelman, Marc, Borras, Saturnino M., et al. 2018. Emancipatory rural politics: confronting authoritarian populism. *The Journal of Peasant Studies* 45(1), 1–20.

Scott, David. 1995. Colonial governmentality. *Social Text* 43, 191–220.

Seligson, Mitchell A. 2002. The renaissance of political culture or the renaissance of the ecological fallacy? *Comparative Politics* 34(3), 273–292.

Shi, Tianjian. 2008. China: democratic values supporting an authoritarian system. In Yun-han Chu, Larry Diamond, Andrew J. Nathan, and Doh Chull Shin, eds. *How East Asians view democracy*. New York and West Sussex: Columbia University Press.

Shi, Tianjian. 2014. *The cultural logic of politics in Mainland China and Taiwan*. Cambridge University Press.

Sigelman, Lee 1981. Question-order effects on presidential popularity. *The Public Opinion Quarterly* 45(2), 199–207.

Silver, Brian D., and Dowley, Kathleen M. 2000. Measuring political culture in multiethnic societies: reaggregating the World Value Survey. *Comparative Political Studies* 33(4), 517–550.

Sing, Ming. 2004. *Hong Kong's tortuous democratization: a comparative analysis*. London: Routledge Curzon.

Skocpol, Theda. 1979. *States and social revolutions: a comparative analysis of France, Russia and China*. Cambridge: Cambridge University Press.

Skocpol, Theda. 1997. The Tocqueville problem: civic engagement in American democracy. *Social Science History* 21(4), 455–479.

Smelser, Neil J. 2013. *Theory of collective behaviour*. London: Routledge.

Smith, Anthony D. 1995. *Nations and nationalism in a global era*. Cambridge: Polity Press.

Smith, Anthony D. 1998. *Nationalism and modernism: a critical survey of recent theories of nations and nationalism*. London and New York: Routledge.

Sniderman, Paul M. 2011. The logic and design of the survey experiment. In James N. Druckman, Donal P. Green, James H., Kuklinski, and Arthur Lupia, eds. *Cambridge handbook of experimental political science*. New York: Cambridge University Press.

So, Alvin. 2015. The making of Hong Kong nationalism. In J. Kingston, ed. *Asian nationalisms reconsidered*. New York: Routledge.

So, Alvin Y. 1999. *Hong Kong's embattled democracy: a societal analysis*. Baltimore, MD: Johns Hopkins University Press.

So, Alvin Y. 2005. 香港人身份的形成與轉變 [The formation and transformation of HongKonger's identity]. In 文化, 族群與社會的反思 [Reflections on culture, ethnic group and society]. Kaohsiung City: Liwen.

Somin, Ilya. 2016. *Democracy and political ignorance: why smaller government is smarter*. 2nd ed. Stanford, CA: Stanford Law Books, an imprint of Stanford University Press.

Soo, Zen. 2020. Nearly 600,000 vote in Hong Kong pro-democracy primaries. *The Washington Post*, July 12, 2020. https://www.washingtonpost.com/world/asia_pacific/over-200000-vote-in-hong-kongs pro democracy-primaries/2020/07/12/b0f3d296-c40f-11ea-8908-68a2b9eae9e0_story.html

Spivak, Gayatri. C. 1988. Can the subaltern speak? In P. Williams, ed. *Colonial discourse and post-colonial theory: a reader*. Harlow: Pearson Education.

Stancil, Paul. 2017. Substantive equality and procedural justice. *Iowa Law Review* 102(4), 1633–1690.

Steinhardt, H., Christoph, Linda C. Li, and Jiang, Yihong. 2018. The identity shift in Hong Kong since 1997: measurement and explanation. *Journal of Contemporary China* 27, 261–276.

Steven, Andrew. 2014. Beijing says no to open elections in Hong Kong. *CNN*, September 5, 2014. https://edition.cnn.com/2014/08/31/world/asia/hong-kong-elections/index.html

Street, John. 1994. Political culture—from civic culture to mass culture. *British Journal of Political Science*. 24(1), 95–113.

Strumpf, Dan, and Yu, Elaine. 2021. Hong Kong voters widely shun election for Beijing-approved legislators. *The Wall Street Journal*, December 19, 2021. https://www.wsj.com/articles/hong-kong-voters-widely-shun-election-for-beijing-approved-legislators-11639927626

Sui, Cindy. 2019. The murder behind the Hong Kong protests: a case where no-one wants the killer. *BBC News*, October 23, 2019. https://www.bbc.com/news/world-asia-china-50148577

Tang, Sisi. 2012. Hong Kong protests education plan, calls it Chinese propaganda. *Reuters*, July 29, 2012. https://www.reuters.com/article/cnews-us-hongkong-china-protest-idCABRE86S07820120729

Tang, Wenfang. 2009. Rule of law and dispute resolution in China: evidence from survey data. *China Review* 9(1), 73–96.

Tang, Wenfang. 2014. The worshipping atheist: institutional and diffused religiosities in China. *China: An International Journal* 12(3), 1–26.

Tang, Wenfang. 2016. *Populist authoritarianism: Chinese political culture and regime sustainability*. New York: Oxford University Press.

Tang, Wenfang. 2018. The "surprise" of authoritarian resilience in China. *American Affairs* 2(1), 101–117.

Tang, Wenfang. 2021. Understanding authoritarianism: review essay. *American Affairs* 5(2), 139–153.

Tang, Wenfang. 2024. Democratic authoritarianism: a study of Chinese political orientations. In Yang Zhong and Ronald Inglehart, eds. *China as number 1? Merging values of a rising power*. Ann Arbor: University of Michigan Press.

Tang, Wenfang, and Hu, Yue. 2023. Detecting grassroots bribery in an authoritarian society: a survey experimental approach. *Journal of Contemporary China* 32(140), 207–224.

Tang, Wenfang, and Lin, Jingjing. 2020. The CPC as a populist authoritarian party: an impressionable years analysis. *China: An International Journal* 18(1), 26–45.

Tang, Wenfang, and Parish, William L. 2000. *Chinese urban life under reform: the changing social contract*. Cambridge: Cambridge University Press.

Tang, Wenfang, and Yu, Dong E. 2015. Public policy satisfaction in urban China. *East Asian Policy* 7(2), 63–77.

Tang, Wenfang, Hung, Jennifer S. Y., and Ho, Brian Y. Y. 2022. Indigenization of political identity in postcolonial Hong Kong. *Frontiers in Political Science* 4, July 15. https://www.frontiersin.org/journals/political-science/articles/10.3389/fpos.2022.837992/full.

Ting, Chun C. 2013. The Star and the Queen: heritage conservation and the emergence of a new Hong Kong subject. *Modern Chinese Literature and Culture* 25(2), 80–129.

Tocqueville, Alexis de. 1835. *Democracy in America*. New York: Vintage.

Tong, Elson. 2018. Reviving Article 23 (Part I): the rise and fall of Hong Kong's 2003 national security bill. *Hong Kong Free Press*, February 17, 2018. https://hongkongfp.com/2018/02/17/reviving-article-23-part-i-rise-fall-hong-kongs-2003-national-security-bill/

Torode, Greg, and Pomfret, James. 2022. "Colonial wine from new, authoritarian bottles": Hong Kong re-tools sedition law. *Reuters*, January 12, 2022. https://www.reuters.com/world/asia-pacific/colonial-wine-new-authoritarian-bottles-hong-kong-re-tools-sedition-law-2022-01-11/

Triandis, Harry C., Carnevale, Peter, Gelfand, Michele, et al. 2001. Culture and deception in business negotiations: a multilevel analysis. *International Journal of Cross Cultural Management* 1(1), 73–90.

Truex, Rory. 2017. Review of *Populist authoritarianism: Chinese political culture and regime sustainability*, by Wenfang Tang. *Perspectives on Politics* 15(2), 617–618.

Tsoi, Grace, and Wai, Lam Cho. 2020. Hong Kong Security Law: what is it and is it worrying? *BBC News*, June 30, 2021. https://www.bbc.com/news/world-asia-china-52765838

Tung, Chee-hwa. 1997. Chief executive's policy address: building Hong Kong for a new era. GHKSAR, HKSAR. https://www.policyaddress.gov.hk/pa97/english/patext.htm.

Veg, Sebastian. 2017. The rise of localism and civic identity in post-Handover Hong Kong: questioning the Chinese nation-state. *The China Quarterly* 230, 323–347.

Venn, Couze. 2000. *Occidentalism: modernity and subjectivity*. London: SAGE.

Verba, Sidney, Kay, Lehman S., and Henry, E. Brady.1995. *Voice and equality: civic voluntarism in American politics*. Cambridge, MA: Harvard University Press.

Verba, Sidney, Nie, Norman H., and Kim, Jae-on. 1978. *Participation and political equality: a seven-nation comparison*. Cambridge: Cambridge University Press.

Vikers, Edward. 2023. The motherland's suffocating embrace: schooling and public discourse on Hong Kong identity under the National Security Law. *Comparative Education* 60(1), 138–158.

Wall Street Journal. 2019. How Hong Kong protesters evade authorities with tech. *The Wall Street Journal*, September 16, 2019. https://www.wsj.com/video/series/in-depth-features/how-hong-kong-protesters-evade-authorities-with-tech/F9955A9E-5A35-452A-806666-18200394FEDB

Wang, Zhengxu. 2006. Exploring regime strength in China. *China: An International Journal* 4(2), 217–237.

Wang, Zhenmin. 2021. White paper underlines Hong Kong's healthy shift away from Western-style democracy. *South China Morning Post*, December 23, 2021. https://www.scmp.com/comment/opinion/article/3160657/white-paper-underlines-hong-kongs-healthy-shift-away-western-style?module=perpetual_scroll_0&pgtype=article&campaign=3160657

Watkins, David, and Biggs, John B., eds. 2001. *Teaching the Chinese learner: psychological and pedagogical perspectives*. Hong Kong: Comparative Education Research Centre, the University of Hong Kong.

Wazir, Zoya. 2021. Activists, families and young people flee Hong Kong. *U.S. News*, September 16, 2021. https://www.usnews.com/news/best-countries/articles/2021-09-16/activists-families-and-young-people-flee-hong-kong

Weber, Max. 2013. *The Protestant ethic and the spirit of capitalism*. New introduction and translation by Stephen Kalberg. Hoboken, NJ: Taylor and Francis.

Webster, David. 2021. Meng for the two Michaels: lessons for the world from the China-Canada prisoner swap. *The Conversation*, September 26, 2021. https://theconversation.com/meng-for-the-two-michaels-lessons-for-the-world-from-the-china-canada-prisoner-swap-168737

Welzel, Christian, and Inglehart, Ronald. 2007. Mass beliefs and democratic institutions. In Carles Boix and Susan C. Stokes, eds. *The Oxford handbook of comparative politics*. New York: Oxford University Press.

Wen, Taomiao. 2021. 盡快確立普通話法定語言地位 [Establishing the legal status of Mandarin as soon as possible]. *Ta Kung Pao*, September 25, 2021. http://www.takungpao.com/opinion/233119/2021/0925/636036.html

Westin, Alan F. 1966. Science, privacy, and freedom: issues and proposals for the 1970's. Part I—the current impact of surveillance on privacy. *Columbia Law Review* 66(6),1003.

Weyland, Kurt, and Madrid, Raúl L. 2019. Donald Trump's populism: what are the prospects for US democracy? In K. Weyland and R. Madrid, eds. *When democracy trumps populism.* Cambridge: Cambridge University Press.

Wikipedia. 2023. 香港立法會. September 8, 2023. https://zh.wikipedia.org/w/index.php?title=%E9%A6%99%E6%B8%AF%E7%AB%8B%E6%B3%95%E6%9C%83&oldid=79414386

Wildavsky, Aaron B., Ellis, Richard J., and Thompson, Michael, eds. 1997. *Culture matters: essays in honor of Aaron Wildavsky*, Boulder, CO: Westview Press.

Wnuk-Lipinski, Edmund. 2007. Civil society and democratization. In Russell J. Dalton and Hans-Dieter Klingemann, eds. *The Oxford handbook of political behavior.* New York: Oxford University Press.

Wong, Timothy. K. Y. 1997. 公民意識與民族認同: 後過渡期香港人的經驗 [Civic awareness and national identity: the experience of the Hong Kong People during the late-transitional period]. Hong Kong: Hong Kong Institute of Asia-Pacific Studies, Chinese University of Hong Kong.

Wong, Tsui-kai. 2019. HK politics 101: a guide to the city's political parties, from the pro-Beijing to the anti-establishment. *Young Post*, February 26, 2019. https://www.scmp.com/yp/discover/news/hong-kong/article/3061031/hk-politics-101-guide-citys-political-parties-pro

World Values Survey Association. 2022. *World Values Survey wave 7*. (Relevant data can be requested via https://www.worldvaluessurvey.org/WVSContents.jsp)

Wright, Rebecca, and Stevens, Andrew. 2019. "Fear is spreading." Employees expose culture of fear at Hong Kong's flagship airline. *CNN*, September 30, 2019. https://edition.cnn.com/2019/09/30/asia/hong-kong-cathay-pacific-fear-intl-hnk/

Wu, Xiaogang. 2016. Hong Kong Panel Study of Social Dynamics (HKPSSD): research designs and data overview. *Chinese Sociological Review* 48(2), 162–184.

Xia, Chuanli, and Shen, Fei. 2018. Political participation in Hong Kong: The roles of news media and online alternative media. *International Journal of Communication* 12, 1569–1590.

Xia, Ying, and Guan, Bing. 2015. 香港政治文化的嬗變 [Changing political culture in Hong Kong]. *中山大学学报(社会科学版)* [*Journal of Social Sciences, Sun Yat-sen University*] 55(6), 159–170.

Xia, Ying. 2016. Contesting citizenship in post-Handover Hong Kong. *Journal of Chinese Political Science* 21(4), 485–500.

Xiao, Guo. J. 1997. 香港的歷史與文物 [Hong Kong history and heritage]. Hong Kong: Ming Pao.

Xinhua News Agency. 2020. "国务院港澳办发言人:关于香港特别行政区实行"三权分立"的说法必须纠正" [Spokesperson of the Hong Kong and Macau Affairs Office of the State Council: the statement that the Hong Kong Special Administrative Region implements the "separation of powers" must be corrected]. State Council of the People's Republic of China, September 7, 2020. http://www.gov.cn/xinwen/2020-09/07/content_5541339.htm

Xu, Sijian. 2021. *Evolutionary governance in China: state-society relations under authoritarianism.* Harvard Contemporary China Series. Cambridge, MA: Published by the Harvard University Asia Center; distributed by Harvard University Press Cambridge.

Yan, Xiao J. 2015. 香港治與亂: 2047 的政治想像 [Hong Kong order and disorder: political imagination of 2047]. Hong Kong: Joint Publishing.

Yang, C. K. 2020. *Religion in Chinese society.* Berkeley: University of California Press.

Yang, Frances Lu, Au, Adelaide Tsz Nok, Wong, Jason Yue Hei, et al. 2022. The deprived or the devil? A content analysis of the media representation of older adults under Covid-19 in Hong Kong. *Ageing & Society*, 1–22, online.

Yang, Qing, and Tang, Wenfang. 2010. Exploring the sources of institutional trust in China: culture, mobilization, or performance? *Asian Politics & Policy* 2(3), 415–436.

Yang, William. 2021. Were Hong Kong's "patriots only" elections a sham? *Deutsche Welle*, December 20, 2021. https://www.dw.com/en/were-hong-kongs-patriots-only-elections-a-sham/a-60195080

Yee, Ringo. 2020. For the UK to champion Hong Kong democracy is sheer hypocrisy. *South China Morning Post*, December 17, 2020. https://www.scmp.com/comment/letters/article/3114138/uk-champion-hong-kong-democracy-sheer-hypocrisy

You, Leping, and Hon, Linda. 2019. How social ties contribute to collective actions on social media: a social capital approach. *Public Relations Review* 45(4),101771.

Young, Robert, J. C. 2020. *Postcolonialism: a very short introduction*. Oxford: Oxford University Press.

Young, Simon, N. M. 2021. The decision of the National People's Congress on improving the election system of the Hong Kong Special Administrative Region. *International Legal Materials* 60(6), 1163–1177.

Yu, Jessn M. 2014. Hong Kong newspapers, pro- and anti-Beijing, weigh in on protests. *Sinosphere Blog*. https://sinosphere.blogs.nytimes.com/2014/10/06/hong-kong-newspapers-pro-and-anti-beijing-weigh-in-on-protests/

Yun, Verna. 2019. Hong Kong's reluctant police officer: "It's not for us to deliver punishment." *The Guardian*, October 29, 2019. https://www.theguardian.com/world/2019/oct/29/hong-kongs-reluctant-policeman-its-not-for-us-to-deliver-punishment (accessed October 17, 2023)

Yung, Betty, and Leung, Lisa Yuk-Ming. 2014. Diverse roles of alternative media in Hong Kong civil society: from public discourse initiation to social activism. *Journal of Asian Public Policy* 7(1), 83–101.

Zeng, Vivienne. 2015. Interview: student leader Nathan Law reflects on Umbrella movement and the road to democracy. *Hong Kong Free Press*, September 28, 2015. https://hongkongfp.com/2015/09/28/interview-student-leader-nathan-law-reflects-on-umbrella-movement-and-the-road-ahead-to-democracy/

Zhao, Yuezhi. 2006. From commercialization to conglomeration: the transformation of the Chinese Press within the orbit of the party state. *Journal of Communication* 50(2), 3–26.

Zhen, Shuji. 2020. 再有終審庭外籍法官請辭香港最高法院洋法官或成歷史 [Another foreign judge in the final trial resigns as a foreign judge of the Supreme Court of Hong Kong may become history]. *Rfi*, September 25, 2020. https://www.rfi.fr/tw/%E6%B8%AF%E6%BE%B3%E5%8F%B0/20200925-%E5%86%8D%E6%9C%89%E7%B5%82%E5%AF%A9%E5%BA%AD%E5%A4%96%E7%B1%8D%E6%B3%95%E5%AE%98%E8%AB%8B%E8%BE%AD%E9%A6%99%E6%B8%AF%E6%9C%80%E9%AB%98%E6%B3%95%E9%99%A2%E6%B4%8B%E6%B3%95%E5%AE%98%E6%88%96%E6%88%90%E6%AD%B7%E5%8F%B2

Zheng, Sarah. 2019. Beijing warns of "signs of terrorism" in violent unrest in Hong Kong. *South China Morning Post*, August 12, 2019. https://www.scmp.com/news/china/politics/article/3022438/beijing-warns-signs-terrorism-violent-unrest-hong-kong

Zheng, Victor W. T., and Wong, Siu-lun. 2002. 香港人的身份同:九七前後的 [The identity of Hong Kong Chinese: before and after 1997]. *Twenty First Century* 73, 71–80. https://www.cuhk.edu.hk/ics/21c/media/articles/c073-200207038.pdf

Zheng, William. 2022. Dozens of Chinese officials punished over latest wave of Covid-19 cases. *South China Morning Post*, March 22, 2022. https://www.scmp.com/news/china/politics/article/3171313/dozens-chinese-officals-punished-over-latest-wave-covid-19

Zhou, Yingnan Joseph, Tang, Wenfang, and Lei, Xuchuan. 2019. Social desirability of dissent: an IAT experiment with Chinese university students. *Journal of Chinese Political Science* 25(6), 1–26.

Zhu, Alex Y. F., Chan, Alex L. S., and Chou Kee, L. 2020. The pathway toward radical political participation among young people in Hong Kong: a communication mediation approach. *East Asia* 37, 45–62.

Zhu, Julie. 2019. Mainlanders in Hong Kong worry as anti-China sentiments swells. *Reuters*, October 30, 2019. https://www.reuters.com/article/us-hongkong-protests-mainlanders-idUSKBN1X90Q8

Zhu, Runping, Krever, Richard, and Choi, Alfred Siu Kay. 2018. The impact of newspaper reports on fear of violent crime in Hong Kong. *Newspaper Research Journal* 39(4), 470–480.

Zolov, Eric. 2014. Introduction: Latin America in the global sixties. *The Americas* 70(3), 349–362.

Index

Note:- Tables and figures are indicated by an italic *t* and *f* respectively

For the benefit of digital users, indexed terms that span two pages (e.g., 52–53) may, on occasion, appear on only one of those pages.

accountability of government 12–13
activator variable 36–39
age
   political attitude and behavior 14
   trust index and 96
Almond, Gabriel 2–3, 6
ancestor worship and geomancy 18–19
Anderson, Benedict 4, 15
antiauthoritarian political culture 3
anti-Beijing dissidents 91
anti-China activists 33
anti-China camp 6
anti-China forces 72–73, 76, 116–117
anti-China groups 79, 104–106, 116
anti-China media 120. *See also Apple Daily*
anti-China pan-democrats 109–110
anti-China political activists 109–110
anti-China political orientation 120
anti-China political socialization 96
anti-China protests 75, 80, 103–106, 110–112
anti-China sentiment 15, 39–40, 51, 73, 79–80, 82–83, 90–91, 112
anti-China social movements 51
anti-civic education protests 111
anti-elitism 3–4
anti-establishment 34
   camp 141
   feelings 17
   orientation and news media 141
   sentiment 28–29, 34
anti-extradition movement 3–4, 20–21, 33, 73, 78, 90–91, 109–110, 111, 130
anti-extradition protests 73, 79–80, 112
anti-Guangzhou-Shenzhen-Hong Kong-express-railway movements 106
anti-imperialist social movements 13
anti-institutionalism 3–4
anti-national education movement 108

Anti-National Education Reform protest 107–108
anti-nation-building project 135
anti-PRC association 64–65
antisocial desirability measures 40
antiwar culture 14
Apple Daily 51–52, 65–68, 99–100, 119, 125–127. *See also* media
   District Council Election campaign 133
   evidence from 129–135
   media slant 136–138, 137*f*
   narrative of 130–134, 131*t*
   as populist paradigm 139–141
"Apple-lization" 126. *See also* media
Article 23 and National Security Law controversies 72–75
Asian authoritarianism 3
Asian Barometer Surveys (ABS) 24, 27, 88
authoritarianism 1–2
autonomy 20

Barometer Surveys 18
Basic Law and Chris Patten Controversies 71–72
Beijing
   -controlled Election Committee 108
   control of Hong Kong 79–80
   interference in Hong Kong's judicial process 79
   political influence 129
belief system of Western superiority 43. *See also* identity construction
Bhabha, Homi K. 43–44
boycotting 116
   behavior 119–120
British colonial legacy 44
British identity for Hong Kong citizens 44
broadcast effect 31. *See also* media

Index

capitalism 1–2
Catholicism 13
ceiling and floor effects 31
celebrity gossip 128
Cheung, Andrew 79–80
chief executive (CE) 75–76
China/Chinese
 civilization 50
 -controlled media 112
 culture and PRC identities 57
 ethnicity 60–61
 identity 44–45
 -language examination 60
 -language media 128–129
 national identity 44
 sovereignty 37–39, 145
Chinese Communist Party (CCP) 16, 52, 83, 107–108, 125, 128, 146
Chinese People's Political Consultative Conference (CPPCC) 128–129, 134
Chris Patten 71–72
civic cooperation and trust 2–3
civic culture 2–3, 7
 democracy and 5
civic political culture 3
civilizations 1–2
civil liberties 12–13
civil society 18
colonial hegemony 43–44
colonial legacy 44
colonial mentality 43
colonial oppression and social inequalities 43–44
colonial rule 43
communism 1–2
comparative political culture. *See* political culture
"Comparative Political Systems" 2–3
competitive elections 81
confrontations 21
Confucian culture 3
Confucianism 1–2, 13, 19
Confucian values 54, 64
Court of Final Appeal 79–80
Covid-19 pandemic 21, 87–88
critical race theory 42
cross-border high-speed rail project, protest 106–107
cross-country comparison method 25
cultural framing 111–112
cultural identity 43–44, 45–46, 50

cultural nationalism 52, 60–61, 64–65
cultural theory 111–112

death penalty and violent crimes 19–20
de-ethnicization policy orientation 44
democracy/democratic 1–2
 and authoritarian societies, political trust in 80–82
 freedom scores and 17–18
 governance 2–3
 political systems 6
 transition in non-liberal societies 3
digital technology and artificial intelligence 13–14
diplomat's privacy violation 112
direct elections 45
dissatisfaction 145
 with political policies 120, 121*t*
 with social policies 119–120, 121*t*
 socioeconomic and political policies 100
district-level variables, political trust 100–101
Dizayi, Saman, A. H. 43
"do nothing" 115–116
"don't know" responses 25
"dumbing down" tendency 128

Eadeh, Julie 112, 113*f*
East-West value preference 49
economic modernization 3
education 14–15, 51, 61–64, 96–98
 and age on cultural nationalism 63*f*
 cultural identity and anti-PRC sentiment 64–65
 cultural nationalism and political nationalism 64–65
election 32
 campaign managers 23–24
elite newspapers 139–141
English-language ability 60–61
environmental conditions, political culture change 12–14
environmentalism 3, 96–98
ethnic and sexual minorities 28
ethnic identity 49, 57, 95
 and political color 99
ethnic networks 112
European colonial powers 42
external efficacy 8
extradition bill, HKSAR government 32, 73

face-to-face interviews 24, 26
face-to-face surveys 30–31
family background 15
Fanon, Frantz 43
fascism 3–4
feminism 42
feng shui 18–19
fixed order effect 31
Freedom House 52–53
    scores 19
freedom of association 12–13
freedom of expression 24–25
    and belief 12–13
freedom of speech 44
functional constituencies 71

gender
    difference, political attitude and behavior 14
    equality 96–98, 145
    religiosity and marital status 98
globalization 42
government
    responsiveness 3–4
    -subsidized elderly care centers 100
Greater Bay Area of Guangdong-Hong Kong-Macau 134

Hall, Stuart 43–44
Handover 79–80, 96, 101, 103–104
heritage preservation movement 106, 107
Ho Chun-yan, Albert 90
Hong Kong
    identity 44–45
    independence 45
    judicial system 79–80
    National Security Law 37–39
    political culture 34
    postcolonial history 82
    scholars 27
    social movements. *See* relative deprivation
Hong Kong Commercial Daily 126–127
Hong Kong Diploma of Secondary Education Examination 60
Hong Kong Economic Journal 126–127
Hong Kong Economic Times 126–127
Hong Kong Journalists Association (HKJA) 128–129

Hong Kong National Security Law (HKNSL) 28, 32, 40–41, 55–56, 73–75, 82, 109–110
Hong Kong Political Culture Survey, 2021 6–7, 9, 17, 21–22, 32–34, 37, 40–41, 49, 51–52, 113–114, 116–118, 144
Hong Kong Special Administrative Region (HKSAR) 71
Huntington, Samuel P. 19
Hu, Yue 37
hybrid construct 43–44

identity construction 43
immigration 19–20
    intention 49–50, 64–65
implicit association test (IAT) 27
imprison 32
income
    gap 11–12
    inequality 11–12
    political attitudes and behaviors 15
indigenization 44, 144–145
    British colonial government 44
    colonialism and Chinese political identity 46
    data and measures of political identity 49–52
    in Hong Kong under British rule 48–49
    immigration policies 44
    levels of political identities in Hong Kong 52–57
    One Country, Two Systems policy 48
    political identity in postcolonial Hong Kong 45–49
    postcolonial identity, competing theories of 42–45
    protest slogan 47*f*
    robustness check 66–68, 67*t*
    sources of political identity 57–66
    traditional culture availability 48
individual/individualism 3
    autonomy 12–13
    freedom to travel 12–13
    group interest and 11
    protest behavior 28
Inglehart, Ronald 9–10
institutional trust. *See also* political trust
    Asian countries and Hong Kong's change over time 89*f*

Index 225

institutional trust (*Continued*)
   change over time 88
   in China before and after weighting 84*f*
   in Hong Kong before and after weighting 87*f*
   local level 85–89
   local political institutions 85
   in Mainland China 87–88
   national level 83–84
   social desirability 85
integrity 12–13
internal efficacy 8
international media and Umbrella movement 108–109
International Social Survey Programme (ISSP) 8–9
interpersonal trust 6
Islamism 1–2, 19

judicial independence 44
July 1st mass demonstration 104–106

Kunyang, Zhang 113*f*
Kuomintang (KMT) 61–64

labor unions 112
Lai, Jimmy 32
Lam, Carrie 75–76, 77*f*, 90
language 15, 50–51, 128
   Chinese-language 60, 128–129
   English-language ability 60–61
   gap 99
   Mandarin-language education 60
law enforcement agencies 80
Law, Nathan 113*f*
Lee Ka-chiu, John 75–76
leftist newspapers 139–141
Legco 78
Legco election 117–118
Legislative Council 78
Leung, Chun-ying 75–76, 90, 107–108
liberal democracies 10–11, 16
   societies 81
   system 81
liberalism 1–2
list experiment 29–32
   broadcast effect 31
   ceiling and floor effects 31
   fixed order effect 31
   ratios of, to direct questioning by political leaning 38*t*
   steps 17
living standard and per capita income 13
Local Action 106
local identity 21
localism 45–46
Loomba, Ania 43–44
loss of identity 43

Mainland Chinese 56
Mandarin 50–51, 99
   ability 57
   -language education 60
marital status, political attitudes and behaviors 15
market capitalism 70
marriage, political attitudes and behaviors 15
mass line 3–4
mass newspapers 139–141
mass society political culture 3
measurement error
   civil society 18
   democracy and freedom scores 17–18
   list experiment 17
   religiosity 18–19
   social desirability 17
   Western political science literature 18
media 116
   consumption 16
   effect 51–52, 96
   environment in Hong Kong 126–128
   freedom in Hong Kong, existing studies on 128–129
   ideological categories of major newspapers in Hong Kong 139*t*
   market 126, 128–129, 143
   narratives of CCP 129–135
   political identity and 65–66
   reader preference 138–141, 140*f*
   self-censorship 16
   slant 136–138, 137*f*
military conflicts 19
Ming Pao 126–127, 138
   as professional paradigm 139–141
minority rights 12–13
missing value conversion 25
multilevel regression analysis 16, 94

national education curriculum in Hong Kong 107–108
National Identity Survey 8–9
national images, selected countries and regions 49
nationalism 3–4
National People's Congress of China 73–75
National Security Law (NSL) 21–22, 34, 41, 73, 103–104, 113–114, 123–124, 148
national vs. global values 50
Nazi Germany 3
negative values 25
non-liberal democracies, political trust 81–82
non-Western society 10–11

Obama, Barack 26, 30
officials and dissidents, trust in 89–91, 90f
OLS regression analysis 119–120, 121t
  coefficients 96
One Country, Two Systems 20, 24–25, 112, 147. See also political identity
  framework 82
  policy 70–71
Opium War 61–64
Oriental Daily 126–127, 128–129, 136, 138–139
Oriental Daily News 51–52, 65–68
Oriental News 99–100

pan-Democrat candidates 76, 109–110, 133
Pang Ka-ho 113f
Pan-Pearl-River-Delta region 134
participant-based political culture 2–3
patriotism 32, 37–39, 145
Patten, Chris 71–72
People's Republic of China (PRC) 48
Pew surveys 24
physical confrontation 107
place of birth and political identity 65
policy dissatisfaction 119. See also dissatisfaction
policy satisfaction 91–101, 93f, 94f, 145
  dependent variables 93–94
  independent variables (sources) 95–96, 97t
  multivariate regression coefficients 94
  political, and its change over time 94f, 94
  social, and its change over time 93f
political action

  channels of 113–118
  sources of 118–120, 121t, 122f, 123f
political activism 2–3, 7, 20–21, 106–107, 110–111, 118
political and ethnic identity 50
political autonomy 107–108
political behaviors 7, 125
political color 95–96
  and ethnic identity 99
political conservatism 129
political contention
  anti-extradition bill movement 109–110
  Anti-National Education Reform protest 107–108
  cross-border high-speed rail project, protest 106–107
  heritage preservation movements 106
  July 1st mass demonstration 104–106
  political action, channels of 113–118
  political participation in Post-British Hong Kong 103–110
  public events in post-British Hong Kong 105t
  social protests, theories of 110–113
  sources of political action 118–120, 121t, 122f, 123f
  Umbrella movement 108–109
political controversies
  Article 23 and National Security Law controversies 72–75
  Basic Law and Chris Patten controversies 71–72
  chief executive controversies 75–76
  judiciary and Law Enforcement controversies 79–80
  Legislative Council controversies 78
political correctness 34, 41, 143
political culture 1
  cross-country and cross-society comparisons of 4–5
  definition 2–3
  environmental conditions 12–14
  of Hong Kong in postcolonial era 20–22
  ideologies and institutions 2
  implications for 146–148
  indicators 5
  individual and state, relationship 10–11
  individual characteristics 14–17
  individual citizen and political system 5
  matters 19–20

political culture (*Continued*)
  measurement 4–12
  measurement errors 17–19
  political efficacy 8
  political identity and nationalism 8–9
  political participation and political activism, modes of 7
  postmaterialism 9–10
  social and political tolerance 5–6
  social justice 11–12
  social trust 6
  study of 2
political democracy 52–53
political dissatisfaction 120
political distrust 20–21
political efficacy 2–3
political identity 144–145
  Chinese state and 48
  crisis 45
  cultural identity and 57
  data and measures of 49–52
  definition 45
  Hong Kong residents' feelings toward Chinese culture and Chinese state 52, 53*f*
  Hong Kong residents' feelings toward people from other countries and regions 52, 54*f*
  indigenization 148
  levels of, in Hong Kong 52–57
  measures of 54, 56*t*
  nationalism and 8–9
  in postcolonial Hong Kong 45–49
  sources of 57–66
  sources of Hong Kong Ethnic and 58*t*
  subdimensions of 9
  Taiwan 55*f*
political institutions/institutional 1–2
  design 12
  environment 12–13
political landscape in postcolonial Hong Kong 70–80
political leaders selection 11
political leaning 117*f*, 119
political mobilization 3–4, 111–112
political nationalism 52, 60–61, 64–65
political obedience 3
political orientations 34, 49, 141
political participation 145
  political activism, modes of 7

  in Post-British Hong Kong 103–110
  precondition for 8
political party
  affiliation 16
  competitiveness 12–13
political resentment 80, 125, 147
political socialization 51, 101
political tension 123
political tolerance 116
political trust 6, 88, 145
  age 96
  Article 23 and National Security Law Controversies 72–75
  Basic Law and Chris Patten Controversies 71–72
  chief executive controversies 75–76
  in democratic and authoritarian societies 80–82
  in democratic societies 81
  dependent variables 93–94
  district-level variables 100–101
  education 96–98
  ethnic identity and political color 99
  gender, religiosity and marital status 98
  Hong Kong chief executives and political activists, rating 92*f*
  independent variables (sources) 95–96
  institutional trust 83–84, 84*f*, 85–89, 87*f*
  judiciary and Law Enforcement controversies 79–80
  in key institutions 89*f*
  Legislative Council controversies 78
  in liberal democracies 84
  Mandarin 99
  measuring, in Hong Kong 82–89
  media 99–100
  officials and dissidents 89–91, 90*f*
  policy satisfaction 91–101, 93*f*, 94*f*
  political landscape in postcolonial Hong Kong 70–80
  protesters 74*f*
  social class 98–99
political vacuum 46, 82, 111–112, 120–123, 147
political values 50
populism 1–2
populist authoritarianism 3–4
postcolonial and postindustrial society 24–25

postcolonial anti-China political
    socialization 101
postcolonial Hong Kong 45–46, 64
    education in 61–64
    political landscape in 70–80
postcolonial identity 43
postcolonial indigenization 46. *See also*
    indigenization
postcolonial societies 43, 46–48
post-globalization era 3–4
post-Handover Hong Kong 45, 79–80,
    108–109, 127, 147–148
postmaterialism 9–10, 13
postmaterialist political culture 3
post–National Security Law era 33, 145–146
pro-Beijing functional constituencies 78
problem-solving channels 115f
pro-China 51–52
    candidates dominance 33
    leftist riots 44–45
    respondents 6
    sentiment 44–45
pro-establishment feelings 34
pro-establishment newspapers 125
property ownership 12–13
protest 114
Protestantism 13
protesting 7
Provisional Legislative Council 71–72
pro-West feelings 57
public
    involvement in political
        decision-making 12–13
    mood 41
    opinion surveys 4, 28
    surveillance cameras 28
Putonghua ability 60, 96

racist attitudes 24
radicalization 107
rational choice theories 111
regime legitimacy 81
relative deprivation 111
religion, political socialization 16
religiosity 18–19, 95
representativeness 12–13
resource mobilization theories 112
respondents' unwillingness 25
reunification 131–132
Reuters surveys 27

right-wing political parties 3–4
rule of law 12–13
Russian Orthodox Church 19

Said, Edward. W. 43
satisfaction. *See also* political dissatisfaction
    with political policies 92
    with socioeconomic policies 92–93, 93f
self-censorship 129, 138
self-determination 45
self-identify 141
self-identity 111–112
sense of justice 11–12
sexual orientation 3
silent revolution. *See* postmaterialism
Sing Pao 126–127
Sing Tao Daily 126–127, 128–129, 136, 138
Skocpol, Theda 4
social/socialism 1–2
    autonomy 111
    class 51, 65, 95, 98–99
    economic development and 12
    hierarchy 3
    indicators 13
    justice 11–13
    movement 123f
    policy dissatisfaction 120
    political tolerance and 5–6
    trust 19
social desirability 82–83, 90–91, 144, 147
    in democratic societies 24
    discussion and implications 39–41
    effects 34–36, 89–90
    in Hong Kong 24–25, 28
    Hong Kong Political Culture
        Survey 32–34
    Hong Kong Public Opinion
        Surveys 27–29
    influence 24
    institutional trust 85
    list experiments 29–32
    political desirability and, traditional
        methods of 25–26
    by political leaning 35f
    in public opinion surveys 17, 23–25
    statistical weighting with an activator
        variable 36–39
    support for politically sensitive
        questions 39f
    tools to, political desirability and 26–27

"social desirability of dissent" 28–29
social protests 110–113
    political opportunities 112
    rational choice 110–111
    relative deprivation 111
    resource mobilization 112
    resource mobilization theories 112
socioeconomic distributions, survey and population by-census 149
sociopolitical identities 43–44
South China Morning Post 128–129
sovereignty 32
special administrative regions (SAR) 103–104
state capitalism 3
statistical weighting 17, 23, 36–39, 40

tabloid journalism 128
Tai Yiu-ting, Benny 90
Ta Kung Pao 126–127
Tang, Wenfang 32, 37
technological development 12
technology, environmental factor 13–14
text analysis 130, 146
    machine-aided 138–139
Tiananmen protests, 1989 71–73, 75, 79–80
traditional culture 49
    Chinese culture 45–46
    practices 13
    values and practices 12
transitional political culture 148
trilingual education in schools 60
trust. *See also* political trust
    in Hong Kong political institutions 92
    in local institutions 93
    in national political institutions 92
Tsang, Donald 75–76, 90
Tung, Chee-hwa 60, 75–76, 90, 104–106

Umbrella movement 72–73, 76, 88, 108–109, 132

Verba, Sidney 2–3, 6, 146–147
vertical comparison method 26
violence 33
visiting government 114
voter turnout 78
voting 7, 116–117

weighting technique 144
Wen Wei Pao 126
Wen Wei Po 126–127. *See also* media
    evidence from 129–135
    media slant 136–138, 137*f*
    narrative of 134–135
    as propaganda paradigm 139–141
Western and Confucian values 54
Western boycotts 73
Western-friendly societies 64
Western liberal democracy 52–53
    cultures 19
    ideas of human rights 44
    political culture 7
    tradition 82
Western liberal values 54–56
Western liberal world 71–72, 75
Western media reports 28
Western political science literature 18
Western-style liberal democracy 19
    society 2–3
Wong Chi-fong, Joshua 107–108, 113*f*
Wong, Joshua 32
World Values Surveys 5, 9–10, 18, 24, 26, 27

Young, Robert, J. C. 43–44

Zhou, Yingnan Joseph 27

www.ingramcontent.com/pod-product-compliance
Ingram Content Group UK Ltd.
Pitfield, Milton Keynes, MK11 3LW, UK
UKHW012052080126
466741UK00013B/136